November 2011

Dear
Michael
& Lois -

Congratulations!

Helping to make 2 Canterbury
your wine country home has
been my pleasure.

I know you love good books
& wine, so this book
should be lots of fun.
Hope the whole family
had many memories
here.

Warmly,
Heidi

DWC

DECANTING WINE COUNTRY

DECANTING NAPA VALLEY

A COLLABORATION OF THE TERROIR

100 Napa Valley Wines with
Pairing Recipes from Restaurateurs,
Wineries, and Professional Chefs

and Article Contributions from
18 Napa Valley Personalities
"Life on the Inside"

MICHELLE HIGGINS

Published in the United States
Printed in China

Distributed by Decanting Wine Country Publications
decantingwinecountry.com

Decanting Napa Valley is a registered trademark of
Decanting Wine Country™

Library in Congress Cataloging-in-Publication Data available.

Higgins, Michelle.
Decanting Napa Valley/ by Michelle Higgins.
Includes index.

ISBN 978-0-615-31455-6
First Edition

Dedication

To my husband Milton
for giving his heart and lending his brain

and for our son Cole
for showing us what courage is

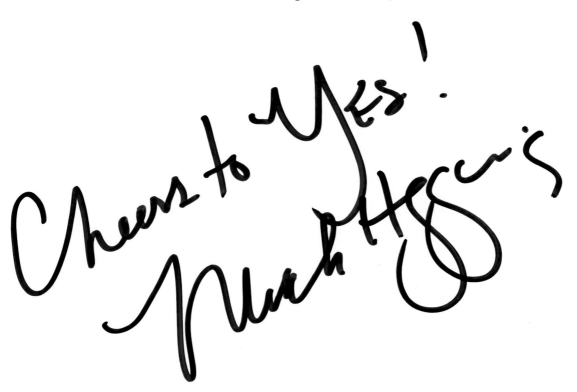

TABLE OF CONTRIBUTORS

THE WONDERS OF THE NAPA VALLEY
PETER L. JACOBSEN

" My own little farm, which I often refer to as a Culinary Dream Works, could not exist without the inspiration and support of the chefs and the many guests that come to their restaurants."

Napa Valley is a wondrous place, in a unique moment, filled with passionate people. This cookbook is about this place, this moment, those people. It touches on the heart of what the Valley and the people who live here, are all about. Interestingly enough, your involvement in reading this cookbook adds to this unfolding story of food, wine, land and people. You are very much a part of this creation.

There is a concept of local adaptation, intended to mean that ideas and opportunities, passion and hard work unfold in their own ways, in a local area, in a specific time. The Napa Valley is such an area and now is, very much, the time.

The Valley has developed as a world class wine growing area over the last 50 years. It started with the land and the hard work of the people who settled it. It continued with the dreams of Robert Mondavi, Miljenko "Mike" Grgich and Robin Lail and other vintners and their vision to create fine wines. Young winemaker Aaron Pott artfully articulates the myriad of ways the vintners and winemakers in this book are expressing their passion for nurturing the land and creating fine wines. These wines can jitter-bug with joy on your tongue or waltz across your palate with grace and refinement. They can be consumed with food, friends and family in a noisy celebration of life or sipped quietly with a loved one appreciating a moment in time that you can call your own.

Along with wine, Napa Valley has grown in stature and sophistication in the world of food. Perhaps it was the Diner in Yountville in the 1960's that created the idea of a destination location for special occasions or for any occasion. A fun place that was crowded with locals and tourists telling stories and visiting friends. Perhaps it was Auberge du Soleil and Domaine Chandon in the early 1970's, serving fine food in an elegant setting. But wherever it started, the food scene has grown dramatically over the years.

The Valley is blessed with culinary pioneers and mentors such as Thomas Keller with his focus on the culinary journey, as a pursuit of perfection, an evolving goal, constantly to be strived for. Such ideas and his dedication have inspired a whole generation of chefs and restaurateurs. The Valley is still very much in this pursuit as it chases the culinary and enological definition of perfection. The chefs and wine makers take their inspiration and challenge from the expectations of the many guests that come to the Valley each year to feast on fun, wine and food.

The Chefs, and the visitors that have enjoyed their creations, have inspired a whole generation of food artisans and specialty produce farmers. My own little farm, which I often refer to as a Culinary Dream Works, could not exist without the inspiration and support of the chefs and the many guests that come to their restaurants. The relationship is one of mutual respect for what we each do and mutual inspiration, as we each pursue our passion for creating great food. Chef Gary Penir discusses how local, regional, national and international cuisine comes together to influence the Chefs in the Napa Valley.

Now the Valley is blessed with its very own institution of higher food and wine education, the Culinary Institute of America at Greystone. It builds on the culinary foundation that is here and helps create the future. It brings young chefs from all over the world, to the Napa Valley. The graduates fit perfectly into the local restaurants and wineries. Some of instructors and graduates, are among the winery chefs featured in this book.. Enjoy their ideas and excitement for food, as you read and create their recipes.

The Valley has also garnered the attention of other world class artisans, witness the fascinating story by Riedel and his family legacy of generations of fine glassware. Each new part, each new person, each new recipe, each new wine, each new visitor is very much a part of this ongoing and dynamic creation we call Napa Valley.

Please enjoy this cookbook as an unfolding story, a passion play written and acted by a cast of characters who want to share their excitement about what they do, with you. Your being here, your caring, your enjoyment, is what inspires the Napa Valley.

PETER L. JACOBSEN,
CERTIFIED MASTER ORGANIC FARMER
JACOBSEN ORCHARDS
YOUNTVILLE, CALIFORNIA
AUTUMN, 2009

THE CULINARY INSTITUTE OF AMERICA
WINE SPECTATOR GREYSTONE RESTAURANT
2555 MAIN STREET
ST HELENA, CA 94574
707-967-1010
WWW.CIACHEF.EDU
SEE STERLING VINEYARDS FOR PAIRING RECIPE

DNV | she Cookbook | 12

The Wine List

A

ACACIA CARNEROS PINOT NOIR
WINEMAKER MATTHEW GLYNN

ARDORE
WINEMAKER MARK HEROLD PH.D.

ARKENSTONE
WINEMAKER SAM KAPLAN

B

BACCHANAL CABERNET SAUVIGNON
WINEMAKER FREDERIC DELIVERT

BEAULIEU VINEYARD
GEORGES DE LATOUR
RESERVE CABERNET SAUVIGNON
WINEMAKER JEFFREY STAMBOR

BUONCRISTIANI SYRAH ROSATO,
CABERNET SAUVIGNON, AND OPC
WINEMAKER JAY BUONCRISTIANI

C

CADE SAUVIGNON BLANC
WINEMAKER ANTHONY BIAGI

CAKEBREAD CELLARS CHARDONNAY
WINEMAKER JULIANNE LAKS

CALDWELL VINEYARD SYRAH ROSÉ,
ROCKET SCIENCE, AND GOLD
WINEMAKER MARBUE MARKE

CLARK-CLAUDON
CABERNET SAUVIGNON
WINEMAKER FREDERIC DELIVERT

CONTINUUM
WINEMAKER TIM MONDAVI

CROSS CELLARS CABERNET SAUVIGNON
WINEMAKER CRAIG BECKER

D

DANCING HARES
WINEMAKER ANDY ERICKSON

DARIOUSH VIOGNIER, SHIRAZ
AND CABERNET SAUVIGNON
WINEMAKER STEVE DEVITT

DAVID ARTHUR
WINEMAKER NILE ZACHERLE

DEL DOTTO PINOT NOIR
AND CABERNET SAUVIGNON
WINEMAKER ROBBIE MEYER

DOLCE
WINEMAKER GREG ALLEN

DOMAINE CARNEROS
LE RÊVE BLANC DE BLANCS
WINEMAKER EILEEN CRANE

DOMAINE CARNEROS
ESTATE PINOT NOIR
WINEMAKER TJ EVANS

DOMAINE CHANDON ÉTOILE
WINEMAKER TOM TIBURZI

E

ETUDE PINOT GRIS AND PINOT NOIR
WINEMAKER JON PRIEST

F

FANTESCA CHARDONNAY
AND CABERNET SAUVIGNON
WINEMAKER HEIDI BARRETT

FAR NIENTE CHARDONNAY
AND CABERNET SAUVIGNON
WINEMAKERS DIRK HAMPSON
AND NICOLE MARCHESI

FAUST
WINEMAKER CHARLES THOMAS

FAVIA
WINEMAKERS ANNIE FAVIA
AND ANDY ERICKSON

G

GHOST BLOCK
WINEMAKER ROB LAWSON

GIRARD ARTISTRY
WINEMAKERS MARCO DIGIULIO
AND ZACH LONG

GRGICH HILLS ESTATE CHARDONNAY
WINEMAKER MIKE GRGICH

H

HARTWELL ESTATE SAUVIGNON BLANC
WINEMAKER BENOIT TOUQUETTE

HILL FAMILY ESTATE ORIGIN
WINEMAKER ALISON DORAN

HOFFMANN, AUM WHITE AND
AUM CABERNET SAUVIGNON
WINEMAKER PETER HOFFMANN

HOPE & GRACE PINOT NOIR
CABERNET SAUVIGNON AND MALBEC
WINEMAKER CHARLES HENDRICKS

J

JOSEPH PHELPS VINEYARDS
VIOGNIER AND INSIGNIA
WINEMAKER ASHLEY HEPWORTH

K

KEEVER VINEYARDS SAUVIGNON BLANC
AND CABERNET SAUVIGNON
WINEMAKER CELIA WELCH

L

LAGIER MEREDITH SYRAH
WINEMAKER STEPHEN LAGIER

LAIL VINEYARDS SAUVIGNON BLANC
AND CABERNET SAUVIGNON
WINEMAKER PHILIPPE MELKA

LAS BONITIAS CHARDONNAY
CONSULTANT GARRET MURPHY

M

MARTIN ESTATE
CABERNET SAUVIGNON AND
ROSÉ OF CABERNET SAUVIGNON
WINEMAKER FREDERIC DELIVERT

MELKA CJ AND MÉTISSE
WINEMAKERS PHILIPPE
AND CHERIE MELKA

MINER CABERNET SAUVIGNON
AND ORACLE
WINEMAKER GARY BROOKMAN

MI SUEÑO LOS CARNEROS
CHARDONNAY AND EL LLANO
WINEMAKER ROLANDO HERRERA

MOONE-TSAI CABERNET SAUVIGNON
WINEMAKER PHILIPPE MELKA

N

NICKEL AND NICKEL DRAGONFLY
CABERNET SAUVIGNON
JOHN C. SULLENGER
CABERNET SAUVIGNON
WINEMAKER DARICE SPINELLI

NEWTON VINEYARD CHARDONNAY
WINEMAKER CHRIS MILLARD

P

PALMAZ VINEYARDS CHARDONNAY
AND CABERNET SAUVIGNON
WINEMAKERS MIA KLEIN
AND TINA MITCHELL

POTT WINE KALIHOLMANOK
AND INCUBO
WINEMAKER AARON POTT

PRIDE MOUNTAIN VINEYARDS
CHARDONNAY
WINEMAKER SALLY JOHNSON

PROVENANCE VINEYARDS
CABERNET SAUVIGNON
DIRECTOR OF WINEMAKING
TOM RINALDI AND
WINEMAKER CHRIS COONEY

Q

QUINTESSA
WINEMAKER CHARLES THOMAS

QUIXOTE PETITE SYRAH
WINEMAKER TIMOTHY KEITH

R

REVANA
WINEMAKER HEIDI BARRETT

REYNOLDS FAMILY STAGS LEAP
CABERNET SAUVIGNON
WINEMAKER STEVE REYNOLDS

ROUND POND ESTATE SAUVIGNON BLANC
WINEMAKER BRIAN BROWN

ROY ESTATE CABERNET SAUVIGNON
AND ESTATE PROPRIETARY RED
WINEMAKER PHILIPPE MELKA

S

SCHRAMSBERG, J. SCHRAM
WINEMAKERS HUGH DAVIES
AND KEITH HOCK

SILVERADO VINEYARDS SAUVIGNON
BLANC AND CABERNET SAUVIGNON
WINEMAKER JON EMMERICH

SILVER OAK CABERNET SAUVIGNON
WINEMAKER DANIEL BARON

SPRING MOUNTAIN VINEYARD
SAUVIGNON BLANC, ELIVETTE
AND CABERNET SAUVIGNON
WINEMAKER JAC COLE

STERLING VINEYARDS MERLOT
WINEMAKER MIKE WESTRICK

ST. SUPÉRY VIRTÚ AND ÉLU
WINEMAKER MICHAEL SCHOLZ

SWANSON VINEYARDS CHARDONNAY,
CABERNET SAUVIGNON, AND MERLOT
WINEMAKER CHRIS PHELPS

V

VIADER
WINEMAKERS DELIA AND ALAN VIADER

VILLA DEL LAGO
CABERNET SAUVIGNON
WINEMAKER GERARD ZANZONICO

VINEYARD 7 & 8
CHARDONNAY, CABERNET SAUVIGNON
AND ESTATE CABERNET SAUVIGNON
WINEMAKER LUC MORLET

W

WAUGH CELLARS
CHARDONNAY, PINOT NOIR
AND CABERNET SAUVIGNON
WINEMAKER RYAN WAUGH

Z

ZD FOUNDER'S RESERVE
PINOT NOIR
WINEMAKER CHRIS PISANI

"By unifying, we provide an unprecedented and uniquely defined food and wine resource."

Grape growers, while master farmers, are still dependent upon the balance of soil, weather, disease and a symbiotic reliance on Mother Earth. Winemakers are skilled craftsmen brilliant in components of science and technology. Most are magicians who — with careful guidance — can direct a wine by sheltering flaws and enhancing beauty. These are the most powerful fundamentals of our landscape in the Napa Valley. These practices scrutinized in the simplest of forms translate into one revered aspect... collaboration. And so I knew that this must be the resounding message in this book. We must convey this "farmer's philosophy" to the wine enthusiast. I must encourage the wineries, restaurants, and professional chefs to come together.

Who better to provide tested pairing recipes than the passionate chefs who create and taste these wines and dishes on a daily basis?

You'll find most chefs offered meat as a main protein since the Napa Valley is referred to as the "King of Cabernet." Quite simply, these are the courses that are paired best with each wine. While creating a template for recipes we deliberately tried to maintain the chef's professional voice (so each has a different approach) but all are uniformly similar. The recipes were developed by professional chefs for the "seasoned" home chef. We recognize our readers love food and wine and because of this they have developed an understanding of cooking, and for the occasional questions, resources such as the internet, are available. One glance and you see many wineries offered full courses and others tasting courses. Our goal is to provide you with flavor profiles that specifically pair well with each varietal and to be more exact, the actual wine itself!

" She attacks everything in life with a mix of extraordinary genius and naive incompetence, and it was often difficult to tell which was which."
Douglas Adams

Who better to write about the wines and share the exact scientific details and tasting notes than the winemakers?

This is a recipe cookbook for the chef, a statistical wine directory for the enthusiast, and in many ways an editorial magazine, in concept, for the reader. It integrates the vision of the winemakers, the taste of the chefs, the palate from the sommeliers, and the 250+ year history of Riedel Crystal. This is modernization.

I asked those who are experts in each field for article contributions with two requests: infuse your own personality and make it approachable for the reader. In total we have 18 contributing writers each speaking about what they know and each revealing who they are through the written word. I regularly laugh when people say to me that this cookbook is such a good idea they wish they had thought of it. In truth, it has been five years in the making.

My series of guidebooks, which have grown over time, are called Decanting Wine Country and include the wine regions of Napa Valley, Sonoma County and Monterey (currently in production). The guidebooks feature exceptional quality travel, food, and wine resources; design-centric they are filled with vibrant photographs and beautifully written biographical copy so the readers can imagine themselves there.

I have so enjoyed bringing together the Napa Valley and will soon have cookbooks featuring the wine regions of Sonoma and Monterey! My sincere thank you to all who contributed to this book.

Here's to "A LOUD AND HEARTY...CHEERS!"

DOMAINE CARNEROS
1240 DUHIG ROAD
NAPA, CA 94559
707-257-0101
DOMAINECARNEROS.COM

The Recipes

The Chefs

Wineries with staff chefs, or family matriarchs, (particularly those with private event spaces), provided specific pairing recipes for their own wines and are noted as **"winery chefs."**

Wineries choosing to be partnered with a restaurant, had the restaurateur create pairing recipes for their wines and are noted as **"restaurateur, chef/owner, or executive chefs."**

Smaller wineries were partnered with one of our private or catering chefs, who crafted the specific pairing recipe and are noted as **"professional chefs."**

The Layout

In order to maintain the integrity of the recipes we chose to print them as they were submitted. Because of this, you'll find there are variations in the recipes in reference to format, layout and terminology. We decided to "embrace this," as collaborating produces many different voices and styles.

DECANTING THE PAIRING MENUS

Wines are placed first, in alphabetical order, by producer. Pairing recipes are placed after each wine, with winemaker and chef acknowledgment following. A full index of recipes categorized by protein, starch, vegetable and sauce are found on page 380.

ACACIA CARNEROS PINOT NOIR
PORK CHOPS WITH PORT, FIGS AND APPLES
WINEMAKER MATTHEW GLYNN, PROFESSIONAL CHEF JOEY ALTMAN

AD HOC
BABY ICEBERG WEDGE SALAD BUTTERMILK DRESSING
CHEF DE CUISINE DAVE CRUZ, BEVERAGE MANAGER JULIA MORETTI

ARDORE
GRILLED RACK OF LAMB, SAVORY BLUE CHEESE BREAD PUDDING, ROASTED CIPOLLINI SAUCE
WINEMAKER MARK HEROLD PH.D., PROFESSIONAL CHEF JOHN VLANDIS

ARKENSTONE
BRAISED SHORTRIBS, RICOTTA AND PANCETTA RAVIOLI, ENGLISH PEAS, YOUNG SPROUTS GARNISH
WINEMAKER SAM KAPLAN, WINERY CHEF NANCY KAPLAN

BACCHANAL CABERNET SAUVIGNON
SEARED RIB-EYE STEAK, SAUCE BORDELAISE, MASHED LA RATTE POTATOES
WINEMAKER FREDERIC DELIVERT, RESTAURATEUR MICHAEL MINA

BEAULIEU VINEYARD GEORGES DE LATOUR PRIVATE RESERVE CABERNET SAUVIGNON
BLACKENED NEW YORK STEAK WITH CHAYOTE AND CORN SUCCOTASH
WINEMAKER JEFFREY STAMBOR, PROFESSIONAL CHEF JOEY ALTMAN

BOUCHON BISTRO
DAY BOAT SCALLOPS WITH PARSNIP PURÉE AND CIDER BEURRE BLANC
CHEF DE CUISINE PHILIP TESSIER, HEAD SOMMELIER GARTH HODGDON

BUONCRISTIANI SYRAH ROSATO
SALMON EN PAPILLOTE
WINEMAKER JAY BUONCRISTIANI, PROFESSIONAL CHEF DOUG WELDON

BUONCRISTIANI CABERNET SAUVIGNON AND BUONCRISTIANI OPC
LIBERTY FARMS CHINESE RED COOKED DUCK TAMALES, PASILLA CHILIES CRÈME FRAÎCHE
WINEMAKER JAY BUONCRISTIANI, CHEF/OWNER GREG COLE ~ COLE'S CHOPHOUSE

CADE SAUVIGNON BLANC
SMOKED ALBACORE TUNA, BABY ARUGULA CONFETTI TOMATOES
WINEMAKER ANTHONY BIAGI, WINERY CHEF KENT NIELSEN

CAKEBREAD CELLARS CHARDONNAY
FATTED CALF CHORIZO, BUTTERNUT SQUASH, GRUYÈRE CHEESE EMPANADAS
WINEMAKER JULIANNE LAKS, WINERY CHEF BRIAN STREETER

CALDWELL VINEYARD SYRAH ROSÉ
OPAH CRUDO HIBISCUS VINAIGRETTE, AVOCADO, YELLOW CREAMED CORN
WINEMAKER MARBUE MARKE, PROFESSIONAL CHEF GARY PENIR

CALDWELL ROCKET SCIENCE AND CALDWELL GOLD
WAGYU BEEF, FISCALINI PEARL TAPIOCA, CABERNET SAUCE
WINEMAKER MARBUE MARKE, CHEF/OWNER KEN FRANK ~ LA TOQUE RESTAURANT

CLARK-CLAUDON CABERNET SAUVIGNON
GRILLED CRISPY SKIN WILD SALMON WITH CREAMED CORN, BABY BOK CHOY AND BUERRE ROUGE SAUCE
WINEMAKER FREDERIC DELIVERT, CHEF STEPHEN BARBER, LARK CREEK RESTAURANT GROUP ~ FISH STORY

CONTINUUM
PORCINI-DUSTED WILD ALASKAN HALIBUT WITH BELUGA LENTILS AND PORCINI JUS
WINEMAKER TIM MONDAVI, WINERY CHEF SARAH PATTERSON SCOTT

CROSS CELLARS CABERNET SAUVIGNON
DAUBE DE BOEUF WITH CÈPE MUSHROOMS
WINEMAKER CRAIG BECKER, WINERY CHEF JAMES CROSS

DANCING HARES
FILET MIGNON, CHANTERELLES, FINGERLINGS, TOMATO CARPACCIO, CABERNET SAUVIGNON SYRUP
WINEMAKER ANDY ERICKSON, PROFESSIONAL CHEF JOHN VLANDIS

DARIOUSH VIOGNIER
CARAMELIZED DIVER SCALLOPS, CAULIFLOWER PURÉE, TOASTED ALMONDS, BALSAMIC REDUCTION
WINEMAKER STEVE DEVITT, CHEF/OWNER RICHARD REDDINGTON ~ REDD RESTAURANT

DARIOUSH SIGNATURE SHIRAZ AND DARIOUSH CABERNET SAUVIGNON
HORSERADISH CRUSTED BRAISED SHORTRIBS
WINEMAKER STEVE DEVITT, CHEF/OWNER RICHARD REDDINGTON ~ REDD RESTAURANT

DAVID ARTHUR
BRAISED WILD BOAR WITH POTATO GNOCCHI
WINEMAKER NILE ZACHERLE, EXECUTIVE CHEF CRAIG DIFONZO ~ CANTINETTA PIERO

DEL DOTTO PINOT NOIR
PAN SEARED DUCK BREAST WITH CONFIT CRESPELLES, CARAMELIZED BRUSSELS SPROUTS AND SOUR CHERRY JUS
WINEMAKER ROBBIE MEYER, EXECUTIVE WINERY CHEF JOSHUA SCHWARTZ

DEL DOTTO CABERNET SAUVIGNON
INVOLTINI OF VEAL STUFFED WITH PORCINI AND SPINACH, BLACK TRUFFLE CREAM, HAND ROLLED FETTUCCINE
WINEMAKER GERARD ZANZONICO, EXECUTIVE WINERY CHEF JOSHUA SCHWARTZ

DOLCE
APPLE TART WITH BLUE D'AUVERGNE CHEESE, MAUI ONION AND SMOKED BACON
WINEMAKER GREG ALLEN, WINERY CHEF ABI MARTINEZ

DOMAINE CARNEROS LE RÊVE BLANC DE BLANCS
WARM MAINE LOBSTER AND ROASTED SWEET POTATO SALAD
WINEMAKER EILEEN CRANE, CHEF/OWNER KEN FRANK ~ LA TOQUE RESTAURANT

DOMAINE CARNEROS ESTATE PINOT NOIR
SEARED SONOMA ARTISAN FOIE GRAS WITH FRESH CORN POLENTA AND CHANTERELLES
WINEMAKER TJ EVANS, CHEF/OWNER KEN FRANK ~ LA TOQUE RESTAURANT

ÉTOILE DOMAINE CHANDON
SEARED DAY BOAT SCALLOPS, BRAISED PORK BELLY, UNI TANGERINE
WINEMAKER TOM TIBURZI, CHEF DE CUISINE PERRY HOFFMAN ~ ÈTOILE RESTAURANT

ETUDE PINOT GRIS AND PINOT NOIR
SOFTSHELL CRAB BLT, CRISPY PORK BELLY, BRIOCHE, CALABRIAN CHILI AIOLI
WINEMAKER JON PRIEST, PROFESSIONAL CHEF GARY PENIR

FANTESCA CHARDONNAY
BACON WRAPPED PORK TENDERLOIN, FAVA BEANS, ONIONS, CIDER JUS
WINEMAKER HEIDI BARRETT, CHEF/PARTNER EDUARDO E. MARTINEZ ~ MARKET

FANTESCA CABERNET SAUVIGNON
BRAISED BEEF CHEEKS RAVIOLI APERTO
WINEMAKER HEIDI BARRETT, PROFESSIONAL CHEF JOHN VLANDIS

FAR NIENTE CHARDONNAY
STEAMED BLACK COD ROLLS WITH SWEET MANGO AND HERBS
WINEMAKERS DIRK HAMPSON AND NICOLE MARCHESI, WINERY CHEF ABI MARTINEZ

FAR NIENTE CABERNET SAUVIGNON
WHOLE ROASTED QUAIL STUFFED WITH HATO MUGI, SAUTÉED FOIE GRAS, PORCINI MUSHROOMS
WINEMAKERS DIRK HAMPSON AND NICOLE MARCHESI, WINERY CHEF ABI MARTINEZ

FAUST
PAN SEARED PHEASANT BREAST RATATOUILLE AND CRISPY POLENTA CAKE
WINEMAKER CHARLES THOMAS, PROFESSIONAL CHEF JOHN VLANDIS

FAVIA
ROASTED PORK AND DUCK CONFIT CASSOULET
WINEMAKERS ANNIE FAVIA AND ANDY ERICKSON, PROFESSIONAL CHEF VINCENT NATTRESS

GHOST BLOCK
SPICED NEW ZEALAND LAMB LOIN, FENNEL FRONDS, WHITE PEPPER FOAM, CAULIFLOWER PURÉE
WINEMAKER ROB LAWSON, PROFESSIONAL CHEF GARY PENIR

GIRARD ARTISTRY
MUSTARD GLAZED VEAL CHOP WITH BLACK-EYED PEA SUCCOTASH
WINEMAKERS MARCO DIGIULIO AND ZACH LONG, EXECUTIVE CHEF STEPHEN ROGERS ~ **PRESS**

GRGICH HILLS ESTATE CHARDONNAY
JASMINE AND WILD RICE WITH TOASTED ALMOND AND DRIED SUMMER FRUIT
WINEMAKER MIKE GRGICH, EXECUTIVE CHEF IGNACIO ALSARO ~ RUTHERFORD GRILL

HARTWELL ESTATE SAUVIGNON BLANC
SEARED FENNEL CRUSTED AHI TUNA, SUMMER SQUASH CARPACCIO
WINEMAKER BENOIT TOUQUETTE, EXECUTIVE CHEF NASH COGNETTI ~ TRA VIGNE RESTAURANT

HILL FAMILY ESTATE ORIGIN
GRILLED JERK CHICKEN, ROASTED VEGETABLES, AND DRIED FRUIT INFUSED RICE
WINEMAKER ALISON DORAN, WINERY CHEF PETER JACOBSEN

HOFFMANN, AUM WHITE AND AUM CABERNET SAUVIGNON
GOAT CHEESE TARTLET, HERB SALAD, WHITE TRUFFLE OIL
WINEMAKER PETER HOFFMANN, PROFESSIONAL CHEF JOHN VLANDIS

HOPE & GRACE PINOT NOIR
GRILLED WOLF FARMS QUAIL, SPRING MORELS AND GARDEN FAVA BEANS
WINEMAKER CHARLES HENDRICKS, PROFESSIONAL CHEF JOHN VLANDIS

HOPE & GRACE CABERNET SAUVIGNON AND HOPE & GRACE MALBEC
PAVÉ OF BLACK ANGUS NEW YORK SHIITAKE MUSHROOM SALSA
WINEMAKER CHARLES HENDRICKS, PROFESSIONAL CHEF JOHN VLANDIS

JOSEPH PHELPS VINEYARDS VIOGNIER
CATALAN SEARED GARLIC SHRIMP
WINEMAKER ASHLEY HEPWORTH, WINERY CHEF STEPHEN PAVY

JOSEPH PHELPS VINEYARDS INSIGNIA
HORSERADISH AND GARLIC PRIME RIB
WINEMAKER ASHLEY HEPWORTH, RESTAURATEUR TYLER FLORENCE

KEEVER VINEYARDS SAUVIGNON BLANC
HEIRLOOM MELON SALAD, PORCINI MUSHROOM, IBERICO HAM, VANILLA-SHERRY VINAIGRETTE
WINEMAKER CELIA WELCH, EXECUTIVE CHEF SEAN O'TOOLE ~ BARDESSONO

KEEVER VINEYARDS CABERNET SAUVIGNON
ROASTED CALIFORNIA WHITE BASS, PORCINI, SPICED BLACK MISSION FIG, WATERCRESS
WINEMAKER CELIA WELCH, EXECUTIVE CHEF SEAN O'TOOLE ~ BARDESSONO

LAGIER MEREDITH SYRAH
SYRAH GRAPE VINE TEA SMOKED DUCK SALAD
WINEMAKER STEPHEN LAGIER, WINERY CHEF NAIKANG KUAN

LAIL VINEYARDS SAUVIGNON BLANC
SALT-ROASTED SALMON TOSTADAS, TOMATILLO-AVOCADO SALSA
WINEMAKER PHILIPPE MELKA, CHEF/OWNER CINDY PAWLCYN ~ MUSTARDS GRILL

LAIL VINEYARDS CABERNET SAUVIGNON
OAK WOOD GRILLED PORK CHOP, FLAGEOLET AND WILD MUSHROOM RAGOUT
WINEMAKER PHILIPPE MELKA, PROFESSIONAL CHEF JOHN VLANDIS

LAS BONITAS CHARDONNAY
AN EXPRESSION OF SQUASH: AERATED, ROASTED AND ESCABECHE
CONSULTANT GARRET MURPHY, EXECUTIVE CHEF AARON LONDON ~ UBUNTU

MARTIN ESTATE CABERNET SAUVIGNON AND ROSÉ OF CABERNET SAUVIGNON
SLOW ROASTED KOBE BEEF ROULADE
WINEMAKER FREDERIC DELIVERT, RESTAURATEUR MICHAEL MINA

MELKA CJ
NEW YORK STRIP LOIN PERSILLADE, BEET TARTARE, CRISPY EGG YOLK
WINEMAKERS PHILIPPE AND CHERIE MELKA, PROFESSIONAL CHEF GARY PENIR

MELKA MÉTISSE
BRAISED LAMB SHANKS WITH CABERNET ONION CONFIT, BROCCOLI RABE AND TUSCAN BEANS
WINEMAKERS PHILIPPE AND CHERIE MELKA, PROFESSIONAL CHEF PETER HALL

MINER CABERNET SAUVIGNON AND MINER ORACLE
STEAK TARTARE, TRUFFLE OIL, SHAVED PARMIGIANO-REGGIANO, GRILLED TOASTS
WINEMAKER GARY BROOKMAN, CHEF/PARTNER TODD HUMPHRIES ~ MARTINI HOUSE

MI SUEÑO LOS CARNEROS CHARDONNAY
ORGANIC FRESH CORN AND LOBSTER CHOWDER
WINEMAKER ROLANDO HERRERA, CHEF/PARTNER ANGELA TAMURA ~ ZUZU RESTAURANT

MI SUEÑO EL LLANO
BARBEQUED FLAT IRON STEAK WITH ROSEMARY CHIMICHURRI
WINEMAKER ROLANDO HERRERA, CHEF/PARTNER ANGELA TAMURA ~ ZUZU RESTAURANT

MOONE-TSAI CABERNET SAUVIGNON
COLORADO RANGE FED BISON WILD MUSHROOM POTATO TERRINE, NAPA VALLEY RED WINE SAUCE
WINEMAKER PHILIPPE MELKA, CHEF/OWNER KEN FRANK ~ LA TOQUE

NICKEL AND NICKEL DRAGONFLY CABERNET SAUVIGNON
RIBBONED LAMB SKEWERS, MINT INFUSED MUSTARD DIPPING SAUCE
WINEMAKER DARICE SPINELLI, WINERY CHEF ABI MARTINEZ

NICKEL AND NICKEL JOHN C. SULLENGER CABERNET SAUVIGNON
TOASTED PECAN AND ENGLISH STILTON DEMI NAPOLEONS
WINEMAKER DARICE SPINELLI, WINERY CHEF ABI MARTINEZ

NEWTON VINEYARD CHARDONNAY
DUNGENESS CRAB WITH SHAVED FENNEL AND MADEIRA GELÉE
WINEMAKER CHRIS MILLARD, CHEF DE CUISINE PERRY HOFFMAN ~ ÉTOILE RESTAURANT

PALMAZ VINEYARDS CHARDONNAY
SEARED SEA SCALLOPS AND FRISÉE SALAD WITH HOLLANDAISE DRESSING
WINEMAKERS MIA KLEIN AND TINA MITCHELL, WINERY CHEF AMALIA PALMAZ

PALMAZ VINEYARDS CABERNET SAUVIGNON
SAUTÉED SQUAB BREAST WITH TALEGGIO POLENTA IN PORCINI BROTH
WINEMAKERS MIA KLEIN AND TINA MITCHELL, WINERY CHEF FLORENCIA PALMAZ

POTT WINE KALIHOLMANOK AND POTT WINE INCUBO
HONEY GLAZED LOIN OF LAMB, GOAT CHEESE POTATO GRATIN AND CIPPOLINI ONIONS
WINEMAKER AARON POTT, WINERY CHEF STEPHEN HUTCHINSON

PRIDE MOUNTAIN VINEYARDS CHARDONNAY
BELLWETHER FARMS GOAT CHEESE, ROASTED MARCONA ALMOND, BLOOD ORANGE SALAD
WINEMAKER SALLY JOHNSON, WINERY CHEF JASON SKELLY

PROVENANCE VINEYARDS RUTHERFORD CABERNET SAUVIGNON
GRILLED RED CURRY LAMB SKEWERS WITH TOMATO CHUTNEY
RECTOR OF WINEMAKING TOM RINALDI AND WINEMAKER CHRIS COONEY, PROFESSIONAL CHEF JOEY ALTMAN

QUINTESSA
SEARED BEEF TENDERLOIN, BING CHERRIES, MUSTARD GLAZED MUSHROOMS, FENNEL SALAD
WINEMAKER CHARLES THOMAS, EXECUTIVE CHEF ERIK VILLAR ~ THE LAKE HOUSE CALISTOGA RANCH

QUIXOTE PETITE SYRAH
SPRING LAMB SHOULDER AND YOUNG PEA RISOTTO, MEYER LEMON GREMOLATA
WINEMAKER TIMOTHY KEITH, CHEF/OWNER HIRO SONE ~ TERRA

Revana
Lamb Loin, Cardoons, Potato Gnocchi
Winemaker Heidi Barrett, Executive Chef Robert Curry ~ Auberge du Soleil

Reynolds Family Stags Leap Cabernet Sauvignon
Roasted Squab Breast, Braised Cabbage, Sun Dried Tomato Bulgur Wheat
Winemaker Steve Reynolds, Professional Chef John Vlandis

Round Pond Estate Sauvignon Blanc
Grilled Flatbread with Brie, Fresca Pear Salsa, Estate Olive Oil Drizzle
Winemaker Brian Brown, Winery Chef Hannah Bauman

Roy Estate Cabernet Sauvignon
Darjeeling Tea Scented Squab, Dried Cherries, Butter Poached Baby Radishes
Winemaker Philippe Melka, Restaurant Chef Christopher Kostow ~ Meadowood Napa Valley

Roy Estate Proprietary Red
Herb Crusted Rack of Lamb with Roy Estate EVOO
Winemaker Philippe Melka, Winery Chef Shirley Roy

Schramsberg, J. Schram
Housemade Smoked Salmon Pierogies
Winemakers Hugh Davies and Keith Hock, Chef/Owner Matt Spector ~ JoLe

Silverado Vineyards Sauvignon Blanc
Salmon, Halibut, and Scallop Ceviche with Coconut
Winemaker Jon Emmerich, Chef /Owner Cindy Pawlcyn ~ Go Fish

Silverado Vineyards Solo Cabernet Sauvignon
Mongolian Pork Chops
Winemaker Jon Emmerich, Cindy Pawlcyn Catering

Silver Oak Cellars Cabernet Sauvignon
Moroccan Spice Lamb Sausage Pizza
Winemaker Daniel Baron, Winery Chef Dominic Orsini

Spring Mountain Vineyard Sauvignon Blanc
Olive Oil Poached Thai Snapper, White Bean Sauce, Artichokes, Clams
Winemaker Jac Cole, Robert Curry Executive Chef ~ Auberge du Soleil

Spring Mountain Vineyard Elivette and Cabernet Sauvignon
Braised Beef Ribs, Horseradish Potatoes, Blue Cheese Cream Spinach
Winemaker Jac Cole, Professional Chef Doug Weldon

Sterling Vineyards Merlot
Wild Mushroom Lasagna with Ricotta and Bellwether Farms Crescenza Cheese and Spinach
Winemaker Mike Westrick, Executive Chef Polly Lappetito ~ Restaurant at CIA Greystone

St. Supéry Virtú White Meritage
Heirloom Carrot Soup with Crispy Carrot Confetti
Winemaker Michael Scholz, Professional Chef Gary Penir

St. Supéry Élu
Roasted Venison, Wild Blackberry Sauce, Creamy Porcini Polenta
Winemaker Michael Scholz, Chef/Owner Bob Hurley ~ Hurley's Restaurant

Swanson Vineyards Chardonnay
Silk Handerchiefs al Pesto
Winemaker Chris Phelps, Chef/Partner Donna Scala ~ Bistro Don Giovanni

Swanson Cabernet Sauvignon Alexis and Swanson Merlot
Beef Tenderloin, Mushroom Orzo, Crispy Beet Chips and Horseradish Crème Fraîche
Winemaker Chris Phelps, Professional Chef Graham Zanow

Viader
Tortilla Española with Garlic Aioli
Winemakers Delia and Alan Viader, Winery Chef Mariela Viader

Villa Del Lago Cabernet Sauvignon
Beef Tenderloin Wrapped in Speck with Pasticcio al Fromaggio, Chanterelles and English Peas
Winemaker Gerard Zanzonico ~ Executive Winery Chef Joshua Schwartz

Vineyard 7 & 8 Chardonnay
Pancetta Wrapped California Wild Halibut, Warm Potato and Tomato Salad, Salsa Verde
Winemaker Luc Morlet, Winery Chef Peter Hall

Vineyard 7 & 8 Cabernet Sauvignon and Estate Cabernet Sauvignon
Braised Oxtail, Escarole and French Fingerling Potatoes
Winemaker Luc Morlet, Chef/Owners Curtis Di Fede and Tyler Rodde ~ Oenotri

Waugh Chardonnay
Maine Lobster, Celery Root Purée and Preserved Meyer Lemon Vinaigrette
Winemaker Ryan Waugh, Professional Chef John Vlandis

Waugh Pinot Noir and Waugh Cabernet Sauvignon
Grilled Salmon, Crispy Risotto Cake, Haricots Verts, Cabernet Sauvignon Sauce
Winemaker Ryan Waugh, Professional Chef John Vlandis

ZD Founder's Reserve Pinot Noir
Glazed Duck Breast Quinoa, Cipollini Onions, Celery Root, Black Trumpet Mushrooms
Winemaker Chris Pisani, Executive Chef Patrick Kelly ~ Angèle

The 250+ Year History of Riedel Crystal

It was a cold, clear day in 1946 when Claus Riedel made his leap to freedom. Jumping from a train on the Brenner pass not only marked an incredible turning point in Claus's life, but was a defining moment in the history of the Riedel family: the start of the modern era of the glassmaking dynasty.

The Riedel family and its affiliation with glass can be traced back to **Johann Christoph Riedel,** who became known as the "Ur Riedel" meaning the original Riedel.

In 1723, Johann Christoph Riedel was murdered as he returned from his travels as a glass trader, the two murderers believing him to be carrying a lot of money. Johann Christoph's story became famous, being retold all around Bohemia, from generation to generation. The circumstances of his death are identical to the murder described by Friedrich Schiller in "The Cranes of Ibykus", written in 1895, and it is thought that the terrible story may have inspired the great author. The Riedel story of glassmaking, however, goes back over 250 years, when the first Riedel glassworks was established in a northern Bohemian forest.

Johann Carl Riedel, (1701-1781) 2nd generation, was a gilder and glasscutter. He operated his own workshop refining glassware.

It was Johann Christoph's grandson, **Johann Leopold Riedel (1726 -1800) 3rd generation,** who proved to be an entrepreneur along the lines of the modern day Riedels. Working his way up through the ranks of his cousin's glassworks, the young Riedel excelled as a glassmaker, but this was just at the time when the glassware market fell dramatically, and they had to close the glassworks. Before too long, with the help of a loan and an upturn in the market, the furnace was stoked up again. By 1756, the loan repaid, and the business successful, Johann Leopold was allowed by the local Count to run the business independently under lease, and thus the first Riedel glassworks was born at Zenckner in Antoniwald, just at the same time that the Seven Years War began.

Riedel Crystal
[Rhee-dl Kris-tl]

noun. 1. Manufacturer of exceptional stemware and wine decanters 2. The originator of the concept of having many different glasses with characteristics designed to enhance specific types of wines (pronounced "rhee-dl" rhymes with needle).

" Eleven generations, each contributing and moving the legacy forward. I am honored to share their family story."   MH

Hardly was the new glassworks finished in 1775, and production flourishing, when a new crisis loomed on the horizon - the Bavarian War of Succession, where the Prussians went marauding through the countryside, torching other glassworks in the Jizera mountains. Johann Leopold's typical Riedel character showed through, as he ignored all personal danger and threats to his business, and sheltered several families from Prussian-occupied towns and villages in the area.

After the death of his father Johann Leopold's eldest son **Anton Leopold Riedel (1761-1821) 4th generation,** continued the main branch of the Riedel family. He took over the Neuwiese glassworks with a similar verve for the business as his father. Prosperous times were interrupted by the Napoleonic Wars, which crippled international trade, leading to a stagnation in sales, and ultimately a depreciation in currency. Anton Leopold then set about experimenting with various production methods, and new forms of distribution. A glass enhancement works was his next project, where he put his two sons in charge, one of whom, Franz Xaver Anton Riedel (1786-1844) **5th generation,** demonstrated an extraordinary talent for engraving, and became a gifted glass artist. When Anton Leopold died in 1821, his son Franz Xaver faced rosier times - the economy was picking up and the fashionable Biedermeier style with its romantically idealized watercolors, suited the Bohemian glass makers well - they were heading for a new boom.

Franz Xaver, proved to have the typical Riedel head for business, as well as a tremendous amount of artistic flair - a rare combination! Franz Xaver Anton's era can be seen as a link between the old forest glassworks and modern industrial production as we know it today. The demand for fancy beads, buttons and jewelry, known as "notions" became widespread, and soon the production for these notions was running at full capacity. Better glass quality and the development of interesting new colours such as yellow and green uranium glass put him firmly on the cutting edge of the glass industry.

Franz Xaver Anton had a flourishing stable business, but no male heir, only his beloved daughter Anna Maria, and in those patriarchal days, bequeathing a business to a woman was unthinkable. So in 1830, Franz Xaver Anton brought his 14 year old nephew Josef into the business.

Josef Riedel The Elder (1816 -1894) 6th generation, works his way up through the company, willingly taking on any chore in order to immerse himself fully in the workings of a glassworks. Four years before the death

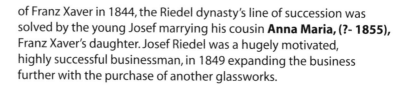

of Franz Xaver in 1844, the Riedel dynasty's line of succession was solved by the young Josef marrying his cousin **Anna Maria, (?- 1855),** Franz Xaver's daughter. Josef Riedel was a hugely motivated, highly successful businessman, in 1849 expanding the business further with the purchase of another glassworks.

Josef Riedel became known as the Glass King of the Jizera mountains, and everything was going well in his life until his beloved wife Anna Maria was to die in 1855 at the age of 36, leaving four children. Such was his grief, that Josef could not remain in Antoniwald, but instead re-located to his new works in Unter-Polaun, where he threw himself into his work. In 1859, Josef married Johanna Newinger, and in 1866 he began the construction of another works next to the one in Wilhelmshöhe to replace the original Antoniwald Zenkner works.

There was no stopping the Glass King. The business expanding further and further and his four sons, Otto, Hugo, Wilhelm and Josef (the fourth son was from his second marriage) began working in this large-scale business, although Josef Senior showed no signs of slowing down himself. He introduced gas furnaces, which were fed by coal and therefore put an end to the strip logging of forests. The Glass King was decades ahead of his time. He did not stop working until his death in 1894, leaving his son Josef Junior a glass empire unrivalled the world over.

Josef Riedel, The Younger (1862-1924) 7th generation, obviously had a very hard act to follow. He decided to plough his own furrow and not try to emulate his father as such, concentrating on other areas of the business, where he could become established in his own right. One thing he shared with the Glass King was a great love for glass, and dedication to innovation. Josef Junior succeeded in developing a machine that mechanized the drawing-out rods and tubes necessary for the production of beads from one to four millimeters - a milestone in the history of glass production.

Walter Riedel (1895 - 1974) 8th generation, experienced the greatest imaginable highs and lows: from being one of Europe's greatest industrialists, he was to endure ten years internment in Russia. On his return from service as an artilleryman in Italy in World War One, Walter began to work in his father's company, taking the helm on Josef's death in 1924.

There was a global depression in the 1920s culminating in the crash of the New York Stock Exchange in 1929, after which national protectionism in Germany spread, with exports shrinking and unemployment growing. Walter commanded a great presence, and his achievements were many and varied.

Shortly after the war broke out, Walter began making fine, spinable fiberglass for the production of rope wool. Another industrialist, Werner Schuller developed a new method for spinning fiberglass without platinum, which was patented.

The Ministry of Aviation recognised a military application for this material, and more or less coerced Riedel and Schuller to enter a joint venture to produce it. The Ministry then asked Walter if he could produce a 76 centimetre glass screen, when at that time, the maximum achievable was only 38 centimeters, and no one thought it possible to produce a screen of more than this. Three weeks after being asked, Walter turned up in Berlin with a 76 centimeter tube, astonishing the military with his technical wizardry, for which ironically he was later to pay with ten years of his life.

The end came for the Riedel company in May 1945, when the Russians marched into Polaun from the north and Czech partisans swept in from the south. Walter Riedel received an order from the new Czechoslovakian government to continue to run the now nationalized company - the entire Riedel fortune was claimed by the state - two hundred years and eight generations of work disappeared virtually overnight. Sixteen days after the US dropped the atomic bomb on Hiroshima, Walter Riedel was taken into custody, and was sent to a camp in Eastern Siberia, thereafter being transferred to Russia as a "forced contractor," where at first he helped to rebuild Russian glass factories. When his five-year contract was up, Walter tried to leave, but the Russians had other plans. He appealed to the Austrian Embassy in Moscow, only to be arrested as a spy for allegedly telling the Embassy about his work - he was sentenced to 25 years imprisonment. After Stalin's death and German Chancellor Adenauer's great efforts on behalf of prisoners of war, however, he was able to return home in 1955.

Claus Josef Riedel (1925-2004) 9th generation, made his great leap to freedom, ending up in Austria, where finally the Riedel fortune took a turn for the better.

Claus had landed 17 kilometers from the village where one of his fellow prisoners lived. He walked to the village through the snow in his thin cotton prison uniform, until he reached the village, where he was given a warm welcome. The head of the local glassworks, Swarovski, had heard that there was a Riedel in town and asked to see him. Swarovski had been taught the art of glass making by Claus's great grandfather Josef, and took Claus under his wing like a son, even sending him to university to study chemistry.

Claus Riedel, now married to Italian Adia, whom he had met in Italy during the war, moved around doing various jobs between 1951 and 1956, ending up in Innsbruck, Austria. This was around the time that the Swarovskis were approached to take over a glass works in the small town of Kufstein near Innsbruck in Austria, but they declined as the production of stemware did not fit their profile. Claus had no capital to buy the works, but the Swarovskis advanced him the money, and Claus took over the bankrupt Tiroler Glashütte, today's Riedel factory.

After a period of readjustment, Walter threw himself into the new business with his son, but they had quite different ideas in terms of priorities - Claus was very keen on the production of stemware and Walter preferred high output items. This led to an inevitable conflict. Such conflict between the two generations was considered very healthy in the Riedel family, leading to the family motto - "stoke the fire, don't save the ashes."

The Riedel glassworks had a brand new direction - unadorned, delicate, fine wine glasses. In his 1961 catalogue, Claus Riedel displayed for the first time his vision of glasses specially made to enhance specific styles of wine, distinguishing the Riedel company more than ever before, as to date fashion in stemware had been dictated purely by aesthetics, not function. The handmade Sommeliers Series was launched in 1973, introducing the revolutionary new concept to the wine trade and changing the world of wineglasses forever. In his research into how the shape of a glass affects the wine inside, Claus discovered one major factor - that virtually every glass people drank wine from was too small to do justice to the wine. The Sommeliers Series was showered with prizes from around the world.

Georg Josef Riedel (born 1949) 10th generation, further developed Claus's theories, producing grape-specific glasses, and mechanizing the production of fine wine glasses with his Vinum series, making Riedel glasses far more affordable to wine lovers the world over. A milestone in the modern Riedel company is the founding of a Riedel company in the United States, which came about following an encounter between Robert Mondavi and Georg Riedel, showing real commitment to the US market.

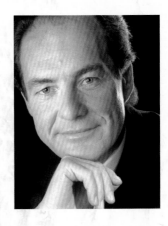

While Claus was a talented designer, as recognised by the National Olympic Committee when they commissioned him to design and produce vases for the 1968 Olympic Games, his son Georg brought a calming, analytical eye to the business, soon spotting weaknesses in the corporate structure. As Georg took over more and more of the strategy for the business, Claus gradually became less involved, until Georg took the helm of the company in 1987. Georg has made it his life's work to develop specific glasses to enhance individual wines, travelling around the world to carry out workshops with experts in their field to develop a whole array of glasses from Tinto Reserva to the Single Malt glass. As the world of wine continues to chance, Riedel will always have scope to develop yet more glasses.

Maximilian Josef Riedel (born 1977) 11th generation, who runs the Riedel company in the US, has already very much made his mark in the world of wine glasses, with the development of Riedel O - stemless wine glasses, which are wine specific. This relaxed approach to glassware has already achieved amazing success, showing that there is always room on the market for new ideas and innovation.

Georg's tremendous talent for strategic thinking led to the Riedel acquisition of the German glass company FX Nachtmann in 2004. Georg took this momentous decision for the Riedel company because he sees potential for incredible growth in the machine-made glass sector. There will always be a market for fine, hand-made glasses, but on the machine-made side of things, there is far more competition and it is vital to remain ahead of the game. The three brands now in the Riedel stable - Riedel, Spiegelau and Nachtmann will be positioned clearly in the market place. Georg is living up to the impressive past of his ancestors through sheer determination, in, dedication and forward-thinking to ensure the continued success of the Riedel Company for generations to come. A springboard has been created for penetration into markets all over the world, and the Riedel company is now poised for the next leap...

The Contributors

" Each year, I conduct dozens of glass tastings in the U.S. I always start by saying... "I'm Georg Riedel and I'm here to complicate your life." This usually gets a laugh. "

The Riedel glass tasting is a practical, sensory exercise that answers the question: Does the shape of the glass influence the perception of the wine? For the thousands of people who attend our glass tastings (even the biggest skeptics) the answer is a resounding "yes."

When I first started preaching the gospel that wine glass shape matters to wine enjoyment, there were far more skeptics than believers, but I was just getting started. We had been making varietally specific stemware since 1973, and in 1986 I introduced the Vinum collection, which is still our best-selling collection. A very pivotal event in Riedel's success in the U.S was a meeting I had on October 17, 1989 with Robert Mondavi in London. Now, at that point, we were still not well known in America and I was hoping this meeting might change that.

We were both invited by Harrod's Department Store to do a joint tasting where Mondavi would show his wines and I would show my glasses. As it turned out, we first met the morning of the presentation at the Connaught Hotel. I introduced myself to him and we talked for a few minutes; I think he must have been a bit jet-lagged as he did not make much of an impression on me at that moment. I explained what the glasses do for wine and how the shape of a glass could change how people tasted the wines; how some could show more tannins while other shapes would highlight the wine's harmony and balance. I tried to explain, although perhaps not so successfully, that it was the perception of the wine that would change, not the actual wines. But Mondavi was not impressed, perhaps even a little angry, and finally said, " I've never heard such nonsense." That was not the reaction I was looking for.

Later that evening everything changed. The night was a total delight. During the tasting it became apparent that it was almost as if his wines were made to sit in our Vinum glasses. Mondavi must have agreed, because when I was speaking to the audience he interrupted my speech and yelled out, "Can you taste the difference? This is amazing!" I couldn't believe it, but I was thrilled he admitted it because if Mondavi, the most important winemaker in America, at that time, believed our glasses could make his wines taste better then I knew others would certainly pay attention and follow.

"Georg Riedel first met with Robert Mondavi in the 1970's a meeting that proved monumental for the Napa Valley and an entire industry evolved."   MH

In January 1990, I went with Angelo Gaja, who at the time was representing Mondavi, to California where I met Mondavi's sons, Michael and Tim. I took this opportunity to talk with them about our glasses. Tim agreed to do a glass tasting with me and invited the winery's technicians, winemakers and management to participate as well. It was clear he had the idea I was a little nuts -- he even told me he originally thought "there is a difference between a water glass and wine glass, but not that much." After our tasting Tim had changed his mind -- in fact, he didn't even join us for lunch. The reason? He was too amazed. He stayed behind continuing to taste the wines from our glasses. He believed!

After these two events, the Mondavi family decided to change all of their glassware to Riedel as they recognized that our glasses showed their wines in the best possible light. They became the first winery in North America to use only Riedel glasses and they became very good customers and great friends.

So by now, you may be wondering how Riedel glasses "work." By creating glasses that deliver the typical components of a grape variety, the glass highlights balanced flavors, maximizes fruit and integrates acidity or tannins into the overall pleasure of wine enjoyment. A person interested in wine is led by color, bouquet and taste, but often the glass is not considered as an instrument to convey the message of the wine. Riedel recognizes the complex role that size and shape play in expressing the character of a fine wine. Our glasses are created in workshops, not on a drawing board. It is an organoleptic, rather than engineering, feat. Most of our glasses have been developed in workshops with winemakers and sommeliers and reflect a consensus of great palates.

Bouquet: When wine is poured, the bouquet immediately starts to evaporate and its aromas fill the glass in layers according to their density and gravity.

Taste: Every wine has its own blend of fruit, acidity, minerals, tannin and alcohol that are based on the grape variety, climate and soil in which it is grown.

Shape: To fully appreciate the different grape varieties and the characteristics of individual wines, it is essential to have a glass whose shape is fine-tuned for the purpose. The shape is responsible for the quality and intensity of the bouquet and the flow of the wine.

Size: The size of the glass affects the quality and intensity of aromas. Simply put, red wines generally require large glasses, white wines medium-sized glasses and spirits small glasses (to emphasize the fruit character and not the alcohol).

Serving Quantities: The glass should never be over-filled.
Red wine: three to four ounces; white wine: three ounces; spirits: one ounce.

My glasses are the "loudspeaker" for the winemakers and their vineyards. Because they give so much thought and heart in making wine, we are not allowed to miss anything. From the earth to the senses, I want to make sure the chain isn't interrupted. I want to make the best possible glass to show off the greatness, complexity and beauty of wine.

DECANTING FOR PLEASURE
MAXIMILIAN RIEDEL

" Many times I have been asked if the decanter makes a difference, the way the glass shape does. It does, but not in the same way. "

Riedel has been producing decanters for hundreds of years. Decanting is the key that opens the door to wine enjoyment. There are two reasons we decant wines. One, in the case of an older wine, to separate it from its sediment. Two, in young wines, to increase the oxygenation, which in turn then reveals more complexity and opens up the aromas and flavors. It is the latter reason that is of great interest to me.

Decanting a young wine is like putting it through a time machine — to a future where the tannins are supple and integrated, the bouquet fully developed, the acidity balanced and the flavor long and satisfying. If you are among the fortunate few who have an extensive cellar where wine slowly reaches its maturity, you can let Mother Nature take its course. For the rest of us, decanting brings the wine forward so that we don't sit around saying to each other, "I wonder what this will taste like in five years?" or "Awfully tight!"

Few people take the time to decant, even though it is to their benefit (and their guests'). Most simply pop the cork a few minutes before sitting down to dinner, whether it is an everyday or celebration wine. Yet decanting young wines takes no more than a minute and is richly rewarding. Some people feel it will be viewed as pretentious, but I think it makes your guests feel special—you did something extra for them. Other people complain that they want to show off the bottle and let their guests look at the label -- but that is precisely why Riedel makes a wine bottle coaster (though even a saucer would do). I think the underlying reason is simply that no one has demonstrated to them the enormous difference that decanting imparts on a wine. Drinking is believing. For anyone who holds that decanting is just another snobby wine ritual, I challenge you to buy two bottles of the same wine. Decant one and serve the other from the bottle -- then draw your own conclusion.

" Maximilian Riedel shares with great pride his family business. And he is also a very talented and innovative designer in his own right." MH

In the last few years, Riedel has pushed the envelope in designing decanters, creating dramatic sculptural shapes that seem to soar off the table. Because Riedel owns all of our factories, we have the freedom to challenge our glass artisans to create whatever Georg and I dream up. Sometimes it can take a year to fine-tune the design, but we think the end result is worth it. Although our decanters have esthetic appeal, they are built first for function -- to unlock the mystery of a wine otherwise imprisoned in a bottle. Further, it is important to understand the different functions that a decanter serves -- and which one fits a particular wine.

If you are decanting a very old wine to separate it from its sediment, then you want a decanter with a very small surface area. In that case, the structure is simple. However, for a young wine, you want to introduce as much oxygen as possible and several of our new decanters (EVE, Face to Face and Flamingo) do just that.

It is not simply the large surface area that oxygenates the wine—it is the active physical act of swirling the wine within the decanter and then pouring it. We've all sat in restaurants swirling and swirling our wine in a vain attempt to get it to show its potential. The EVE decanter double-decants your wine as it flows through the coiled shape. Serving wine becomes a performance as the decanter's twists and turns require the same movement by you—turning the decanter in a slow 360 degree rotation to 'charge' the decanter and allow the wine to pour. We recently had a laboratory in Germany test the efficacy of the EVE decanter and the findings were surprising -- even to us. The EVE introduced seven times more oxygen into the wine than pouring from the bottle.

Decanting off the sediment of an old wine is a gentle, slow process, but decanting young wines should be vigorous. Don't be afraid to upend the bottle into the decanter. Swirl the decanter until you see a foam cap on top. Our Face to Face decanter is a striking design, but the real purpose of the two inward looking faces is to act as paddles to aerate the wine.

Wine enjoyment begins the moment a bottle is uncorked. How you handle the wine from there on can significantly affect the level of pleasure you derive from it — and Riedel has always been committed to extracting the last iota of pleasure out of a bottle of wine. That means not just having the right wine glass, but decanting it properly as well. The right decanter, used in the manner for which it is designed, will open the door to a wine's enjoyment.

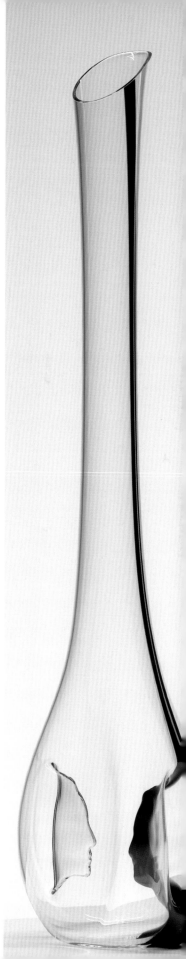

" Using a structured method of tasting can deepen our understanding and appreciation of wine."

As Sommeliers we learn to taste wine analytically. Starting with our most basic senses, sight, smell, and taste - we begin to assess wine, often with the intention of concluding the appellation, grape varieties, vintage and quality level of the wine. Beyond this sensory evaluation, a strong knowledge of wine theory can help to understand what all of this information really means. We begin by focusing on the appearance of the wine. Looking at the wine closely, we consider details such as the brightness, color, clarity, concentration of color, viscosity, sediment and the variation in color from the center to the rim of the wine.

The Brightness level can help us assess age. A youthful wine is often very bright - or even brilliant; a mature wine may be slightly dull. The Color can provide an indication of the growing climate, grape varieties, wine-making methods and age of the wine. A white wine may be clear, pale green, straw, golden, amber or brownish in appearance. A red wine may be purple, ruby, red, garnet, brick or even brownish. Warmer climates, thicker grape skins, longer macerations and more oak influence generally produce more color in wine. Age and oxidation will eventually turn wines brown.

The Clarity and Concentration of Color can help us assess climate, the thickness of the grape skins and the amount of time the juice spent on the skins. Cooler climates generally produce lighter, more translucent wines. Warmer climates cause thicker grape skins and thus, darker or even opaque wines.

Finding Sediment in our wine can give us an indication that a wine has aged and possibly reached maturity. Viscosity can tip us off to higher alcohol or residual sugar levels in a wine. Glycerin, a natural by-product of fermentation, will add viscosity - as will higher sugar levels. We check this by swirling the wine and looking at the "tears" or "legs" on the side of the glass. The higher the alcohol and/or residual sugar, the slower the tears will form and fall. Thicker red grape skins may also cause staining of the tears.

Rim variation can help indicate the age of the wine - or even the grape variety. As I mentioned, brown is an indication of more age and oxidation. Certain grapes will also provide very unique rim colors. For example, Nebbiolo usually has an orange rim and Malbec usually has an intensely bright purple rim.

Next we'll enjoy the aromatic qualities of the wine. We gently swirl our glass to help vaporize some of the wine's alcohol and release more of its natural aromas before smelling the wine.

"Dennis Kelly is the Head Sommelier at The French Laundry and he is able to – quite flawlessly – engage and educate the reader at the same time." MH

Initially we look for obvious flaws like cork taint (chemical compounds 2,4,6-trichloroanisole), barnyard aromas (a spoilage yeast called brettanomyces), reduction (hydrogen sulfide), burnt match aromas (sulfur dioxide), volatility (volatile acids which smell like nail polish remover) and oxidation (sherry-like aromas created by exposure to oxygen). We then assess the fruit, earth, oak and other secondary aromas. It is important to understand that while we can smell hundreds of unique scents, our taste perception is limited to sweet, sour, salt, bitter and umami. It is the combination of smell and taste that allows us to discern flavor.

White wine offers citrus fruits like lemon, lime, grapefruit and tangerine - orchard fruits including apple, pear and quince - and stone fruits like peach, apricot and plum. In red wine I find red fruits including cranberry, raspberry and strawberry - and black and blue fruits such as blackberry, cassis and blueberry. Fruits like cherries, plums and currants can be either red or black. The fruit aromas in wine can smell fresh, baked or dried... super-ripe, just-ripe, or under-ripe.

Earth aromas and flavors may include organic components like plant materials - or inorganic components such as minerals. Common examples of organic earth aromas might include wet leaves, grass and hay. Minerality can translate into the glass in the form of chalk, slate, iron, gravel and granite just for starters.

The most commonly used Oak species are French and American oak. French oak imparts subtle baking spices including cinnamon, nutmeg, allspice and clove while American oak contributes forward vanilla, dill, coconut, and sawdust aromas. A higher percentage of new oak usage will usually result in a more obvious influence on the wine.

Additional secondary aromas may include floral, herbaceous and spice aromas. Common floral aromas include rose petals (Barolo), violets (Margaux), honeysuckle (Viognier), lime blossoms (Riesling) and potpourri (Gewurztraminer). Herbaceous qualities are often found in grape varieties such as Sauvignon Blanc, Cabernet Franc and Cabernet Sauvignon. As I mentioned, spice can come from oak - or it can be varietal as is the case with Pinot Gris, Gruner-Veltliner and Zinfandel.

Finally we can taste the wine. We start with a small sip and let it roll around our tongue. I prefer to focus on the structure of the wine during the attack phase (the initial impression that the wine makes on your palate). The structure includes the body (weight), as well as the residual sugar (dryness or sweetness), alcohol, acidity, and tannin levels of the wine. These components form tactile impressions, but not necessarily true flavors like fruit or spice.

Next is the mid-palate. In this phase we are looking to discern the flavor profile of the wine. This will include the fruit, earth and oak flavors and perhaps some spice.

The wine's finish is the length the flavor impression lasts after it is swallowed. At this point I also consider the balance and complexity of the wine. Ideally all of these components will be harmonious and seamless, with no component more prominent than the others. A highly complex wine will offer endless layers of flavors throughout the tasting experience.

As we become more comfortable with these concepts, we tend to get more satisfaction and enjoyment out of wine. And really .... isn't that what wine tasting is all about?

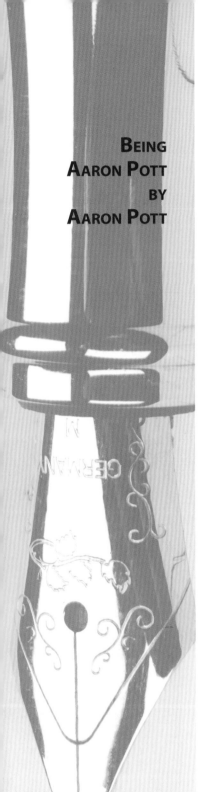

BEING
AARON POTT
BY
AARON POTT

"Aaron was asked to write because he is a gifted and unconventional wine writer as evident in his monthly column in *The Atlantic Journal*. He is also a brilliant winemaker creating numerous vintages of Quintessa, Blackbird and his own label Pott Wine."   MH

" Does it bring me pleasure? If the answer is "yes", then you can start thinking about why, and then you can start understanding what you like in wine and not what other people tell you to like."

The question that I get asked more often than any other is, "How do you taste wine?" The answer to this question is not an easy one. I have been making wine for over 20 years now and the exercise of tasting, of sensory analysis has become so automatic and precise that I rarely deconstruct it to think where it comes from. I have made an effort to try and pick apart what I look for and have come up with a list of ten attributes which I find very important.

Typicity: "Mile Davis' sessions were not typical of anybody else's sessions. They were totally unique."

Herbie Hancock

Typicity is not an English word but it should be. In French they call it Typicité, my dog-eared Larousse dictionary describes it as "The ensemble of characteristics that make a food product unique." If you are drinking a Pinot Noir, typicity is what helps us recognize it as a Pinot Noir. It is also what tempers the urge to overdo a wine, to obliterate its natural characteristics. Typicity is best served when the winemaker translates flawlessly the poetry of the vineyard into the wine without fuss and ornament.

Sense of Place: "People also leave presence in a place even when they are no longer there."

Andy Goldsworthy

What makes great wines great? The simple answer is that great wines come from great vineyards. These vineyards through their unique sites, climates, soils and history produce wines that are great and speak most clearly of where they are from. Typicity and sense of place are intertwined: a wine with a sense of place has typicity and wine that shows typicity shows a sense of place.

Complexity: "Armageddon is not around the corner. This is only what the people of violence want us to believe. The complexity and diversity of the world is the hope for the future."

Michael Palin

Complexity is the simplest element of wine to explain. It merely means that there are a lot of different flavors and aromas in a wine that are unique. Wine can be complex and bad but wine cannot be simple and great. The key to complexity is integration, which allows wines that are complex to seem like one seamless experience with many different singular sensations. Imagine a train ride through a varying and beautiful countryside, where we are never at a loss for things to look at and never crack the spine on that book we brought.

Integration: "This production of Cinderella, it's very integrated. The step-mother is played by a man, and we have Asians, blacks, whites, gay boys, straight boys. It's all wonderful."

Eartha Kitt

Integration is when all of the complex elements come together. In wine we don't want any hard edges or anything that dominates too much. We want wines to have integration not only of the many complex aromas and flavors but also tannin integration. All wine has a shape when you put it into your mouth, from the very first drop on your palate you get sensations of texture, density and flavor. Ideally they should intensify in value gradually and taper off into a long finish. The less there are holes and interruptions in the symmetry of these perceived sensations the more we have integration.

Elegance: "Elegance is not the prerogative of those who have just escaped from adolescence, but of those who have already taken possession of their future."

Coco Chanel

Surprisingly, elegance in wine is a controversial subject. The Oxford English Dictionary defines it perfectly as "refined grace in form." Elegant wines can be light in body but they can also be weighty. Elegant wines don't necessarily need to be complex but most certainly are integrated. Elegance can be the type of aromas that we get in the nose or the supplest of velvety tannins that meld perfectly into the wine. I remember Chateau Latour winemaker Jean-Louis Mandrau describing a wine as "little Jesus in velvet underpants," or a friend's description of a lovely Italian Refosco as, "Audrey Hepburn on a Vespa." Man! That is elegant.

Aaron Pott
Continued

Length: "The moment at which two people, approaching from opposite ends of a long passageway, recognize each other and immediately pretend they haven't. This is to avoid the ghastly embarrassment of having to continue recognizing each other the whole length of the corridor."

Douglas Adams

Length is just a question of time. The time that the positive sensations of the wine stay on your palate, the length of time that flavor is perceived after the wine has been swallowed. An hour after a wonderful lunch and a bottle of 1990 Le Bon Pasteur, I remember emitting a horrendous satisfied belch and discovered that the dense black fruit flavor of the wine was still perceptible in my mouth.

Balance: "What I dream of is an art of balance, of purity and serenity devoid of troubling or depressing subject matter - a soothing, calming influence on the mind, rather like a good armchair which provides relaxation from physical fatigue."

Henri Matisse

Integration is the coming together of all the separate elements of wine but balance is the elegant duel of opposites. Flavor and Oak, quality of tannins whether they are dry or sweet in perception and alcohol are among the many things that we look at to see whether a wine is balanced. The ideal example of this crossing of swords is the duel between acid and perceived sweetness. The smallest excess in acidity can make wines seem thin and dry, while the lack of acidity makes wines seem tired, cloying and lacking in freshness.

Power: "When power leads man toward arrogance, poetry reminds him of his limitations. When power narrows the area of man's concern, poetry reminds him of the richness and diversity of existence. When power corrupts, poetry cleanses."

John F. Kennedy

Power is the perceived intensity of many wine components. When it is balanced and integrated it is a good element. When it is monolithic and lacks complexity, it is boring and ponderous. In my opinion power is overrated in wines. One can have wonderful wines that are complex, elegant, pleasurable and balanced with great length but that are not powerful. Powerful wines can be elegant as well.

Texture: "The web, then, or the pattern, a web at once sensuous and logical, an elegant and pregnant texture: that is style that is the foundation of the art of literature."

Robert Louis Stevenson

Texture is a quality that the tannin gives to wine. The important thing to realize about tannin is that it differs in quantity and quality in wines. A wine can be very tannic but have very good quality tannin, what we in the trade would call "fine grained." That is to say that perception of the tannin is not dry but dense. Fine-grained tannins support wines like flying buttresses hold up great cathedrals. Wide-grain tannins give us the feeling that we have little wool sweaters that have been individually hand-knit for each of our teeth; they dry at the gum line. Tannins help with perceived density and extend length. Dry wide-grain tannins in young wines stay dry forever and never come around with age. Wines with fine-grained tannins soften well with age and are excellent for long-term storage.

Pleasure : "Why not seize the pleasure at once? How often is happiness destroyed by preparation, foolish preparation!"

Jane Austen

In the end the only question is: Do I like this? I have had many wines that for whatever reason I have personally loved. Maybe it was the beautiful vineyard, maybe the presence of a special person, or a myriad of other reasons that influence the taste of a wine. When I am clouded by outside sentiments I call this the "Cassis Effect" after the small seaside town in southern France. It is a stunning place, a small port town that has immense cliffs nearby that fall abruptly into the Mediterranean. The wine is always fantastic there as you sip it on the terrace of a restaurant looking out over the masts of sailboats in the harbor. I have made the mistake of serving it to friends here in the States after exporting it back and found it to be severely lacking, leaving only the taste of the subtle bitterness of friendly chiding.

Does it bring me pleasure? If the answer is "yes", then you can start thinking about why and then you can start understanding what you like in wine and not what other people tell you to like.

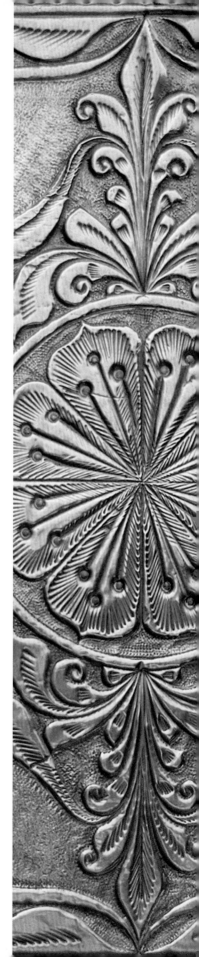

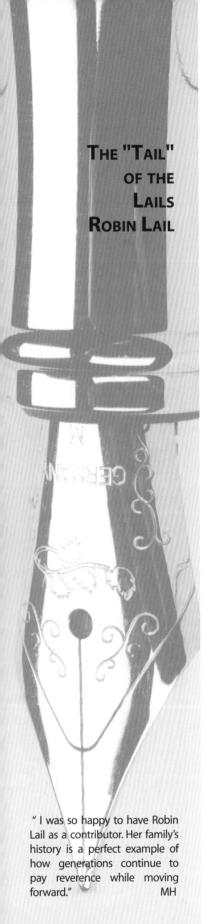

John Daniel, Jr. often said...
" Napa Valley can produce wines
which are second to none in the world."

Lail Vineyards, founded in 1995, and led by its managing partner, Robin Daniel Lail, sits atop a foundation of 130 years of Napa Valley winemaking history and tradition. The company traces its roots back five generations to the founding of Inglenook Vineyards in 1879, by Robin's great grand-uncle, Captain Gustav Niebaum.

Niebaum was born in Helsinki, Finland in 1842, and began his lifetime love affair with the sea at twelve. Graduating from the Nautical Institute at nineteen, he enlisted in the Russian navy and was stationed in the Pribilof Islands until the time of the Alaskan Purchase in 1867. Niebaum then joined a trading company in San Francisco dealing in seal furs. Extensive travels in Europe included many visits to the great winemaking regions of France and Germany, and a new avocation – wine.

After several years, Niebaum determined to enter the wine business and bought property in Napa Valley and founded Inglenook Vineyards. It would be safe to say that he was obsessed with excellence in all that he did, and the wine business was no exception.

A great innovator, he pioneered double sorting, bottling in glass, developing and marketing a brand, meter-by-meter vineyard planting and numerous other contributions to the industry. By the 1890's his wines were winning gold medals in Paris.

Following his death in 1908, the winery was taken over by John Daniel, Sr., Niebaum's nephew. The wine business was in steep decline due to a serious recession, phylloxera in the vineyards and the rise of the prohibitionists culminating in Prohibition (1920-1933).

John Daniel, Sr. replanted the vineyards at Inglenook and the grapes were boxed and sold during Prohibition as the winery was closed.

" I was so happy to have Robin Lail as a contributor. Her family's history is a perfect example of how generations continue to pay reverence while moving forward." MH

Third generation John Daniel, Jr. began working in the vineyards in the summers of his high school and college years. On the repeal of Prohibition he re-opened Inglenook. The wines made during Daniel's tenure are legendary today. Critics and winemakers alike ponder what is behind the vivid liveliness of wines he made in the 1940's and 1950's.

Daniel's vision in the wine business was an extension of Niebaum before him. He and his protégé, Robert Mondavi, were extremely important to the reconstruction of the wine business. He was the first to put Napa Valley as an appellation on a bottle of wine, a co-founder of the Vintners Association, and repeated Chairman of many industry organizations. He was a pillar of the industry, not only in Napa Valley, but in California as well.

The winery was sold in 1964 and many thought the young dynasty was over. However the weaving of the tapestry began again in 1970 when Robin Daniel Lail took over the management of her family vineyards upon the death of her father. The settlement of Daniel's estate made additional changes and by 1974 the only vineyard remaining was Napanook in Yountville.

In 1977 Robin began a five-year apprenticeship with Robert Mondavi during the course of which she was instrumental in building the first Napa Valley Wine Auction in 1981. Mondavi became her mentor in the business and introduced her to Christian Moueix with whom she subsequently co-founded Dominus at Napanook in 1982.

The following year she co-founded Merryvale Vineyards and served as President of the firm for eleven years. While it was her hope that one of these ventures would carry forward the Inglenook legacy, neither did so for a variety of reasons.

In 1995 the Lail family sold their interests in these other wineries which were extraordinary training grounds. They turned to the rich history of their inherited tradition. Robin, her husband Jon, and their daughters Erin and Shannon carry forward the baton into the 21st Century and have reached into the sixth generation, naming their Grave style Sauvignon Blanc "Georgia" after Erin's first daughter.

Today Lail Vineyards produces the J. Daniel Cuvée Cabernet Sauvignon, Georgia and two sister wines, Blueprint Cabernet Sauvignon and Blueprint Sauvignon Blanc.

John Daniel, Jr. often said, "Napa Valley can produce wines which are second to none in the world." His children and grandchildren revel in the family tradition of producing wines of brilliance.

"These are the vintners do not have a tasting room of their own, and crave exposure and advocacy."

In the late 1990s, my husband Garret and I realized just how many amazing Napa winemakers there were who produce phenomenal wines, yet are just under the radar of the national press and the general wine-public.

Many times these are the vintners who work for renown labels, and produce their own handcrafted projects on the side. They are creative mavericks, whether they are newcomers to Napa Valley or were raised here amongst the vines. These are the vintners who do not have a tasting room of their own, and who crave exposure and advocacy. Their wines are so much like the heirloom tomatoes found at our local farmers market...our vintners begin their odyssey with grapes that have been carefully and lovingly farmed, and magically craft them into wine.

At the same time, we always felt that consumers across the United States who are truly passionate about wine have a real desire to dig deeper; to know more, to understand the ever-changing connections between the winemakers, the wineries, the vineyards and the people that make up the under-current of Napa Valley.

We wanted to find a way to bring these talented winemakers and passionate clients together. In 2002, with the help of family and friends — and with Garret's background in food and wine and mine in design — we took the plunge. Vintner's Collective is a select group of boutique Napa Valley Vintners who share a bonded tasting room space. The germination of our idea coincided nicely with the growth of the City of Napa as a destination in its own right. By this I mean, as opposed to a blur on Highway 29 while driving to what locals call 'Up Valley.

We were lucky enough to build our business in Napa's oldest commercial building. Built in 1875, the exterior is Italianate

"Kim and Garret Murphy restored Napa's oldest building and are in the center of Napa's renaissance." MH

architecture, and the inside was home to a former saloon and brothel. This place is as much a part of who we are as the wine and people it brings together! From two employees in 2002, we've grown to a staff of eleven. What a thrill!

While built on a philosophy of advocacy, our commitment to the highest quality wines has kept our exclusive group of vintners to a small number. Among our Vintners are Melka Wines, Mi Sueño Winery, Buoncristiani Family Winery, Clark-Claudon, and Vinoce Vineyards.

We are our customer's friends and enthusiastic guides, opening Napa Valley's doors to them. Napa seems to be on everyone's lips these days, with an explosion of world-class restaurants opening steps from Vintner's Collective, on or near the Napa River.

There is an energy growing here, from restaurants such as La Toque, Ubuntu, Fish Story and Tyler Florence Rotisserie, to nightlife and small shops. We have always had a collection of charming inns and B&B's but now larger luxury resorts such as The Westin Verasa have opened. It is a "boomtown" once again, and makes us reminisce about the immigrants, miners and cowboys of old. Many people came by river, and brought dreams of fortune and gold.

We're looking forward to the day that visitors can take a ferry up from San Francisco, hop off at the Riverfront, taste amazing wines at Vintner's Collective, and finish with an unforgettable meal.

Our city is on the rise! In 2002, we fell in love and restored Napa's oldest stone building, which we are lucky enough to call home. We look forward to many years of unfolding its old stories. Vintner's Collective now has two wine clubs and our own online store. We also host candle-lit winemaker dinners and release parties in our beloved, old building. Recognizing the need to help our friends and clients, we have grown to include a concierge service and our very own Napa guesthouse, which we call La Casita Bonita. (The pretty one!) At the end of the day, Vintner's Collective has a true love story with the city of Napa, where it all began.

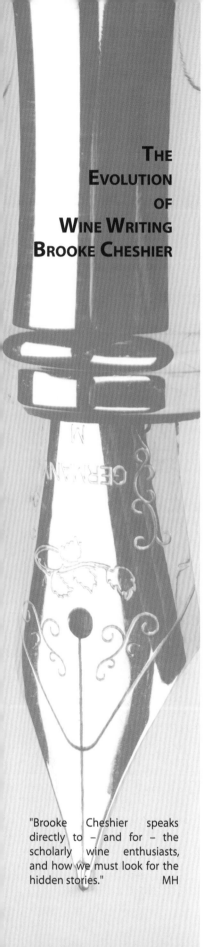

"Brooke Cheshier speaks directly to – and for – the scholarly wine enthusiasts, and how we must look for the hidden stories." MH

" I still believe writing about the world's great winemaking talents – in Napa Valley, Bordeaux, Austria, Australia or even Israel – is the best way to show gratitude for their existence."

"Great wines open up the possibilities," New York Times wine critic Eric Asimov said recently. I believe great wine writing does, too. Every wine has a story to tell, with a plot that often hinges on the hardworking men – and women – dragging the hoses, punching down the caps and tending to their barrels like babies.

There are the Doug Fletchers pioneering stainless steel fermentations in the Napa Valley, and the Sara Saffirios honing centuries-old winemaking traditions up in the fog-shrouded hills of Barolo. She is the second generation of females to coax the most bewitching Nebbiolos out of her grandfather's ten-acre calcareous-clay vineyard, and the world should get to know the artistry she infuses into her wine. Of course, every winery has a story it wants to convey. It is the job of the wine writer to find the authentic story, which may or may not be the fairy tale spun by a good PR company.

Thanks in large part to wine blogging, wine writing today is not just tasting notes, scores and PR shelf talkers. This new guard of wine writers works to uncover the history, culture, and politics of wine – all of the angles that make it so fascinating to so many people. Not that they (we) are the first to do it.

As a blogger, I take my cues from the great wine journalists, from Frank Prial, Petie and Don Kladstrup, Eric Asimov and Alice Feiring. Old guard? Perhaps. But they're strong swimmers and certainly not in danger of being swept away by the new surge of bloggers. In fact, Asimov and Feiring now pen two of my favorite blogs. I also emulate less traditional folk, like interactive-designer-by-day-and-wine-cyberstar-by-night Alder Yarrow. The man credited with pioneering the wine blog concept, Alder is a straight shooter who believes wine reminds us that we are human. "And celebrates just how magical that is." Wine blogs like Alder's Vinography inspire readers to start their own conversations and create their own wine stories.

"Wine is as close as we get to true alchemy. The transformation of grapes into wine is a proxy for the fulfillment of our hopes and dreams And when we taste wine in all its flavors and aromas we are using our bodies and minds at their peak of complexity. Wine reminds us that we are human, and celebrates just how magical that is."

Alder Yarrow
Vinography.com

And they remind me that wine writing does, indeed, matter. It matters because my mother back in Arkansas doesn't know the messy, sweaty, sticky, muscle-tearing work it is to take grapes from the vine, to harvest, haul hoses, move barrels and clean tanks. But she loves to read about it on Verge Winery's blog. Because even the manliest men in St. Paul eventually tire of artisan ales and when they do, they can turn to Star Tribune blogger, Bill Ward, of Ward on Wine, for help.

It matters because poets like Terry Theise remind us that "wines which slide smoothly onto the palate and dance in sync with food are the wines which, paradoxically, have the most to say to us." It matters because my friends know that a good frozen dinner can transport you to a Parisian bistro if you pair it with non-vintage Champagne from Canard-Duchêne. And because Diane over at Napa Farmhouse 1885 has the most beautiful, faintly lavender-scented cookie recipe on her blog, and I know just the Napa Valley dessert wine to pair with it. Wouldn't you like to know, too?

"In old wine, life is given back to us with all the bad stuff removed; no fights, no illnesses, no misery. Only the stately passings of seasons, again and again. Only the love, the strange indifferent love without affection, the love you hear between the notes and the sentiment."

Terry Theise
Reading Between the Vines

I still believe writing about the world's great winemaking talents – in Napa Valley, Bordeaux, Austria, Australia or even Israel – is the best way to show gratitude for their existence. And I still believe that luxuriating in the flavors, smells, textures, preparations and presentations of wine is one of the most beautiful ways to put the eyes, ears, nose, mouth and hands God gave us to good use. Wine writing pulls back the curtain and invites us to see the blistered hands and swollen backs that go into creating such beauty. The stories of these generous, often sunburned, faces are layered and layered…just like so many of my favorite wines.

"I can never emphasize enough that a great wine starts from the roots up. My work does not begin at harvest when the grapes arrive at the winery door. I tend to my grapes year round, monitoring their every stage of development. I envision wine as a wheel, with the vineyard as the hub from which - like spokes - emanate the grapes, the terroir, climate, manual labor, story, winemaking and, last but not least, the many passionate people, all joining in a perfect radius."

Frederic Delivert
Martin Estate Winemaker

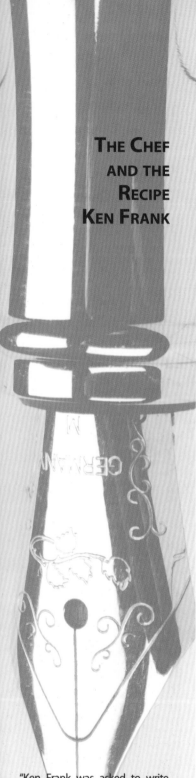

THE CHEF AND THE RECIPE
KEN FRANK

" It typically takes a good week for a dish to mature to the point that I sense it's a "keeper" or not. I know it's a keeper when I start wondering why it took me so long to think of it."

Cooking and sharing food is at the core of our humanity, necessary for our survival but also holding the potential for great pleasure. No doubt, the pleasure has always driven me. Creativity in the kitchen, the freedom to try things your own way, is essential. Over time, great cooks develop a strong sense of personal style, without which eating would be so dull. To be able to express this creativity through cooking and share it with others is deeply satisfying.

Creativity is a loaded word, easily taken too seriously. I always tell people, "every combination has already been tried, you're just doing your own version." I certainly wasn't the first person to layer slices of duck breast with slices of toasted apple and fan them on a plate with some Calvados sauce. Nonetheless, when I put it on my menu in 1976 with a little asterisk denoting that it was a "creation" of the chef, it was a pretty novel idea and I got a lot of credit for it.

So where do recipes come from? Where do you get the idea that sparks your imagination? Certainly the most direct way to come up with a recipe is to pick up a cookbook for inspiration. I consider a book to be worthy if it has even just one good idea. You might wonder is that stealing? It's only stealing if you copy the formula for Coca Cola and try to make a profit. Ideas can come from anywhere. I get ideas from talking with people about meals they've enjoyed, from pictures, eating in restaurants famous and not, and once in a rare while, just out of the blue. The best chefs, truly comfortable with their métier, are eager to share their "secrets." I've always been of a mind that if someone can take one of "my" dishes and make it better, more power to them.

An idea starts with the assumption that something seems like it would taste good. From there it burrows into the mind, filtering through a web of taste memories and experiences. If it's a really good idea it will persist until the mind spits out version 1.0.

By now I can begin to taste it mentally. No need to start cooking yet, but I'm onto something. Typically the idea will rattle around a few more days in my head, refining itself. If the idea matures to the point of craving, it's time to start making room for it on the menu.

Even when something is ready for the menu, there's really no need to write anything down yet, unless there's a component like a dough or batter that would need to be measured. My kitchen has always run on a thread of oral history with the older cooks passing along our way of doing things to the newer ones. Sure, we eventually get around to writing recipes down when they've long been perfected, but in the early stages we just talk about how and then do it.

Now it's time to practice. Cooking isn't rocket science, it takes lots and lots of practice. Every night as we make something over and over the little touches, some technical, others aesthetic, that make something really good begin to come into focus. It typically takes a good week for a dish to mature to the point that I sense it's a "keeper" or not. I know it's a keeper when I start wondering why it took me so long to think of it.

S..L..O..W
FOOD
MOVEMENT
TINA AND CHRIS
CARPENTER

"As this cookbook grew, I knew we must include The Slow Food Movement. Christopher and Tina Carpenter have been instrumental in promoting this philosophy and the amazing success of the national movement." MH

" Napa Valley Slow Food kicked off its activities in 1998. Since that time, we have held over 50 events in the Napa Valley, highlighting a diverse collection of farmers, food producers, culinary artists and their associated restaurants and beverage producers..."

We live in a world of speed! Our success is measured by how quickly and how efficiently we are able to accomplish tasks. Our careers and our business success is not only mandated by quality but also often predicated on being the first out of the gate and the winner at the end of the race. Many of us have two jobs, a family and organizations in which we belong and are active.

This is the reality of our culture. With this reality there are consequences.

Stress is a real and debilitating disease. There is our willingness, sometimes unconsciously, to allow the breakdown and sacrifice of our individual relationships as we pursue our career goals. We sometimes sacrifice how we treat our children and ourselves nutritionally, and how we interact with our communities. We forget the aspect of our community that provides our food as we seek the path of least resistance at the grocery store. Slow Food was formed as a means to explore an alternative and timeless method of approaching these aspects of our lives.

This isn't an easy proposal, we know. Chris is a winemaker and is the Chairman of Slow Food USA's National Board of Directors. Tina operates two businesses and we have two beautiful daughters who need our attention. Needless to say, we are busy. But we have made a real effort to spend an hour to two each day cooking and eating our evening meal together. It doesn't always happen, and we occasionally order a pizza. But the time spent together at the table lets us regroup and center ourselves. And we really look forward to this time each day quite a bit. There is a real joy in slowing oneself down and doing it with a nice meal and a good bottle of wine. We truly believe that if a majority of folk made this a part of their day, we wouldn't see as much of the stress-related problems and crimes we hear about, our children's nutritional and emotional lives would be richer and our communities would be more attuned to the individuals who reside in them. It's about a willingness to rediscover the joys of the table and the flavors of our local farmers and food artisans, and in turn, gain an understanding of how quickly our lives begin and end and what we miss if we speed through it all.

Napa Valley Slow Food kicked off its activities in 1998. Since that time, we have held over 50 events in the Napa Valley, highlighting a diverse collection of farmers, food producers, culinary artists and their associated restaurants, and beverage producers. We have engaged in discussions on food system issues and created awareness around our local food culture. We continue to evolve and become an organization that now looks to the future on how our environment and the political system are interconnected with our food system, our farmers and their methods of production and ultimately how all of these factors affect us as humans and our future generations. It's an amazing time to be involved in these issues, and we hope that through the efforts of all our members and our leadership team we can truly make a difference.

" Tasting anything is specific to the individual and no one is wrong, everyone just tastes differently..."

The evolution of cuisine over the past century has made a profound impact in the way we do things today. Although some chefs are making a move toward specific micro-regional farms and purveyors, most still use major corporations to source their products.

In California and other major agricultural areas we are truly fortunate to walk out our back door and have incredibly fresh local organic products at our fingertips. The use of local and seasonal ingredients gives a personality to the flavors of a region. We see this all over the world and it is becoming much more prevalent in the United States. This strong movement towards micro- regional farming and the advancement in technology has made a definitive change in cuisine forever.

Having just returned from a month-long food and wine tour of almost the entire country of Spain, I feel I have a much better understanding of how important farming and technology are for the evolution of cuisine worldwide. The amount of attention that is paid to the quality of a specific ingredient produced from a specific person and region is unprecedented. This quality driven mindset is seen across the entire country, which in turn puts more pressure on producers to keep increasing quality. The sheer quantity and diversity of products you see just driving along the roads is incredible. It felt like almost every square inch of the country was planted with some kind of food crop. Great food can only be produced from great quality ingredients so I believe the future of cuisine needs to start with farming.

The advancement of technology and molecular gastronomy has taken modern cuisine to previously unimaginable heights. Restaurants like El Bulli, as well as a long list of others, have been instrumental in the progression of perception, technique and innovation. Understanding newer techniques such as sous vide, or the use of emulsifiers and hydrocolloids have allowed us to control our execution of cuisine in a much more precise manner. American chefs such as Thomas Keller and Grant Achatz have taken these techniques and exposed them through their restaurants and cookbooks in America. The use of these tools and techniques enable chefs to attempt their personal aspect of perfection.

Even with access to these tools, chefs are still in pursuit of finding the best quality ingredients before they even enter the rear doors of their kitchens.

Another important aspect regarding the future of cuisine is research. Understanding flavor interactions between the guest and the food is so complex on a scientific level. For example, understanding what makes a dry wine taste sweet when you take a sip while eating artichokes. This specific example can be great with a few wines but distasteful with most. Not only is the science behind food interaction complex, but it is also very subjective to the individual. When you add beverages to the equation the different possibilities of outcomes are exponential. Another factor which is important but many times neglected is ambiance. Lighting, room temperature, indoor or outdoor, table setting, staff demeanor, noise, are all influencing the way people perceive the food. Having added knowledge about these factors will serve as a huge advantage to a dining experience.

The last point I would like to touch on is perception. Subconsciously thinking you don't like something or that a certain product is "bad," tricks your brain, so when you taste that product again all your brain can perceive is "bad, bad, bad." The flavor of the product would be more positive if you just had a clear mind. Whenever I go to dine somewhere, whether it is a casual dinner or fine dining, I try to be as open-minded as possible. I stay in the exact moment rather than think of past experiences which could influence the way I taste. After the meal is finished I then reflect on past experiences and how they relate to the current one. If you don't like a specific product after tasting varied preparations, "you" don't enjoy that specific product. I find it incredibly interesting that two different people can taste the same product and come up with tasting notes that are completely different. This is even more prevalent between males and females. Tasting anything is specific to the individual and no one is wrong, everyone just tastes differently.

After earning a bachelor's degree in Food Science, attending the Culinary Institute of America, working in many restaurant kitchens, and intensifying my knowledge in international wine studies, I developed my culinary business with a focus on molecular gastronomy named Cuisine GP. While it sounds advanced, my philosophy is simply to embrace traditional and international flavor profiles from specific regions around the world. Fusing this concept with the use of local producers I try to express the terroir of the Napa Valley. I develop menus by evaluating the wines first, and then, prepare a multi-course meal specifically paired for each wine. I am constantly researching food, tasting wines, and incorporating various cooking techniques to execute my culinary goals. If that means personally hunting down ingredients one by one from small artisan purveyors to achieve my culinary vision, then so be it. This progressive business takes the fine dining experience to a private setting without the environment of a busy restaurant.

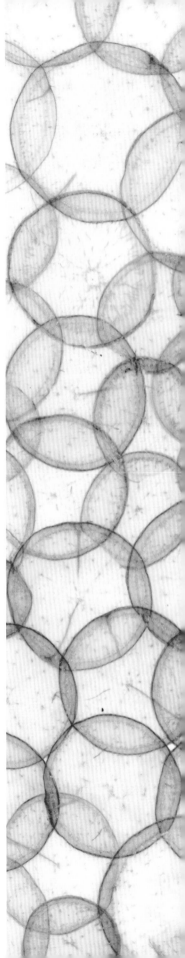

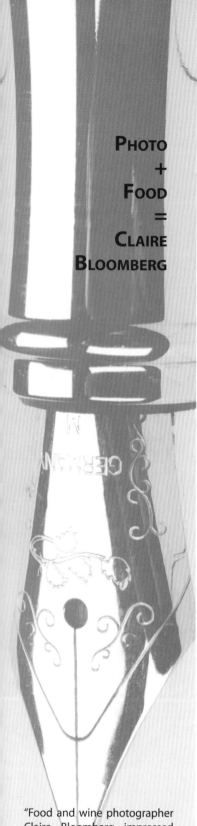

PHOTO
+
FOOD
=
CLAIRE
BLOOMBERG

"First and foremost, you want your food to appear appetizing. When you approach the dish you are shooting with your camera, always have this in mind."

Food photography is an art form that is often misunderstood by the public at large. The common misconception is that all food photographed is "fake food." While some of the photographs in big-budget advertising are not entirely of real food, a large percentage of them are. They depict real food made by real chefs! This is the kind of food photography shown in this book, and thus, my topic.

Your choice of props is critical. As a rule, using blue dishes, blue napkins, or other blue props is not recommended - blue is an appetite suppressant. You should choose props to complement the color in the food you are shooting (such as a red napkin beneath or beside a serving of cherry pie) or keep them extremely neutral (beige, black, gray, or white) so that all the focus remains on the food. Be mindful of your props as you shoot from different angles: they should always be part of (and add to) the overall composition. Remove any props that feel extraneous or which overcrowd the composition.

Lighting is equally important. A large source of diffused light (scattered and causes soft shadows rather than hard-edged ones) works well for most food photography. It creates softness in the appearance

"Food and wine photographer Claire Bloomberg impressed me so much with her photographs that I knew she could advise the novice photographer." MH

of your dish and eliminates distraction due to hard shadows which can shift the viewer's focus from the food. A large window is an excellent source of this type of light. Most often, a source of fill light (that which provides some illumination for the areas of the image in shadow) is needed for the side of the dish not facing the window. A piece of white cardboard, placed standing up facing the dark side of the dish, is an easy way to achieve this fill. You could also use anything that reflects light, such as a mirror or aluminum foil.

Now that your set is ready, turn your dish in every possible direction, looking for the angle that most makes you want to take a bite! Start with the most obviously delicious shot, and keep going with the second most delicious, etc.

For a standard dish (one which is beautiful in and of itself), the straightforward approach (e.g. shooting from slightly above the dish, looking down) works best. You want to put the accent on the details that make the dish mouth-watering. It could be the wisp of steam rising from a bowl of chicken-noodle soup, the perfect piece of melting cheese on a sandwich, or the beautifully balanced bite of steak with a smidgen of potato.

In some dishes that are very pattern like you will want to shoot a bird's-eye view. This approach also works well with dishes that could look unappetizing when viewed too closely. Examples of this kind of dish would be those with lots of bones (a whole fish, meaty stews with large shank bones, etc.), those containing offal, and those looking rather sloppy close up (chili, and other one-pot type preparations). If not shot in bird's-eye view, they should be shot as a whole rather than in parts.

If you appreciate good food, your enthusiasm will shine through in your pictures. These guidelines are only a beginning. Always experiment with your food photography. Give yourself enough time to take your art one step beyond where you would usually push it. Even when you think you've turned that dish (or yourself) in every possible direction, there's always one more angle to try.

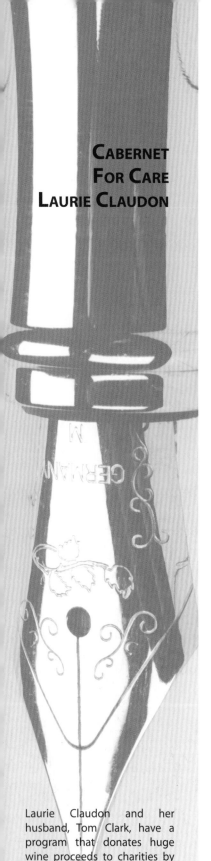

CABERNET
FOR CARE
LAURIE CLAUDON

Laurie Claudon and her husband, Tom Clark, have a program that donates huge wine proceeds to charities by working with both individual enthusiasts and the charities themselves. MH

"Cabernet for Care can be utilized in a variety of ways by both individuals who want to give and charities who are striving to raise funds. Together through Cab for Care we can make a huge difference... one sip at a time! "

Cabernet for Care is a unique philanthropic program which generates funds by unifying Napa Valley's small, hand-crafted wineries directly with charities in need, along with the wine buyer who share a love for exceptional wine and philanthropic missions.

Cabernet for Care was founded to satisfy my families' two passions; exceptional wine growing and meaningful outreach. "Cab for Care" has now grown into a collection of small, artisan winemakers who generously donate up to fifty percent of retail proceeds directly to the charities in need. These are some of Napa Valley's most allocated and sought after producers, all joining with us to make a difference.

Cab for Care is a four pronged program; from the vineyards, to the bottle, to the conscience enthusiast and ultimately to the charity. Through our own label, Clark- Claudon, we have been able to bring hospitals and schools to the poor, hearing to the deaf, wheelchairs to the disabled, joyful experiences to the sick, and meaningful support to medical research.

The seeds for this program began germinating in 1971 when my husband , Tom Clark, and I decided to join the Peace Corps and "honeymoon" in Colombia, South America. That life-altering decision dramatically changed our perspective. It showed us the best and the worst of humanity and infused us with a determination to continue trying to make a difference.

Upon our return from South America, it was a serendipitous opportunity that led us to the Napa Valley with our new baby boy. It was 1974 when we joined in the amazing energy of collaboration among growers and winemakers who shared in the passion of growing the Napa Valley. We loved being part of it and felt an even stronger desire to give back.

As our family grew with the birth of our daughter, Tom founded Clark Vineyard Management and I began outreach to troubled teens and families. Eventually my work led us to kindred spirits, Dick and Anne Grace, and for seven years we worked together philanthropically.

Simultaneously, it was Tom's reputation and the kindness of a stranger that enabled us to lease, develop and eventually purchase vineyard property of our own. When we first hiked the property we knew it could produce world class wine, provide us with a down to earth lifestyle and hopefully enable us to create a wine-driven philanthropic program. The seeds for Cabernet for Care would soon have fertile ground.

While focusing on building our wine business, Tom and I, our children and a group of friends participated in cross cultural out reach in a tiny village in Nicaragua. For ten years we diligently worked to aid those in Nicaragua building sixty homes, improving schools and hospitals, establishing an educational foundation and even building a beloved baseball stadium!

Enriched by many wonderful experiences and very proud of the recognition Clark-Claudon wines had received, we were finally ready to develop Cabernet for Care. Now, almost forty years after the Peace Corps, we often reminisce and marvel at our good fortune in being able to support important causes. To walk the vineyard and know that ultimately our wine will bring joy to wine lovers and hope to the less fortunate is a great joy!

By directly managing Cab for Care, we are able to give all of the intended proceeds directly to the charities. Along with us, many of our vintner partners willingly give fifty percent of their retail price to charity! With the support of Michelle Higgins, and her company Decanting Wine Country, we are able to reach more people and let them know about Cab for Care.

If you are a wine enthusiast who would like to give, or a charity that needs fundraising assistance please visit cabernetforcare.com. Anyone involved in outreach will tell you that the only difference between the giver and the receiver is that the giver often ends up with the joy of the greater gift. Together through Cabernet for Care we can make a huge difference... one sip at a time!

THE ART OF WINE LABELS
JAMES CROSS

"Creating something memorable and innovative at the same time expresses the uniqueness and individuality of that particular wine. The owner's personality is often a major influence on the direction I will take."

For over thirty years, my design firm Cross Associates specialized in corporate identity with offices in Los Angeles, Orange County and San Francisco. In 1994 I sold the firm and moved to St. Helena, with my wife Sue, to retire!

Instead, I returned to my wine roots, consulting with a number of wineries in the Napa Valley. It was way back in the early seventies that I designed labels for Cakebread Cellars, Chateau Chevalier and Fisher Vineyards.

During the past thirteen years since we moved here, I have been fortunate to design a plethora of labels probably as many as 70. Design clients include Lail Vineyards, Schramsberg, Bressler, Calera, Darioush, Crocker and Starr, Kelleher Family Vineyards, Paraduxx, Quixote, Jaffe Estate, Stonestreet, and a number of private labels for members of The Napa Valley Reserve.

Some of my other wine country corporate logo clients include: UC Davis, CIA Greystone and Hyde Park, Rudd Center for Professional Wine Studies, Yountville Appellation, Brix Restaurant, Napa Valley Opera House and the Vintners Hall of Fame. So much for retirement!

"James Cross is as distinguished in person as his work illustrates, and he has been instrumental in the progression of label design throughout the wine industry."   MH

Designing Successful Wine Labels

The wine label has two basic functions or objectives:

to attract the consumer when the bottle is on the shelf
and
to create a good impression when on the table

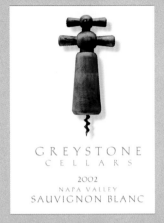

There are legal requirements which the designer must deal
with such as informing the consumer of vintage, varietals, and
appellation, plus the government warning and the size of the bottle.
There is often additional romance text, i.e. "the wine's story."

Interestingly, however, most of the above information is put on the
back of the bottle, freeing up the front for a label
which is more artistic and has more impact.

The toughest problem for the designer is to reconcile the two basic functions
of attraction and impression which are often contradictory. If a label shouts
for attention in the store, it is likely to look unattractive on the table where
the environment is less competitive. It can suggest "the quality of this wine
needs help — it isn't really good enough to stand on its own merits."

On the other hand, an elegant and dignified design can say "Inside this bottle
is quality, the wine will speak for itself." The label is like a certificate of quality.

I explain to my clients that my goal is to create the appropriate
impression on the shelf as well as the table. Creating something
memorable and innovative at the same time expresses the
uniqueness and individuality of that particular wine. The owner's
personality is often a major influence on the direction I will take.

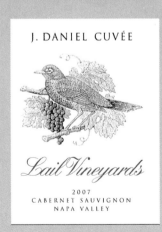

NAPA VALLEY
THROUGH
A LENS
CHARLES O'REAR

" My 25 years with *National Geographic* took me to every state and to more than 20 countries, but California wine country had everything I needed to call it home. "

More than 30 years ago I was dispatched to Napa Valley to produce a photographic story for *National Geographic Magazine.* The resulting 1979 article introduced America's premier wine-growing region to the world. I fell in love with the place and decided to stay. When my non-stop travels wound down in the mid-1990's I found this to be a good decision. The Napa Valley had agriculture, ideal weather, outstanding food, and generous people. And, it was near a major airport.

Since my viewpoint is through the lens of a camera, simple shapes, light, symmetry and colors are what I look for when I shoot. Here in Napa Valley, neatly tended rows of vines, changing seasons and dramatic vistas provide many of the ingredients I need for my photography.

Because the angle and intensity of light, such as a sunset, offer the most dramatic scenes, even today's pocket-sized digital cameras can produce photos comparable to our best film cameras of a decade ago. I seldom set my cameras on automatic, whether it's the focus or exposure, because unusual light often confuses the camera settings. My cameras are set on manual and the results often give great surprises. For example, the color green seldom exposes correctly and, as we all know, the valley is one huge green palette in the summer. Dramatic light from shooting vineyards at sunrise and sunset produces much of my best work.

On a few occasions I resort to strobe lights and almost always those lights are small and compact. When light is low I will "paint" with flashlights much like an artist painting with a brush. For a dozen years I taught this technique at the world-famous Santa Fe Photographic Workshop.

My wine country photography appears in nine books selling more than a quarter million copies, including: *Wine Across America; Beringer--Napa Valley's Historic Estate; Napa Valley; Wine Country; Cabernet; Chardonnay* and others. My photos have also appeared in publications around the world which my agent, Corbis, a small Seattle company owned by Bill Gates, has overseen. Perhaps the most viewed photograph in history is one I took in 2001 in the Carneros region of Napa and Sonoma counties. It is called the "Bliss" photo, and it is the screen saver on all PC computers. The photo shows rolling hills of green grass with a blue sky dotted with white clouds. The photo was not manipulated and at the time it was the real deal. Today those same hills are covered with vineyards.

I am currently working on my newest book about Napa Valley, which will publish in 2010. My past books about the valley have contained popular subjects such as winery doors, wine labels, grape leaves, corkscrew collections, four seasons of a vine, as well as portraits, aerial photos and scenery. The new book will bring surprises with photos never seen before.

For the best photography, always remember rule number one: be in the right place at the right time.

Mr. O'Rear's article shows the accomplishments of a world renowned photographer. What I want to add is that he also shared kindness, inspiration and confidence to make this cookbook possible. Thank you, Chuck.   MH

The Restaurants

IN ORDER OF APPEARANCE

ACACIA CARNEROS PINOT NOIR
PORK CHOPS WITH PORT, FIGS AND APPLES
WINEMAKER MATTHEW GLYNN, PROFESSIONAL CHEF JOEY ALTMAN

Encépagement : Pinot Noir

Appellation : Carneros

Vineyard : 130-acre vineyard estate

Soils : Haire and Diablo series clay loam

Elevation : 60 - 200 feet

Micro-Climate : Marine influence, coolest of the Napa climate regions

Average Vine Age : 10-13 years

Yield : 2 - 4 tons per acre

Philosophy : Acacia winemaking starts in the vineyards well before harvest, with meticulous pruning, careful canopy and cluster management, cover crops between the vine rows, and monitoring of both soil moisture and grape development.

Harvest Details : Hand-harvested and hand-sorted to assure that only ripe, undamaged grapes enter the winery.

Winemaking : To emphasize the unique character of each Pinot Noir clone, we conducted many small-lot fermentations. We increased the wine's complexity by beginning the primary fermentation in stainless steel tanks and then completing both primary and malolactic fermentations in barrels.

Wood Origin: French, Hungarian and American

Oak Regiment: 100%

ACACIA WINERY
2750 LAS AMIGAS ROAD
NAPA, CA 94559
707-226-9991
ACACIAVINEYARD.COM

PINOT NOIR GLASS, O SERIES

"The opulent layers of Burgundy and Satsuma plums, red Bing cherry , and olallieberry fruit character in our Pinot Noir come from grapes grown in the southern, coolest reaches of Carneros. Seductive sun-warmed rose and forest loam nuances mingle with the red fruits, along with teaberry spice from barrel aging. There's a hint of tangerine zest on the long, fruit-imbued finish. " MG

Any Pinot Noir fan knows their way around the famed Carneros wine region and, if lucky enough to be en-route, they head first to Acacia. Set just two miles from San Francisco's San Pablo Bay, Acacia Vineyard is anchored in Carneros, with stellar views of vineyards and the turbulent steel bay. The 130-acre estate was founded in 1979, and is regarded as a pioneer winery in the Carneros appellation. The winery itself is rather handsome, with Cape Cod inspired architecture, and welcomes guests with pre-arranged tastings. Winemaker Matthew Glynn is well known for his abilities to handcraft beautiful wines and oversees the meticulous care given when transforming grapes into wine. Harvest begins only when Matthew and his staff are satisfied the grapes have reached maturity, with the proper balance of flavor and acidity. Acacia winemaking is all about control, gentle handling and allowing the wines to express vineyard character.

ACACIA CARNEROS PINOT NOIR
PORK CHOPS WITH PORT, FIGS AND APPLES
WINEMAKER MATTHEW GLYNN, PROFESSIONAL CHEF JOEY ALTMAN

Pork Chops:

4	double-cut pork chops; bone-in 1½"
tt	salt and freshly ground black pepper
2 T	extra virgin olive oil

Sautéed Apples:

2 T	unsalted butter, (¼ stick)
1 T	light brown sugar
2	apples, peeled, quartered, and cored
½	pint fresh figs, stemmed and cut in half
2 T	minced shallot or red onion
2 T	finely chopped fresh ginger
½ c	chicken stock
½ c	ruby port
tt	salt and freshly ground black pepper

Sweet Potato Purée:

4 T	butter
1	yellow onion, sliced
1 lb	sweet potatoes, peeled, cut in large dice
2 t	minced fresh ginger
1 c	chicken stock
1½ c	heavy cream
tt	salt and pepper to taste

Garnish:

¼ c	chopped chives or green onions

Brining :
In a large bowl or re-sealable plastic bag, combine ½ gallon water, ½ cup kosher salt, and ½ cup granulated sugar. Add aromatics—I like a teaspoon of freshly ground black pepper, 2 bay leaves, ¼ cup fresh thyme sprigs, and a tablespoon of juniper berries. Or add subtle Asian nuances with star anise and sliced ginger. Stir to dissolve the sugar and salt, then submerge the pork chops in the brine, cover the bowl or seal the bag, and refrigerate for one hour. Pat the chops dry before cooking.

Pork Chops:
Season the pork chops liberally with salt and pepper. Heat half the olive oil in a large skillet over medium-high heat. Cook half the chops until well browned, 6 to 7 minutes per side. Repeat with the remaining oil and chops. Transfer the chops to a plate and cover with foil to keep them warm.

Apples:
In a heavy-gauge skillet over medium heat, melt the butter, then stir in the brown sugar. Add the apples and cook until they brown lightly, 1 to 2 minutes. Add the shallots and ginger and cook 2 minutes more. Add the stock and port and simmer until reduced by about half, about 15 minutes.

Sweet Potato Purée:
In a heavy bottom pot, cook the butter and onion on medium-high heat for 5 minutes, stirring frequently. You want the onion to lightly caramelize or brown.
Add the remaining ingredients and bring to a simmer. Lower heat to a low and let cook for 30 minutes, stirring occasionally. Using a colander, strain off excess liquid into a bowl, reserving the liquid to thin out the puree, if necessary. Using a food processor or an immersion (stick) blender, puree potatoes and season with salt and pepper, to taste. Add some of the strained liquid if the puree is too thick.

Plating:
Place a pork chop in the center of each plate, spoon a small mound of the sweet potato puree to the side and top with a few pieces of apple and fig. Drizzle with a few spoonfuls of the sauce, garnish with chives, and serve immediately. Serves 4

ACACIA WINERY
2750 LAS AMIGAS ROAD
NAPA, CA 94559
707-226-9991
ACACIAVINEYARD.COM

AD HOC
BABY ICEBERG WEDGE SALAD BUTTERMILK DRESSING
CHEF DE CUISINE DAVE CRUZ, BEVERAGE MANAGER JULIA MORETTI

Baby Iceberg Wedge Salad:

12 ea	baby iceberg lettuce heads, cleaned and quartered through stem (or 4 large heads)
1lb	Applewood smoked bacon, cut into lardons
8 ea	ripe Roma tomatoes
2 t	chopped thyme
1c + 3T	extra virgin olive oil
1 c	brioche croûtons

For the Buttermilk Dressing:

1	egg yolk
1 c	canola oil
pinch	mustard powder
1 to 2	lemons for juicing
½ c	crème fraîche
½ c	buttermilk
2 T	chopped chives
2 T	chopped parsley
1 T	chopped mint
tt	salt and pepper

For the tomatoes:
Preheat oven to 250 ° F.
Core, remove the stem and score with an "x" on the bottom.
In a pot of boiling water, dip the tomatoes for approximately 30-45 seconds and remove to an ice bath. Once the tomatoes are cooled, peel away the skin and discard.
Halve the tomatoes lengthwise. On a sheet tray lined with foil, place the tomatoes with the cut side up and drizzle the cup of olive oil into the flesh of the tomatoes.
Season with salt and pepper, top with chopped thyme.
Bake for approximately 2 ½ hours, or until the tomatoes have shrunk, but have become very tender and sweet.
Allow to cool on the baking sheet.

For bacon:
Preheat oven to 350º F.
Bake approximately 15-20 minutes. The bacon should be slightly crisped. Keep warm.

For the buttermilk dressing:
Place the egg yolks in a stainless steel bowl with mustard powder and whisk until mustard is fully incorporated. Add oil drop by drop until it has emulsified and begins to thicken. As it becomes more emulsified, continue to add the oil, now as a steady stream, but still slowly. When all of the oil is fully incorporated, add the lemon juice, then whisk in the crème fraîche and buttermilk.
Add the chopped herbs, season to taste.

For the plating:
Season the lettuce with the reserved olive oil, salt and pepper and serve chilled. Top with tomatoes, and bacon, garnish with chives and brioche croûtons.
Serve with buttermilk cream dressing. 8 servings

AD HOC
6476 WASHINGTON STREET
YOUNTVILLE, CA 94599
707-944-2487
ADHOCRESTAURANT.COM

ARDORE

NAPA
2005
VALLEY

ARDORE
GRILLED RACK OF LAMB, SAVORY BLUE CHEESE BREAD PUDDING, ROASTED CIPOLLINI SAUCE
WINEMAKER MARK HEROLD PH.D., PROFESSIONAL CHEF JOHN VLANDIS

Wine Making Facts :

Encépagement : 100% Cabernet Sauvignon

Appellation : Napa Valley

Average Vine Age : 9 Years

Yield : 2.5 tons per acre

Alcohol Level : 14.8%

Total Production : 600 cases

Philosophy : Picking grapes at optimal maturity.

Fermentation : Ambient cold soak, thermal extraction, pressing before dryness, no extended maceration, malolactic in barrels.

Harvest Details : Fourth week in October

Fermentation : Hot and short

Maceration : 14 days maximum

Percent new Barrels : 100%

Wood Origin : France

ARDORE
CELANI FAMILY VINEYARDS
2230 BIG RANCH ROAD
NAPA, CA 94558
877- ARDORE1
CFVINEYARDS.COM

SOMMELIERS, BORDEAUX GRAND CRU

" Brighter dusty red and wild blackberry fruit and sweet tobacco. Very good smoke and sweeter oak are still integrating with good complex medley of herbs and fruit with some smoke undertones." MH

Vicki and Tom Celani are a couple with a deep appreciation for ancestral roots; both in their family legacy and in their own vineyard. When they fell in love with the Tuscan-style estate at the foothills of the Vaca Mountain range, they affectionately named the flagship wine Ardore. From its premier vintage release the wine world was swirling. Celani produces estate Chardonnay, Merlot, and Cabernet Sauvignon. They also have a little magical input from winemaking legend Mark Herold, who shares the couple's philosophy for producing intense, highly extracted, terroir-driven wines. "The greatest compliment I could receive is to have a perfect stranger tell me that his Ardore is the best wine that he—or she—has ever tasted." Tom says passionately.

ARDORE
GRILLED RACK OF LAMB, SAVORY BLUE CHEESE BREAD PUDDING, ROASTED CIPOLLINI SAUCE
WINEMAKER MARK HEROLD PH.D., PROFESSIONAL CHEF JOHN VLANDIS

Lamb Marinade:
½ c	red wine
2 t	minced garlic
2 t	minced shallots
1 T	herbs de Provence
1 c	olive oil
1 t	salt
½ t	ground black pepper

Blue Cheese Bread Pudding:
½	sour dough bread loaf, diced
2 c	half and half
5 oz	blue cheese
2 oz	roasted garlic purée
¼ c	thinly sliced scallions
8	large eggs

Roasted Cipollini Sauce:
3 c	Cabernet Sauvignon
1 sl	applewood smoked bacon
1	roma tomato
2	thyme sprigs
5	black peppercorns
2	shallots, peeled and sliced
1 t	chopped garlic
32 oz	veal stock
24	Cipollini onions

Lamb:
2	Rack of lamb

Marinade:
Combine all ingredients and pour over the lamb. Marinate at least 4 hours.
Heat grill and cooked to desired temperature. Let rest 15 minutes before slicing.

Blue Cheese Bread Pudding Method:
In a sauce pot bring half and half to a simmer. Beat eggs and slowly add 1 cup of the
half and half to the eggs, continuously stirring. Whisk the remaining egg back into
the half and half. Add the rest of the ingredients and season with salt and pepper.

Preheat oven to 325º F.
Butter eight 6 oz. ramekins. Spoon mixture into ramekins and place in a deep baking dish
and fill with hot water half way up the sides of the ramekins. Cover and bake for 45 minutes.

Roasted Cipollini Sauce Method:
Render bacon in a saucepan over medium heat. Add the shallots and cook until lightly browned.
Add garlic and cook 15 seconds.
Add the wine thyme, bay leaf and peppercorns.
Reduce by 2/3 and add veal stock and continue to cook until sauce has reduced by half.
Strain, season, add the cipollinis and keep warm.

Roasted Cipollinis Method:
Preheat oven to 325º F.
Place cipollinis on a large piece of foil. Season with salt and pepper, 2 ounces red wine and 1 ounce olive oil. Seal the pouch and roast until tender.
Approximately 30 minutes. Remove from the pouch, peel and slice into julienne strips. 2 servings

Wine Making Facts :
Encépagement : Cabernet Sauvignon, Cabernet Franc, Merlot, Petite Verdot
Appellation : Howell Mountain
Soils : Rocky Volcanic Tufa & Aiken Loam
Elevation : Hillside 1400 - 1650 feet
Average Vine Age : 11 Years
Yield : 2 Tons/Acre
Alcohol Level : 14.5%
Total Production : 400 Cases
Philosophy : Handcrafted wines from Arkenstone 24 separate organically farmed vineyard blocks.
Harvest Details : Blocks harvested at peak ripeness beginning on September 29th until October 28th.
Facility : Underground Winery Cave
Fermentation : Stainless Steel and Barrel
Wood Origin : 100% French Oak
Oak Regimen : 22 Months
Percentage of New Barrels : 70%
Bottling Formats: 750ML and 1.5L

"This well-structured dark garnet-colored beauty reveals sweet aromatics of macerated cherries, brambleberries, cassis, figs, and black licorice. Enticing underlying notes reveal shaved black truffle, rich earth, sage, clove, and stony minerality. Obsidian displays supple tannins, and focused acidity, culminating in an extremely long and delicious finish." SK

ARKENSTONE VINEYARDS
335 WEST LANE
ANGWIN, CA 94508
707-965-1020
ARKENSTONE.COM

VINUM XL
CABERNET SAUVIGNON GLASS

ARKENSTONE
BRAISED SHORTRIBS, RICOTTA AND PANCETTA RAVIOLI, ENGLISH PEAS, YOUNG SPROUTS GARNISH
WINEMAKER SAM KAPLAN, WINERY CHEF NANCY KAPLAN

Short Ribs:
4	beef short ribs, 2" bone-in
4	carrots, rough chopped
4	stalks celery, rough chopped
1	yellow onion, rough chopped
4	large cloves of garlic
2	bay leaf
2 T	tomato paste
1 t	black peppercorns
2	sprigs thyme
4 c	red wine
4 qts	chicken stock
6 T	vegetable oil

Ravioli Filling:
2 c	fresh ricotta cheese
6 T	small diced prosciutto
1 t	minced shallots
1 t	chopped fresh thyme
4 T	grated parmesan cheese

Garnish:
2 c	freshly shelled English peas
2 c	pea sprouts
1	Meyer lemon, zested
1 t	lemon juice
	extra virgin olive oil
	Kosher salt and pepper

Procedure:
Season ribs and heat a 6 quart sauce pot add vegetable oil. Sear short ribs, remove.
Reduce to medium heat, add carrots, onion, celery, and garlic. Sauté for two minutes add tomato paste, and stir constantly so tomato paste does not burn, but allow to get rusty red.
Deglaze pan with red wine and add short ribs back to pot. Allow liquid to reduce by half and then add chicken stock, black peppercorns, and bay leaf.
Bring to a boil, lower heat and cover with a lid. Cook until short ribs are tender and ready to fall off the bone. Remove ribs and reduce your braising liquid down to sauce consistency. Strain then season to taste before cooling sauce, and setting aside for later use.

Ravioli filling:
Combine all ingredients together and mix thoroughly, season to taste with salt and pepper.
Set aside for filling pasta later.

Pasta:
Combine flour, semolina, salt in bowl of a stand mixer. Mix on low with dough hook attachment and once combined increase to medium speed and add egg yolk. Mix until combined, stream in ice cold water slowly. Test to see if more water is needed by feeling dough.
Knead dough for about 5 minutes then remove and wrap in plastic and rest for at least one hour.

Pasta machine: Roll the dough out to the next to lowest setting. Trim rough edges and mark 2 inch square increments to cut for ravioli. Place a full teaspoon of filling in center of dough and brush dough with egg yolk wash. Fold over one corner to the opposite side to form a triangle. Press all edges together to seal. Trim all edges to make a neat triangle.
Set aside on parchment paper sprinkled with semolina.

Garnish preparation and serving;
Warm short ribs in sauce over low heat, then cook ravioli in a pot of boiling salted water for 3 minutes. Blanch English peas, drain, place in ice bath and then in melted butter with a small amount of water, season with salt and a small amount of fresh thyme. Plate by placing peas first, short rib on top then mix sprouts with lemon zest, juice and olive oil, season and place on top. 2 servings

BACCHANAL CABERNET SAUVIGNON
SEARED RIB-EYE, SAUCE BORDELAISE, MASHED LA RATTE POTATOES
WINEMAKER FREDERIC DELIVERT, CHEF/OWNER MICHAEL MINA

Wine Making Facts :
Encépagement : 100% Estate grown, blend of 95% Cabernet Sauvignon, 5% Merlot
Appellation : Rutherford
Vineyard : Puerta Dorada Vineyard
Soils : Well-drained alluvial fans
Elevation: Napa Valley floor
Average Vine Age : 12 years
Yield: 3 tons/acre or less
Alcohol Level : 14.8%
Total Production : 963 case
Philosophy : Handcrafted from small lots without high-tech interventions, the purest expression of Rutherford terroir.
Harvest Details : Late September to early October
Winemaking: Segregated by clones and picking date.
Fermentation : Separately in custom French oak casks and 500-litre barriques to soften the tannin, sculpt, structure, and focus the unique flavor and character of each lot.
Aged : 30 months in new and neutral French oak
Facility : Estate grown, produced and bottled
Maceration : Ranged from 40 to 45 days
Wood Origin : France

BACCHANAL
PO BOX 390
RUTHERFORD, CA 94573
707-967-0300
MARTINESTATE.COM

VINUM, BORDEAUX-CABERNET MERLOT

"Wildly aromatic, Bacchanal is bursting with blackberry, cherry and plum, with lingering clove and pepper nuances. Its refined tannin structure is complemented by the silky mouth feel and subtle earth, light mocha and perfectly ripe fruit flavors. " FD

In 1996, San Francisco entrepreneurs Petra and Greg Martin discovered a 19th century ghost winery surrounded by the unthinkable: unplanted Rutherford land. The building was rich with history (Georges de Latour made his first legendary Beaulieu Vineyards' vintage here in 1908). And, for the past decade, the couple has invested significant hours into restoring this turn-of-the-century property to its former glory. Today, their limited production, 100-percent estate grown, produced and bottled wines are catching due attention. In every vintage, the Martins produce only what their eight-acre Puerta Dorada Vineyard can yield.

BACCHANAL CABERNET SAUVIGNON
SEARED RIB-EYE, SAUCE BORDELAISE, MASHED LA RATTE POTATOES
WINEMAKER FREDERIC DELIVERT, RESTAURATEUR MICHAEL MINA

Meat:

4 ea	portions rib eye – cut into blocks
2 T	grape seed oil
1	bay leaf
6	thyme sprigs
2 T	unsalted butter

Bordelaise sauce:

¼ c	canola oil
6	shallots, sliced
2	bay leaves
1/2	bunch fresh thyme
1 T	whole black peppercorns
¼ c	red wine vinegar
1 c	Cabernet Sauvignon
1 qt	veal demi-glacé

Vegetable:

1 lb	La Ratte potatoes, preferred
1 c	heavy cream
2 T	unsalted butter
	freshly ground black pepper

Optional garnish:

	minced roasted shallots

Meat:
Season the meat well with salt and pepper. Heat a large skillet over medium high flame. Add 2 tablespoons grape seed oil and heat until it just begins to smoke. Add the rib-eye cooking 1 minute on two sides only. When you flip the meat add the bay leaf, thyme and butter to the pan. Baste the meat as it cooks on the second side. Remove the meat and let it rest for 2-3 minutes before serving. At this point the meat will not be cooked through. Slice meat in half and then place cut side down on a hot grill for about 45 seconds to 1 minute. Two slices per serving.

Bordelaise sauce:
Heat a large saucepan over medium-high flame and coat with the oil. When it's hot, add the shallots cooking until they caramelize, about 3 minutes. Add the wine to the pan and simmer until reduced to au sec. Add the demi-glacé, herbs and peppercorns to the pan and bring to a light simmer. Continue cooking for about 20 minutes until a sauce consistency is reached. Add the vinegar to taste; you may not need it all. Strain through a fine mesh strainer and hold warm.

To make the mashed potatoes:
Put the potatoes (unpeeled) in a large pot and cover with cold water, season with about 1 tablespoon of salt. Bring to a boil over medium heat, and then reduce to a gentle simmer. Cook until there is no resistance when a fork is inserted into the potatoes, about 15 minutes. Warm the heavy cream in a small pot over low heat. Drain the potatoes and while they're hot, peel and pass them through a food mill or potato ricer into a large mixing bowl. Mix with the warm cream and butter until the correct consistency is achieved. Season and reserve warm. 4 servings

BACCHANAL
PO Box 390
RUTHERFORD, CA 94573
707-967-0300
MARTINESTATE.COM

BEAULIEU VINEYARD GEORGES DE LATOUR PRIVATE RESERVE CABERNET SAUVIGNON
BLACKENED NEW YORK STEAK WITH CHAYOTE AND CORN SUCCOTASH
WINEMAKER JEFFREY STAMBOR, PROFESSIONAL CHEF JOEY ALTMAN

Wine Making Facts :

Encépagement : Primarily Cabernet Sauvignon, blended with classic Bordeaux varietals such as Petit Verdot and Malbec

Vineyard : BV's Rutherford and Calistoga ranches in the central and northern parts of Napa.

Soils : Rocky, loam to clay loam

Elevation : Valley floor to 300 feet

Micro-Climate : Climatic Region III. Located in the central to the northern end of Napa Valley, this region receives the least influence from the marine night fog and by afternoon winds which are tempered by the afternoon sun.

Average Vine Age : 20 years

Yield : 3-4 tons per acre

Alcohol Level : 14.8%

Harvest Details : Hand harvested in the cool of the morning

Winemaking : We selected grapes from vineyards with distinctly different terroirs and then used the art of blending to create a wine with layer upon layer of delicious flavors. After the grapes were destemmed and crushed, we fermented the must in stainless steel tanks until dry. We then pressed the wines and transferred them to 60-gallon oak barrels for aging.

Maceration: 2-day cold pre-fermentation maceration. Selected lots went through extended maceration.

Wood Origin: Hungarian, American and French

"Smooth and velvety, the wine brims with dark cherry, blackberry and plum character. Hints of rose, chocolate and toasty oak weave through the enticing aromas and mouth filling flavors, finishing with warmth and spice." JS

BEAULIEU VINEYARD
1960 ST. HELENA HIGHWAY
RUTHERFORD, CA 94573
800-373-5896
BVWINES.COM

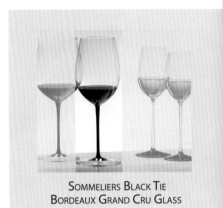

SOMMELIERS BLACK TIE
BORDEAUX GRAND CRU GLASS

Hands down, there is simply no other winery in Napa Valley that has influenced America's wine industry more or has the historical reverence as BV. In 1900, when Georges de Latour's wife, Fernande, first laid eyes on the land that would become their original Rutherford vineyard, she named it "beau lieu," or "beautiful place." Shortly thereafter, de Latour bought the four-acre ranch and founded Beaulieu Vineyard with the vision of making Napa Valley wines that would rival those of his native France. De Latour quickly made a name for himself by importing Phylloxera-resistant rootstock from Europe to the recently-ravaged fledgling California wine industry. He also began selling wine to the Catholic Church, establishing a strong relationship that would allow Beaulieu Vineyard to become the only Napa Valley winery to remain in business during Prohibition. In 1938, he traveled to France returning with André Tchelistcheff the famed viticulturist and enologist. Tchelistcheff introduced cold fermentation for white wines, malolactic fermentation for reds, and aging red wines in small, French oak barrels. In 1936, he also tasted what the family referred to as their own "family wine." So distinctive in character, it alone coined the terms: Private Reserve, flagship wine and, no surprise, cult wine. Now, BV is also a leader in clonal research. We should all be thankful that Georges de Latour recognized "beau lieu" or our beautiful place.

Beaulieu Vineyard Georges de Latour Private Reserve Cabernet Sauvignon
Blackened New York Steak with Chayote and Corn Succotash
Winemaker Elizabeth Delouise, Professional Chef Joey Altman

1	chayote squash	1 T	ground cumin
2	ears of corn, shucked, silk removed	1 T	sweet paprika
1	red onion, sliced in ¼ inch rounds	1 T	garlic powder
5	scallions, trimmed	1 t	cayenne pepper
2 T	minced garlic (about 10 medium cloves)	4	rib-eye steaks, 10 to 12 ounce, 1-inch thick
6 T	butter, softened	1	chipotle chile in adobo, minced
2 T + 1	chile powder	1 t	adobo sauce
3 t	kosher salt	2 t	fresh lime juice
1 t	freshly ground black pepper	2 t	extra virgin olive oil, plus enough to lightly coat vegetables
½ c	chicken stock		

Succotash:
Slice the chayote lengthwise into ¼-inch thick slabs. Coat the chayote slices, corn, red onion, and scallions lightly with olive oil and sprinkle with a little salt and pepper. Grill the vegetables over a medium-hot grill or on a stove top grill pan until they show grill marks and the onions have softened. Transfer the vegetables to a cutting board. When they are cool enough to handle, cut the chayote and red onions into ¼-inch dice, cut the onions into ¼-inch slices, and cut the kernels from the ear of corn.
Sauté the minced garlic in 2 tablespoons of the butter in a large skillet over medium-high heat until the garlic softens. Add the grilled vegetables, the diced red and yellow peppers, 1 teaspoon of the chile powder, 1 teaspoon of the salt, and 1/4 teaspoon of the pepper. Sauté until the vegetables are tender, about 5 minutes. Add the chicken stock and cook over high heat, stirring occasionally, until only enough stock remains to coat the succotash. Taste and adjust seasonings. Set aside.

Steak Rub:
To make the steak rub, stir together the remaining 2 tablespoons chile powder, cumin, paprika, garlic powder, cayenne pepper, the remaining 2 teaspoons salt, and ¾ teaspoon black pepper. Rub the mixture generously on all sides of the steaks.

Chipotle Butter:
Mix together the remaining 4 tablespoons butter with the chipotle chile and adobo until well blended. Slowly drizzle and stir in the lime juice until it is incorporated. Season with salt to taste.

Cooking:
To cook the steaks, heat two large, heavy skillets over medium-high heat and turn on the exhaust fan. (Alternatively, cook the steaks in two batches in one pan.) Add 1 tablespoon of oil to coat each pan. Lay 2 steaks into each pan and leave for about 2 minutes without moving them to sear the outside. Turn the steaks to sear the second side, then reduce the heat to medium and cook the steaks until they are dark and your desired doneness, about 10 minutes total and an internal temperature of 125˚F to 130˚F for medium-rare. Transfer the steaks to a cutting board and let stand 5 minutes.

Serve:
Slice the steaks on a bias into ¼-inch thick slices and lightly sprinkle with salt. Mound the succotash on plates and lay the steak slices over it. 4 servings.

1883

BEAULIEU VINEYARD
1960 ST. HELENA HIGHWAY
RUTHERFORD, CA 94573
800-373-5896
BVWINES.com

BOUCHON BISTRO
DAY BOAT SCALLOPS WITH PARSNIP PURÉE AND CIDER BEURRE BLANC
CHEF DE CUISINE PHILIP TESSIER, HEAD SOMMELIER GARTH HODGDON

For the Parsnip Purée :
2 lb	parsnip, peeled and roughly chopped
1 qt	whole milk
¼ lb	butter
tt	salt and pepper

For the Beurre Blanc :
1 qt	apple cider
2	shallots, sliced
6	peppercorns
2	bay leaves
1c	cold butter, cut into cubes

For the Scallops:
16	Day Boat scallops
½ c	hazelnuts, toasted and lightly crushed

For the Apples:
2	apples, peeled, halved, and cored
3c	white wine
1c	water
1c	sugar
1	bay leaf
2	cloves
1	star anise

For the Parsnip Purée :
Cover parsnips in milk and butter.
Simmer gently until very tender.
Strain out liquid, set aside to reheat.
Place parsnips in Robot Coup (or mesh colander) and purée until smooth.

For the Beurre Blanc :
Place cider in a heavy stainless steel pot.
Add shallots, peppercorns, and bay leaves.
Reduce cider to a syrup.
Slowly whisk in butter.
Strain through a fine mesh chinoise.
Keep warm until use.

For the Apples :
Make a poaching liquid with water, wine, and sugar in a heavy pot.
Add bay leaf, clove, and star anise to liquid. Place apples into the liquid.
Poach apples until just tender.

Plating :
Reheat parsnip purée.
Sauté apples in whole butter.
Arrange purée on plate, apples four scallops and beurre blanc. 4 servings

BOUCHON BISTRO
6534 WASHINGTON STREET
YOUNTVILLE, CA 94599
707-944-8037
BOUCHONBISTRO.COM

BUONCRISTIANI

2007 NAPA VALLEY SYRAH ROSATO

BUONCRISTIANI SYRAH ROSATO
SALMON EN PAPILLOTE
WINEMAKER JAY BUONCRISTIANI, PROFESSIONAL CHEF DOUG WELDON

Wine Making Facts :
Encépagement : Rosé of Syrah
Appellation : Napa Valley
Yield : 3 tons per acre average
Alcohol Level : 14.1 %
Total Production : 235 Cases
Philosophy : Handcrafted from small blocks, harvested
at optimum ripeness based on flavor and texture
Harvest Details : October 9th to the 14th, 2008
Winemaking: Components were fermented in 40%
stainless steel and 60% neutral French oak barrels,
Fermentation : Primary fermentation was allowed
to complete to dryness, while secondary
fermentation was suppressed to preserve
crisp acidity and vibrant fruit.
Barrel Fermented in 40% stainless steel and 60% neutral barrels.
Barrels : French oak barrels, aged 5 months

BUONCRISTIANI FAMILY WINERY
PO BOX 6946
NAPA, CA 94581
707-259-1681
BUONWINE.COM

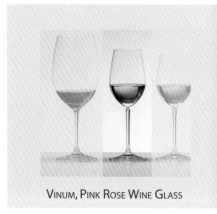

VINUM, PINK ROSE WINE GLASS

"Vibrant aromas of wild cherry, raspberry, orange zest, jasmine, roses, and white pepper excite the senses. Bright flavors of kiwi, strawberry, cherry, and Christmas spices are supported by bone dry tart acidity, leading to a clean, crisp, mouth watering finish." JB

Unlike many Napa Valley winemaking families, the Buoncristiani brothers were born and raised on local soil. Now they're taking that soil and using it to create a new vision in winemaking. Rather than inheriting a family vineyard estate, the four young brothers – Matthew, Jason, Aaron, and Nathan – have built a first-generation, self-made brand that reflects their Italian winemaking heritage. With grandparents from Tuscany, the boys learned from their father, an avid home winemaker, the skills to turn their passion into a profession. Along the way they've earned their credentials working with such prestigious names as Melka, Caldwell, Rudd, and Hess.

BUONCRISTIANI CABERNET SAUVIGNON AND BUONCRISTIANI OPC
LIBERTY FARMS CHINESE RED COOKED DUCK TAMALES, PASILLA CHILIES CRÈME FRAÎCHE
WINEMAKER JAY BUONCRISTIANI, CHEF/OWNER GREG COLE ~ COLE'S CHOP HOUSE

BUONCRISTIANI FAMILY WINERY
PO BOX 6946
NAPA, CA 94581
707-259-1681
BUONWINE.COM

Wine Making Facts :
Cabernet Sauvignon
Appellation : Napa Valley (Mt Veeder,
Yountville, Coombsville, Howell Mountain)
Yield : 3 tons per acre average
Alcohol Level : 15.0%
Total Production : 324 cases
Philosophy : Handcrafted from small
blocks, harvested at optimum ripeness
based on flavor and texture.
Harvest Details : Oct 24 - Nov 11 , 2005
Winemaking: Blend is 93% Cabernet
Sauvignon, 5% Malbec, and 2%
Merlot, kept small lots separate until
marrying the components during
the second year of barrel aging.
Fermentation : Cold soaked 3 days,
punched down 3-4 times daily, extended
maceration post fermentation, basket
press, kept free run separate.
Maceration : 25 days maceration
Oak Regimen: 100% French Oak
Aged: Barrel for 20 months
Percentage of New Barrels : 80%

Wine Making Facts :
OPC Proprietary Red
Appellation: Napa Valley (Mt Veeder,
Yountville, Coombsville, Howell Mountain)
Yield : 3 tons per acre average
Alcohol Level : 14.5%
Total Production : 1,849 Cases
Harvest Details : October 12th
to November 11th, 2005
Winemaking: Blend is 42% Cabernet
Sauvignon, 36% Syrah, 15% Merlot, and
7% Malbec. Kept small lots separate
until marrying the components during
the second year of barrel aging.
Fermentation: Cold soaked 3 days,
punched down 3-4 times daily, extended
maceration post fermentation, basket
press, kept free run separate.
Maceration: Averaged 21 days maceration
Oak Regimen : 100%
Maceration: Averaged 25 days maceration
Oak Regimen: 100% French Oak
Aged: Barrel for 20 months
Percentage of New Barrels : 50%

" Deep aromas of cassis, blackberry, dark chocolate, black pepper, ripe berries, toffee, almond and caramelized oak captivate attention. Intense flavors of ripe black cherry, cassis, caramel, and fudge are supported by integrated French oak, ripe tannin and a mouth-coating mid palate. Ripe dark berries, cedar spice, chocolate and amazing texture all please the palate for well over a minute on the ultra-fine lengthy finish. " JB

" Complex aromas of vibrant wild berry, black cherry, toffee, clove, milk chocolate and exotic spices excite the senses. Intense flavors of ripe blackberry, boysenberry, caramel, and mocha are supported by integrated French oak, round tannin and a mouth-coating mid palate. Mixed red and black fruit, cedar spice, and baker's chocolate continue to gush forth during the ultra fleshy velvet-textured long finish. " JB

VITIS, CABERNET SAUVIGNON WINE GLASS

BUONCRISTIANI SYRAH ROSATO
SALMON EN PAPILLOTE
WINEMAKER JAY BUONCRISTIANI, PROFESSIONAL CHEF DOUG WELDON

Vegetables:

12	asparagus spears, cut on the bias
1	leek, split in half, cut in ½" lengths
2 T	butter

Papillotes:

4	salmon fillets, boneless, skinless
4 pieces	aluminum foil or parchment paper, 12 inches by 18 inches

4	Yukon gold potatoes, small, boiled and cooled, sliced ¼ inch
8 T	butter
4 t	truffle oil
2 t	lemon juice
¼ c	Sauvignon Blanc

Method:

Cut asparagus tips on the bias in 2 to 3 inch lengths.
Cut the remainder of the asparagus spears on the bias, in ¼ inch lengths; discard the woody ends.
Trim the dark leaves from the leek and discard.
Cut the white and light green section of the leek in half from root to tip and then cross cut into half inch pieces.
Sweat leeks slowly in 2 tablespoons butter, until just tender; season.

Preheat oven to 450° F.
Season the salmon fillets with salt and pepper.
Placing off center, to allow foil to be folded over when complete, layer 1 tablespoon butter, 4 potato slices, ¼ portion of leeks, ¼ portion asparagus spears, top with salmon and another tablespoon of butter.
Place ¼ portion of the asparagus tips around the sides of the salmon in each foil papillote.
Add 1 teaspoon truffle oil, ½ teaspoon lemon juice, and 2 tablespoons of wine to each papillote.
Fold the foil over to create a pouch; crimp ends tightly.
Leave enough room so the foil does not touch the fish when closed.
Traditionally papillotes are half moon shaped with tightly crimped edges.
Place pouches onto sheet pan and bake for 10 minutes; remove and rest 2 minutes.
When serving, place the pouch onto the plate and carefully open to release the steam. 4 servings

BUONCRISTIANI CABERNET SAUVIGNON AND BUONCRISTIANI OPC
LIBERTY FARMS CHINESE RED COOKED DUCK TAMALES, PASILLA CHILIES CRÈME FRAÎCHE
WINEMAKER JAY BUONCRISTIANI, CHEF/OWNER GREG COLE ~ COLE'S CHOP HOUSE

Red Cooking Liquid:

¾ c	soy sauce
¾ c	orange juice
¼ c	red wine
1 T	sesame oil
2 T	ginger, chopped
3	garlic cloves
1	star anise
1 T	sugar
1 lb	duck breast, boneless, skinless

Filling:

2 t	sesame oil
1 c	onions, fine chopped
2 t	garlic, minced
2 t	ginger, minced
1	orange, zested and minced
1 c	red cooking liquid

1 lb	duck breast, cooked, fine diced

Masa Dough:

4 oz	butter, softened
1½ c	masa flour (corn flour)
1 t	salt
¾ c	chicken stock
12	dried corn husks

Pasilla Chile Cream Garnish:

2 tsp	olive oil
2 T	pasilla chile dried, finely ground
2	limes, juice and zest
1/2 t	salt
1 c	crème fraîche (sour cream substitute)

Red Cooking Liquid:
Combine all ingredients except duck and bring to a simmer in skillet.
Add duck and poach breasts for 30 minutes. Do not overcook.
Remove from heat and cool duck in liquid. Remove the duck breast and fine dice. Strain, reserve liquid.

Filling:
Heat sesame oil in a sauté pan, add onions and cook until clear.
Add garlic and ginger and cook for two minutes.
Add diced duck meat and reserved red cooking liquid and bring to simmer.
Continue cooking until liquid reduces and mixture is thick. Remove from heat and cool.

Masa Dough:
Whip butter until soft and fluffy.
Blend in masa flour, salt and chicken stock, mixing until dough holds together.
Wrap tightly in plastic wrap until ready to use.

Pasilla Chile Cream Garnish:
Combine chile, lime juice and zest, salt and crème fraîche.
Mix well and chill.

Tamale:
Soak dried corn husks in water overnight. Lay a corn husk out flat.
Spread evenly, 3 tablespoons masa dough, in a rectangular shape, onto the corn husk.
Place 2 tablespoons duck filling in center and fold to form a packet; side to side and end to end.
Arrange in a steamer, lining a collapsible vegetable steamer with extra corn husks.
Cover and steam for 50 minutes. Serve with Pasilla Chile cream. 12 servings

COLE'S CHOP HOUSE
1122 MAIN STREET
NAPA, CA 94559

SAUVIGNON BLANC

CADE

2008 NAPA VALLEY

CADE SAUVIGNON BLANC
SMOKED ALBACORE TUNA, BABY ARUGULA, CONFETTI TOMATOES
WINEMAKER ANTHONY BIAGI, WINERY CHEF KENT NIELSEN

Wine Making Facts :

Encépagement : Sauvignon Blanc

Appellation : Napa Valley

Vineyard : Multiple sites

Soils : Multiple Soil series

Elevation: Multiple elevation

Average Vine Age : 10 years

Alcohol Level : 13.8 %

Total Production : 5,900 cases

Philosophy : Dealing with small artisan growers
to craft a classic Napa Valley Sauvignon Blanc

Harvest Details : Harvested from August 23rd to
September 20th 2009

Facility : CADE Estate winery

Fermentation : 25% Barrel Ferment, 35% stainless steel drum
Ferment, 35% stainless steel tank Ferment 5% concrete ferment

Maceration : 10% 24 hour skin contact

Wood Origin : 100% French oak

*"Enticing aromas of green melon, wet stones, cantaloupe, cut grass
and vanilla bean are followed on the palate with flavors of guava,
rose petal, gooseberry and vanilla. The 7% Semillon fleshes out the
mid palate and adds a nice layer to the finish. " AB*

CADE WINERY
360 HOWELL MOUNTAIN ROAD
ANGWIN, CA 94508
707-965-2746
CADEWINERY.COM

VINUM SAUVIGNON BLANC WINE GLASS

Marinade:

8 oz	piece of local Albacore tuna
¼ c	brown sugar
¼ c	kosher salt
¼ c	soy sauce
4	bay leaves
1 T	mixed peppercorns
4 c	CADE Sauvignon Blanc
1	lemon sliced
	water

Plating:

4 oz	smoked Albacore tuna
4 oz	baby Arugula
1 T	fresh lemon juice
1 t	honey
1 t	Dijon mustard
⅛ c	extra virgin olive oil
8	assorted heirloom cherry or pear tomatoes
	kosher salt and cracked black pepper

Marinade for Albacore Tuna:
Combine the sugar, salt, soy, bay leaves and mixed peppercorns in a non-reactive container. Add wine, tuna, and enough water to cover. Wrap tightly with plastic and refrigerate overnight.

Smoker method: Prepare a smoker with fruit wood chips, cherry or apple. Smoke the fish at low temperature, 185° for approximately 2 hours. Remove and allow to cool on a rack.

Dressing method: Combine lemon juice, honey and Dijon and whisk to blend. Season with salt and pepper. Whisk to dissolve the salt. Slowly drizzle olive oil whisking constantly to create an emulsion. Set aside.

Plating method: Set plates out. Toss arugula in a bowl with a small amount of dressing. Taste and add more dressing if needed. Greens should be lightly dressed. Place a handful of greens on each plate, top with a ¼-inch slice of Albacore. Place cherry tomatoes around. Finish by grinding pepper over top. 4 servings

Cakebread
Cellars

NAPA VALLEY

Chardonnay

2007

ALCOHOL 14.3% BY VOLUME

CAKEBREAD CELLARS CHARDONNAY
FATTED CALF CHORIZO, BUTTERNUT SQUASH, GRUYÉRE CHEESE EMPANADAS
WINEMAKER JULIANNE LAKS, WINERY CHEF BRIAN STREETER

Wine Making Facts :

Encépagement : 100% Chardonnay

Appellation : Napa Valley

Vineyard : Sourced from 28 vineyards throughout Napa Valley

Elevation: Between 10 ft and 175 ft.

Yield : Generally 3 tons/acres range

Alcohol Level : 14.3%

Philosophy : All of the fruit is farmed sustainably with a portion certified under the Napa Green Program.

Harvest Details : Night harvested grapes

Facility : Cakebread Cellars

Fermentation : 85% barrel fermented, 15% stainless steel tank fermented followed by oak aging.

Maceration : No skin contact, 100% whole cluster

Wood Origin : 100% French Barrel fermented; topped in same barrel post primary fermentation

Aged: sur lees for 8 months with periodic stirring for approximately 120 days.

Bottling Formats: 750 ml and 1.5 l

"Vibrant citrus blossom, ripe apple, sweet melon and white peach aromas, with subtle buttercream, baked bread and toasty oak scents adding complexity. Rich, fresh and creamy on the palate, with beautiful underlying structure, the wine delivers sleek, succulent, ripe peach, yellow apple and lemon zest flavors buoyed by a vein of refreshing minerality, which enlivens the crisp, flavorful finish. " JL

CAKEBREAD CELLARS
8300 ST. HELENA HWY
RUTHERFORD, CA 94573
800-588-0298
CAKEBREAD.COM

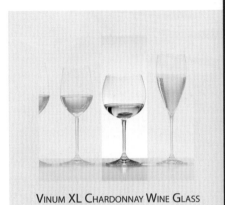

VINUM XL CHARDONNAY WINE GLASS

½ lb	fresh chorizo sausage, preferably Fatted Calf, removed from casing	3 c	butternut squash, peeled, fine dice
2 T	olive oil	1 c	gruyère cheese, grated
1	onion, fine dice	1pk	puff pastry
		1	egg wash

Preheat oven to 400° F.
Sauté sausage (preferably Fatted Calf Chorizo, see resources) and onion in olive oil ; break up sausage into small pieces. Add the butternut squash and cook until squash is tender, about 5- 7 minutes. Remove from the heat, stir in the cheese and allow to cool. Roll out the puff pastry on a lightly floured surface to a 1/8" thick. Cut out 3 ½" circles from the dough. On a floured work surface, brush the dough with beaten egg. Place a heaping teaspoon of filling off to one side. Fold the edge over and seal the edge with the tines of a fork. Set on a sheet pan lined with parchment paper. Brush the tops with the remaining egg. Bake until golden brown, about 15 minutes. 12 servings

2009

Syrah Rosé

CALDWELL

ESTATE GROWN

CALDWELL VINEYARD SYRAH ROSÉ
OPAH CRUDO, HIBISCUS VINAIGRETTE, AVOCADO, YELLOW CREAMED CORN
WINEMAKER MARBUE MARKE, PROFESSIONAL CHEF GARY PENIR

Wine Making Facts:

Encépagement : 100% Syrah Rose

Appellation : Napa Valley

Vineyard : 100% estate-owned vineyard in
Coombsville, Napa Valley

Soils : Stoney Aiken clay sub soil of volcanic ash

Elevation : 500 feet

Average Vine Age : 6 years

Yield : 2 Tons per Acre

Alcohol Level : 13.4%

Total Production : 530 cases

Harvest Details : Grapes picked at optimal ripeness within
micro-blocks at varied times during the harvest from
September 30th to October 30th

Facility : Cave winery

Fermentation : Tank Fermentation

Bottling : Format 750 mL

CALDWELL VINEYARD
169 KREUZER LANE
NAPA, CA 94559
707-255-1294
CALDWELLVINEYARD.COM

SOMMELIERS, ROSÉ WINE GLASS

"Fresh strawberries and rose petals dominate this bright nose. The nose is laced with red raspberry, lavender and hints of bubble gum. A bright raspberry attack is followed by a juicy, full mouth of red cherry, ripe plum, and blood orange, which gives way to a long finish of wild blueberries and notes of candied cinnamon." MM

Hollywood has already taken note of John Caldwell's story: how he single-handedly (legal or not) became the first Californian to discover and import rootstocks and grapevine clones from France. In 1984, after stumbling upon the clonal research program at Château Haut Brion, Caldwell eventually brought back over 60 clones of different varietals. Soon after, at a time when phylloxera was decimating Napa Valley's vineyards, these clones captured the attention of emerging wineries such as Harlan, Spottswoode, and Abreu. They are now referred to as the "Caldwell Clones" and today, in a Bordeaux-style vineyard, the clones are industry standard.

ROC
KET
SCIE
NCE

BY CALDWELL

2008

CALDWELL VINEYARD ROCKET SCIENCE
WAGYU BEEF, FISCALINI PEARL TAPIOCA, CABERNET SAUCE
WINEMAKER MARBUE MARKE, CHEF/OWNER KEN FRANK ~ LA TOQUE RESTAURANT

Wine Making Facts :
Encépagement : Syrah, Merlot, Cabernet Sauvignon,
Cabernet Franc, Petit Verdot, Tannat, Carmenere
Appellation : Napa Valley
Vineyard : 100% estate-owned vineyard
in Coombsville, Napa Valley
Elevation : 500 ft
Average Vine Age : 12yrs
Yield : 3 Tons per Acre
Alcohol Level : 14.8%
Total Production : 1404 cases
Harvest Details : Micro-blocks at varied
times during the harvest from
October 3rd to October 7th
Fermentation : stainless, barrel, and oak
upright fermented
Maceration : 24 - 32 days on the skins
Wood Origin : 100% French
New Barrels : 60%
Oak Regimen : Aged 20 Months
Bottling Format : 375mL, 750mL, 1.5L

CALDWELL VINEYARD
169 KREUZER LANE
NAPA, CA 94559
707-255-1294
CALDWELLVINEYARD.COM

VITIS, CABERNET SAUVIGNON WINE

"BLACK CHERRY, BLACKBERRY, PIPE TOBACCO AND VANILLA AROMAS LEAD WITH SPICY SAGE, SAVORY AND FRESH HERBS SUPPORTING. THE FLAVORS STRIKE A BALANCE BETWEEN RED FRUITY FLAVORS AND CLOVE AND VANILLA SWEET SPICES WITH EARTHY UNDERTONES ADDING A FURTHER DIMENSION OF DEPTH AND COMPLEXITY."

WINEMAKER MARBUE MARKE

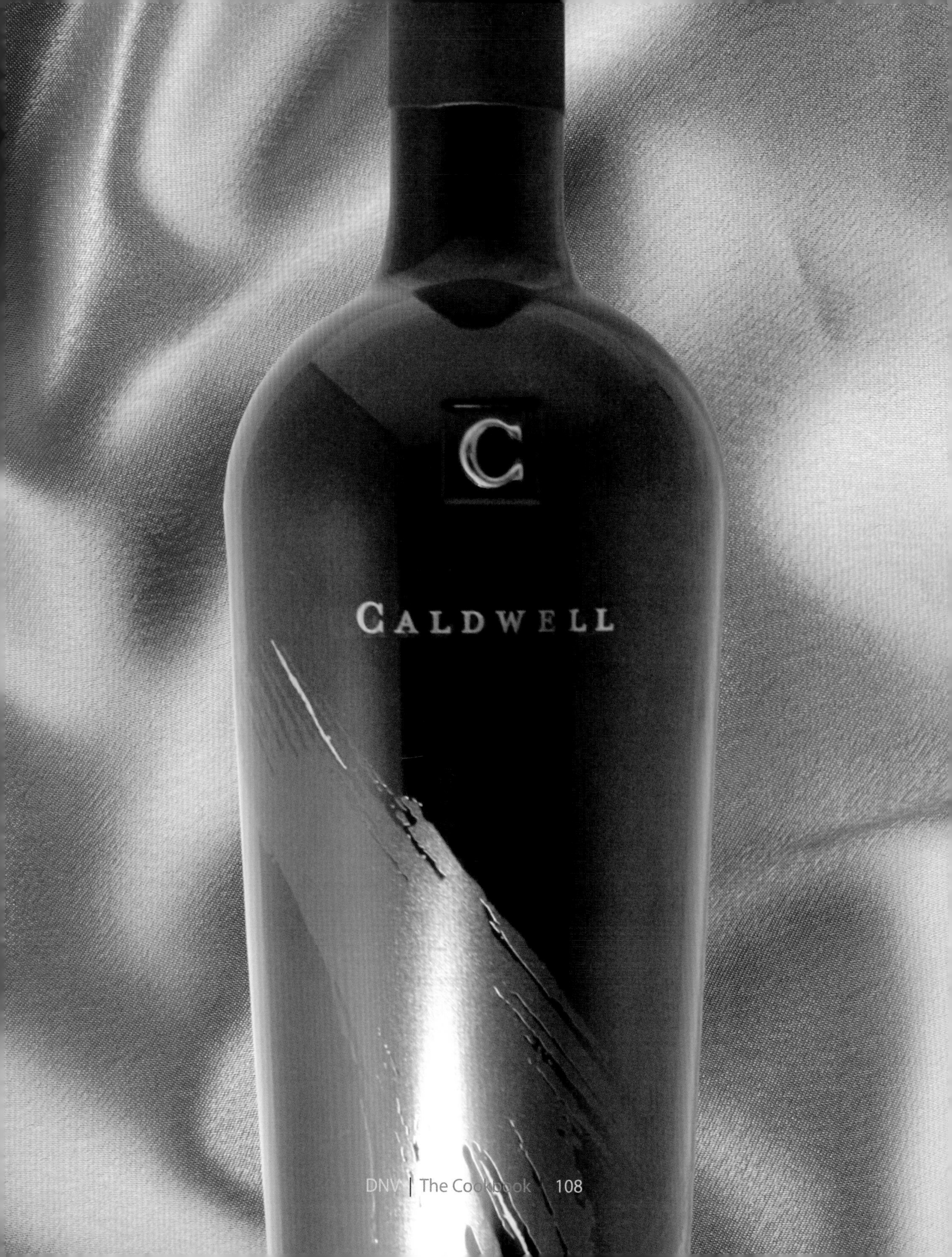
C
CALDWELL

CALDWELL VINEYARD GOLD
WAGYU BEEF, FISCALINI PEARL TAPIOCA, CABERNET SAUCE
WINEMAKER MARBUE MARKE, CHEF/OWNER KEN FRANK ~ LA TOQUE RESTAURANT

Wine Making Facts :
Encépagement : 100% Cabernet Sauvignon
Appellation : Napa Valley
Vineyard : 100% estate-owned vineyard
in Coombsville, Napa Valley
Soils : Stoney Aiken clay with
sub soil of volcanic ash
Elevation : 500 feet
Aspect : Northwest Facing Slope
Average Vine Age : 15 years
Yield : 2.0 Tons per Acre
Alcohol Level : 14.8%
Total Production : 180 cases
Harvest Details : Micro-blocks at harvest
from October 1st to November 9th
Facility : Cave Winery
Maceration : Average 30 days on the skins
Oak Regimen : 24 months
New Barrels : 100% French

CALDWELL VINEYARD
169 KREUZER LANE
NAPA, CA 94559
707-255-1294
CALDWELLVINEYARD.COM

SOMMELIERS BLACK TIE BORDEAUX
GRAND CRU GLASS

"PERFUMED BLACKBERRY, VIOLETS, CHOCOLATE, AND ANISE IN THE NOSE, COMPLEMENTED BY FRESH TOBACCO, VANILLA, AND MINT. RASPBERRY AND BLACK TEA LEADS INTO A BROAD MOUTH OF BLACK CHERRY, BLACK PEPPER, CORIANDER AND CLOVES SURROUNDED BY STRUCTURED TANNINS, WITH BLUEBERRY AND LINGERING MINERALITY."

WINEMAKER MARBUE MARKE

CALDWELL VINEYARD SYRAH ROSÉ
OPAH CRUDO HIBISCUS VINAIGRETTE, AVOCADO, YELLOW CREAMED CORN
WINEMAKER MARBUE MARKE, PROFESSIONAL CHEF GARY PENIR

12	slices Hawaiian opah, (sushi grade)
6 oz	hibiscus viniagrette
24 ea	avocado, balled with a marble size scoop, held in lime juice
2	whipped cream can with two charges
1 c	regular or micro mizuna
1 c	cilantro foam
¼ c	corn nuts, crushed
tt	Hawaiian Black Lava Salt

Hibiscus Vinaigrette:

½ c	lime juice
¼ c	hibiscus leaves, dried
¾ c	extra virgin olive oil
tt	salt
tt	sugar

Yellow Corn Emulsion:

2 ea	yellow corn purée, 2 ears on 1 large cut of box grater
4 T	butter
¼ t	lecithin
tt	salt and pepper

Cilantro Foam:

½	bunch cilantro
2 c	water
2 T	lemon juice
1 T	salt
¼ T	lecithin

Resources:
Le Sanctuaire online

Hibiscus Vinaigrette Method:
Steep hibiscus leaves in lime juice for 20 minutes.
Strain leaves out, reserve the liquid.
Mix salt and sugar until dissolved.
Pour the olive oil in the same container as liquid without whisking.
This is a broken vinaigrette, so just shake in a squeeze bottle prior to plating.

Cilantro Foam Method:
Purée cilantro, water, lemon juice and salt in a blender until it is completely liquid.
Put into a container with lecithin and use a stick blender to achieve the proper foam.

Yellow Corn Emulsion Method:
Over medium heat melt butter into corn purée.
Add lecithin, salt, pepper and blend with an immersion blender.
Strain through a chinois, discard solids.
Pour liquid into whipped cream can and charge with two charges, shake can vigorously.

Opah Method:
Lay slices of opah on a rectangular plate.
Dress and season mizuna with extra virgin olive oil and salt.
Expel a small amount of creamed corn emulsion on each piece of opah.
Season emulsion with black lava salt.
Scatter hibiscus vinaigrette and corn nuts around the fish.
Scatter avocado balls and mizuna around the plate.
Foam cilantro liquid and place around the plate. 4 servings

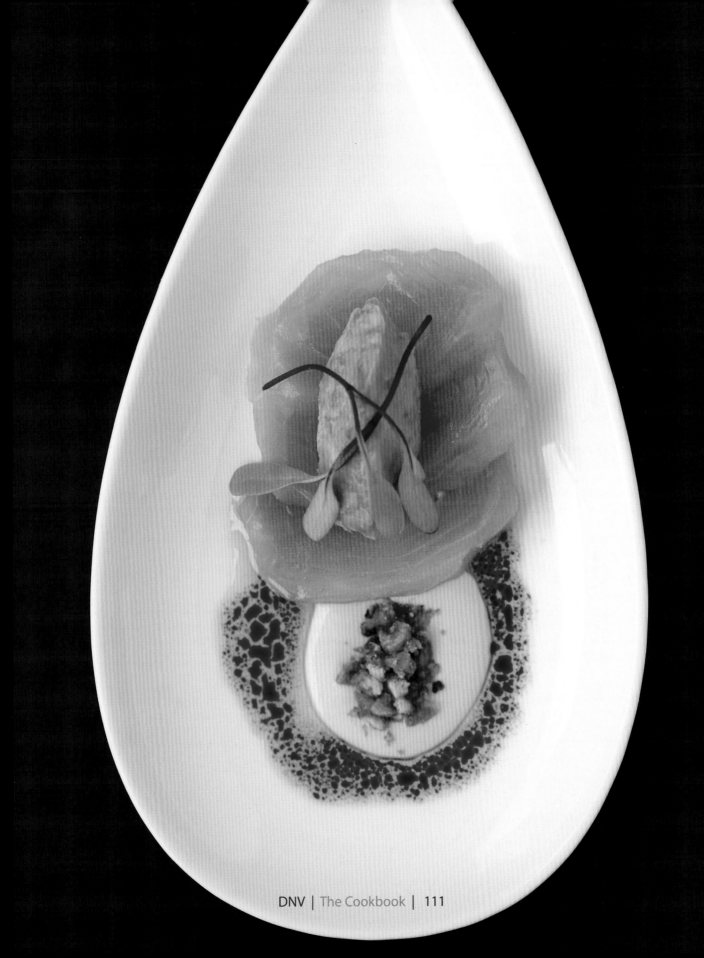

CALDWELL ROCKET SCIENCE AND CALDWELL GOLD
WAGYU BEEF, FISCALINI PEARL TAPIOCA, CABERNET SAUCE
WINEMAKER MARBUE MARKE, CHEF/OWNER KEN FRANK ~ LA TOQUE RESTAURANT

1	thick cut Wagyu New York steak		1 t	butter
1	shallot, finely chopped		¼ c	dry white wine
1 t	bacon, finely chopped		½ c	milk
4 oz	Cabernet Sauvignon		2 T	cream
½ c	veal stock		¼ c	Fiscalini cheddar, grated
¼ c	large pearl Tapioca			Sea salt and black pepper
1 T	white onion, finely diced			

For the tapioca:
Over low heat, sweat the finely diced white onion with butter until translucent and tender. Add the tapioca pearls and stir with butter and onion as if making rice pilaf. Add the white wine and a good pinch of sea salt, simmer for a few minutes, stirring frequently. Add the milk , reduce heat to very low, cover and cook very slowly, never quite reaching a simmer, for about half an hour. Stir from time to time to prevent clumping. Turn off heat and let rest, covered for another 30 minutes. The pearls should now be tender in a creamy sauce. Add 2 tablespoons cream and the grated cheddar cheese and stir while re-heating to melt the cheese into the tapioca. Verify seasoning, adjust as necessary and keep warm.

Cabernet sauce:
Cook the finely chopped bacon and shallot together over medium heat until they just begin to brown nicely. Deglaze with the Cabernet and reduce by 2/3. Add the Veal Stock and reduce slowly over very low heat until the sauce has a nice smooth consistency and the flavors are nicely concentrated. Verify seasoning, adjust as necessary and keep warm.

To serve:
Generously season the steak with salt and black pepper and cook to your desired temperature. After cooking, stand the steak on edge and let it rest in a warm place for about 5 minutes before slicing so that the temperature can equalize through the meat and the fibers can relax to hold in the juices. Slice the steak into 1/3 inch slices, arrange on a warm plate with a serving of the cheesy tapioca, drizzle with Cabernet Sauce and enjoy. 2 servings

LA TOQUE
1314 MCKINSTRY STREET
NAPA, CA 94558
707-257-5157
LATOQUE.COM

CLARK-CLAUDON CABERNET SAUVIGNON
GRILLED CRISPY SKIN WILD SALMON WITH CREAMED CORN, BABY BOK CHOY AND BEURRE ROUGE SAUCE
WINEMAKER FREDERIC DELIVERT, CHEF STEPHEN BARBER ~ FISH STORY, LARK CREEK RESTAURANT GROUP

Wine Making Facts:

Encépagement : Estate Grown Cabernet Sauvignon

Vineyard : Clark-Claudon Vineyard, Napa Valley

Soils : Shattered Sandstone; Bressa Dibble Complex

Elevation : 800 feet to 1000 feet

Micro-Climate : Mediterranean with same heat units as St. Helena, yet divided into cooler nights and mornings and warmer afternoons. Every afternoon a cool breeze moves down the vineyard from the highest Howell Mountain elevations.

Average Vine Age : 25 years

Alcohol Level : 14.2%

Total Production : 500 - 800 cases

Philosophy : Mindful, state-of-the-art farming, and winemaking where farmer, winemaker and nature work together in crafting beautiful expressions of season and place.

Harvest Details : Family & crew, small, 1-3 ton harvest lots, hand picked at night to assure cool fruit with intact skins. Fruit is then triple sorted at winery.

Winemaking : Small lot fermentation and aging with extreme attention to detail.

Fermentation: Primary in stainless steel and secondary in barrels.

Wood Origin: French, Taransaud barrels.

CLARK-CLAUDON VINEYARDS
PO BOX 15
ST. HELENA, CA 94574
707-965-9393
CLARKCLAUDON.COM

SOMMELIERS BORDEAUX GRAND CRU WINE

" This complex beauty invites with dark purple hues and gorgeous aromas of black cherry, plum and cassis with hints of pomegranate. Round and full on the palate, the balanced '07 follows with a stratum of cured meats, floral notes, spicy French oak and shaved dark chocolate leading to a long rich fruit and toasty mocha finish. " FD

Tom Clark and Laurie Claudon settled in Napa Valley, baby boy in tow, in 1974 when the wine-pioneer movement began. Over the next three decades, Napa Valley would emerge as a premier viticultural region. Many wine historians believe this was due in large part, to wines crafted by small artisanal wine producers such as Clark-Claudon. Their highly-allocated wines are consistently off-the-charts; rich, elegant Cabernets with distinct terroir based and varietal characteristics. In 2005, the family added Sauvignon Blanc to their portfolio naming it Wild Iris to resonate a sense of place and obvious passion from the makers. Their steeply terraced, Howell Mountain vineyards are cultivated by Tom's expertise, having spent thirty-six years in vineyard management. But what makes Clark-Claudon so spirited, and what one only discovers after lengthy conversations, is their generous philanthropic nature. "Let's just say we want to help give back…one sip at a time," laughs Laurie Claudon. It began with the Peace Corps and now they fund Cab for Care a program they founded that donates up to fifty percent of wine profits to charitable causes. It is fair to say that the wines produced by Clark-Claudon nurture both the palette and the soul.

CLARK-CLAUDON CABERNET SAUVIGNON
GRILLED CRISPY SKIN WILD SALMON WITH CREAMED CORN, BABY BOK CHOY AND BEURRE ROUGE SAUCE
WINEMAKER FREDERIC DELIVERT, CHEF STEPHEN BARBER ~ FISH STORY, LARK CREEK RESTAURANT GROUP

Ingredients:

4	Salmon fillets, wild and skin on (6- 7oz portions)
4 heads	baby bok choy
4 ears	sweet corn
¾ c	cream
1	lemon
	olive oil
	salt and pepper

Beurre Rouge:

½ c	Cabernet Sauvignon
¼ c	minced shallots
½ t	red wine vinegar
8 T	unsalted butter

Garnish:

Pea shoots on top, dressed with a squeeze of lemon and drizzle of olive oil

To make the Beurre Rouge:
1. Bring wine, shallots, and vinegar to boil in heavy small saucepan.
2. Reduce heat to low and simmer until liquid is reduced to 2 tablespoons, about 5 minutes. Remove pan from heat.
3. Add 8 tablespoons butter, 1 tablespoon at a time, whisking until each is melted before adding next; continue whisking until beurre rouge is thick (do not overheat or sauce may separate).
4. Season with salt and pepper. Hold in warm spot in kitchen.

For the creamed corn:
1. Shuck the corn.
2. In a large bowl, grate the corn on the largest side of a box grater.
3. After you have grated all 4 ears, "milk" the cobs, in the same bowl, by running the back of a knife down them.
4. Place the corn in a small sauce pot and bring to a simmer.
5. Add the cream and continue to cook for 10 minutes.
6. Season with salt and pepper

For the bok choy:
1. Cut each head in half-length wise.
2. Drizzle with olive oil, squeeze of lemon, salt and pepper

To Assemble:
1. Ignite enough charcoal briquettes or hardwood charcoal to fill slightly less than two shoeboxes, and burn until completely covered with thin coating light gray ash, 20 to 30 minutes. Spread coals in single layer to make medium-hot fire (judge by holding outstretched hand 5 inches above coals for 4 seconds; if you cannot make it the full 4 seconds, fire is too hot). Position grill grate over fire and rub cooking area of grate with oil-dipped paper towel.
2. Generously sprinkle each side of salmon fillets with salt and pepper. Place fillets skin side down on grill grate; grill until skin shrinks and separates from flesh and turns black, 2 to 3 minutes. Flip fillets gently with long-handled tongs or spatula; grill until fillets are opaque throughout, yet translucent at very center when checked with point of paring knife, 3 to 4 minutes.
3. Transfer to platter.
4. Meanwhile, grill the bok choy, cut side down to achieve nice grill marks and a little char.
5. Spoon the creamed corn on the plate.
6. Place the bok choy on top of the corn.
7. Place salmon on top of bok choy, skin side up
8. Drizzle sauce around. Serves 4.

FISH STORY
790 MAIN STREET
NAPA, CA 94559
707-251-5600
FISHSTORYNAPA.COM

Wine Making Facts :
Encépagement : 59% Cabernet Sauvignon, 25% Cabernet Franc and 16% Petit Verdot
Appellation : Napa Valley
Vineyard : Over the course of seven decades the Mondavi family has worked with superior Napa Valley vineyards.
Average Vine Age : 36 years
Alcohol Level : 15.1%
Total Production : 1700 cases
Winemaking: The grapes were hand-harvested into small lug boxes, hand-sorted twice then destemmed before being gravity fed to French oak tanks (96%) and some small French oak barrels for fermentation.
Wood Origin : France
Oak Regimen : Aged 19 months in French oak
Percentage of New Barrels : 100%

"The 2006 Continuum is a beautifully luminous, vibrant and persistent wine. Superbly balanced, the 2006 exhibits textbook ripeness with a long velvety finish. Aromas of blackberry, rose petal, leather and Indian spices precede flavors of licorice, cocoa butter and graphite. "
TM

CONTINUUM
PO BOX 112
OAKVILLE, CA 94562
707-944-8100
CONTINUUMESTATE.COM

SOMMELIERS BLACK TIE
BORDEAUX MATURE WINE GLASS

Continuum

Porcini-Dusted Wild Alaskan Halibut with Beluga Lentils and Porcini Jus
Winemaker Tim Mondavi, Winery Chef Sarah Patterson Scott

For the halibut and lentils:

4	Wild Alaskan Halibut fillets, 6 oz each skin on, boned
½ t	porcini powder
tt	kosher salt and pepper
½ lb	Hen of the Woods mushrooms olive oil, Extra virgin
1 c	beluga lentils
¼ lb	pancetta, cut into ¼" dice
2	shallots, finely minced
1	clove garlic, finely minced
1	carrot, ¼" dice, blanched
½ lb	fava beans, shucked, blanched and peeled

For the porcini butter and jus:

½ oz	dried porcini mushrooms, rinsed
1 ½ c	water
¼ t	dried porcini powder
1	shallot, finely minced
1	clove garlic, finely minced
1	stick, unsalted butter, softened
	kosher salt
	pepper
1 t	lemon juice
6 oz	veal demi-glacé
1 t	flat-leaf parsley, chopped
½ t	fresh thyme, chopped

Pat the halibut fillets dry. Refrigerate until ready to cook. In a small bowl, combine the porcini powder with 1 teaspoon of salt and ¼ teaspoon of pepper. Set aside.
Preheat the oven to 425°F.
Clean and tear mushrooms into large petals and toss with extra virgin olive oil. Place on a baking sheet and roast until golden brown and caramelized, about 8-10 minutes. Set aside.

Lentils:
You may substitute French green lentils; pick through the lentils to remove rocks, place in a medium saucepan and cover with 5 cups of cold salted water. Bring to a boil, turn down and simmer until tender, about 25-30 minutes. Drain and set aside. Place the pancetta in a large sauté pan over medium-high heat. Cook until golden brown and crisped. Remove and reserve. Add the shallots and garlic to the pan and cook until tender and translucent, about 3 to 4 minutes. Add the carrots and sauté until tender, 2-3 minutes. Add lentils and fava beans, mushrooms and pancetta. Turn heat off and hold in a warm place.

Porcini butter and jus:
Place the dried porcinis and the water in a small saucepan over medium-high heat. Bring to a boil, turn off and let sit for 30 minutes. Place a fine-meshed strainer over a bowl, strain the mushrooms and their liquid pressing hard. Return liquid to the saucepan over medium heat and reduce to ¼ cup then take off heat and whisk in dried porcini powder until dissolved. Cool to room temperature. Finely mince the porcini mushrooms. Heat two tablespoons olive oil over medium-high heat. Add the shallots and garlic and sauté until tender, about 3-4 minutes. Add the minced porcinis and cook another 2 minutes. Stir in a tablespoon of porcini liquid. Remove from heat and cool to room temperature. In a food processor, combine the porcini mushroom mixture, the stick of butter and season with salt and pepper and ½ teaspoon lemon juice.
Process until well-combined and the mushrooms are very finely chopped.
Place in a small bowl and reserve.

To finish:
Combine the veal demi-glacé and the remaining porcini liquid in a small saucepan over medium-high heat.
Bring to a boil, then turn down and simmer while cooking the halibut. It should reduce to about ½ cup of liquid. Reheat the lentil and vegetables and finish with two tablespoons of extra virgin olive oil and lemon juice.
Heat olive oil in a large sauté pan over medium high heat. Dust the halibut fillets with the porcini and salt mixture. Place in the pan, skin side up and cook for 2-3 minutes. Cover, turn the heat down to low. Cook another 5-7 minutes, or until the fish is cooked through. Whisk three tablespoons of the porcini butter into the veal sauce. Whisk in the parsley, thyme, lemon juice and season. Remove halibut skin. Divide the lentils among plates, top with halibut, (seared side up), and drizzle the porcini jus around the lentils. Garnish with fleur de sel and a scattering of micro arugula. 4 servings

CROSS

2005

OAKVILLE
CABERNET SAUVIGNON
BRIX VINEYARD
NAPA VALLEY

CROSS CELLARS CABERNET SAUVIGNON
DAUBE DE BOEUF WITH CÈPE MUSHROOMS
WINEMAKER CRAIG BECKER, WINERY CHEF JAMES CROSS

Wine Making Facts :

Encépagement : Cabernet Sauvignon

Appellation : Oakville

Vineyard : Brix Vineyard

Soils: Alluvial and clay

Elevation: 210 feet

Aspect : Northwest / Southwest

Micro-Climate : Warmdays /cool nights

Average Vine Age : 14 years

Yield : 1.9 tons per acre

Alcohol Level : 14.5% by volume

Total Production : 180 cases

Harvest Details : Picked on Halloween.

Winemaking: Cold soak, native yeast, pumpovers, fermented dry, post

Fermentation maceration; native ml, 28 months

Fermentation : Native

Maceration : 7 days

"Deep in color and very vibrant. The nose is youthful, intense and quite fine, with excellent fruitiness (black currant, plum cherry), a slight floral character (violet), with spicy overtones (clove, pepper). In the mouth it is full-bodied and smoothly textured, with medium richness, excellent balance, and light tannins and long aftertaste." CB

CROSS CELLARS
1720 SCOTT STREET
ST. HELENA, CA 94574
707-967-8113
CROSSCELLARS.COM

VINUM XL, CABERNET SAUVIGNON

2 lb	beef chuck, cut into 2 inch pieces	2	tomatoes, plum, medium, diced, peeled
½ oz	cèpe mushrooms, dried (substitute porcini)	1	celery stalk, diced
1 T	olive oil, extra virgin	1	bouquet garni (1 Italian parsley sprig, 1 thyme sprig, and 1 bay leaf tied)
2 T	butter		
1	onion, yellow, medium, diced	1 T	AP flour
2	garlic cloves	2 c	red wine
2	carrots, diced		

Place mushrooms in a bowl of boiling water to cover and set aside.

Season beef cubes, sear and set aside.

Sauté onion, garlic, carrots, tomatoes, and celery until vegetables soften (5 minutes).

Return beef to pot and add bouquet garni.

Mix half the wine with the flour making sure there are no lumps and pour into pot.

Add the remainder of the wine.

Cover and simmer for about 3 hours.

Drain mushrooms, rough chop, and reserve liquid.

Strain the reserved mushroom water through a coffee filter and add the liquid to the pot.

Cover and simmer another hour. Remove bouquet garni.

Strain if desired. Season with salt and pepper. 4-6 servings

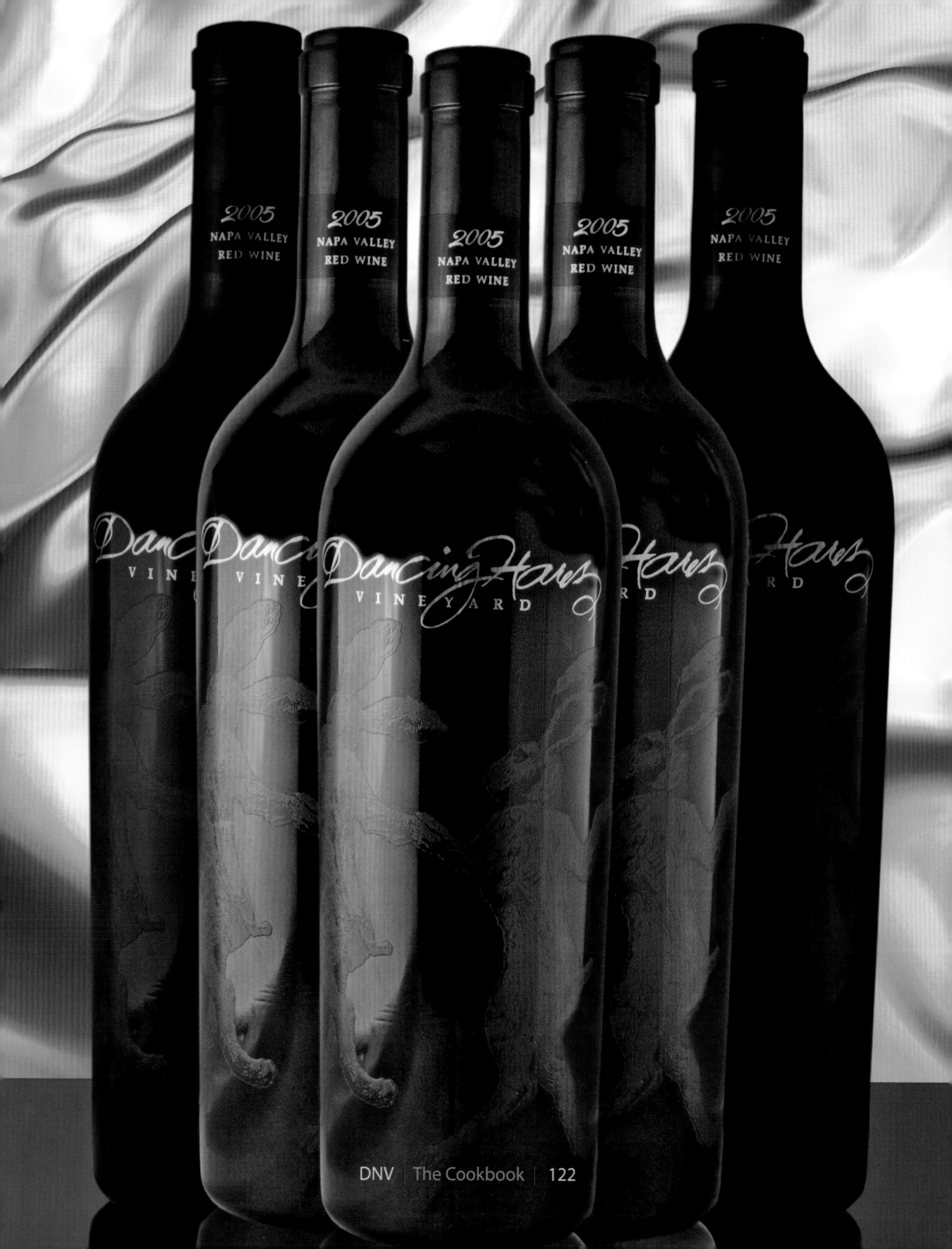
2005
NAPA VALLEY
RED WINE
Dancing Hares
VINEYARD

DANCING HARES
FILET MIGNON, CHANTERELLES, FINGERLINGS, TOMATO CARPACCIO, CABERNET SAUVIGNON SYRUP
WINEMAKER ANDY ERICSSON, PROFESSIONAL CHEF JOHN VLANDIS

Wine Making Facts :
Winemaker: Andy Erickson
Encépagement : Cabernet Sauvignon,
Merlot, Cabernet Franc, Petit Verdot
Appellation : St. Helena, Dancing Hares Vineyard
Soils: Volcanic rock and granite to clay loam
Elevation: Lower 100, upper 450
Aspect : Northwest Facing
Micro-Climate : at the base of Howell Mountain
Yield : 2.5 to 3 tons per acre
Alcohol Level : 14.5%
Total Production : 1100 cases
Fermentation : One-third barrel fermentation,
remainder in stainless steel, native
yeast fermentation.
Maceration : 5-7 day cold soak, long post-
fermentation maceration.
Barrels : 80% French oak
Bottling Format : 750 ml. 1.5 L, 3L, 6L

DANCING HARES VINEYARD
PO BOX 853
ST. HELENA, CA 94574
707-967-8296
DANCINGHARES.COM

SOMMELIERS, BORDEAUX GRAND CRU

" Vibrant aromas of fresh-cut cherries, rose petal, pastry cream, and crushed coriander are very inviting. The palate impression is soft and polished, but with great fruit intensity. The wine shows bright fruit flavors and balanced acidity, with notes of raspberry layer cake, caramel, and toasted almonds. " AE

When Paula Brooks and Bob Cook decided to start a winery — after each had successful careers in the field of high-tech — they went searching for the best and brightest. Their winery, playfully named Dancing Hares, is just under five acres, and lies at the base of Howell Mountain. Together, with winemaker Andy Ericsson and industry masters Michel Rolland and David Abreu, their limited production wine is soon to be all estate grown and aged in a new winery. As traditional in a Bordeaux-style blend, each year Dancing Hares changes the percentage of each varietal during blending and the resulting wine always makes the serious enthusiast dance.

Dancing Hares
Filet Mignon, Chanterelles, Fingerlings, Tomato Carpaccio, Cabernet Sauvignon Syrup
Winemaker Andy Ericsson, Professional Chef John Vlandis

Cabernet Syrup:

3 c	Cabernet Sauvignon
1	slice apple wood smoked bacon
1	roma tomato
1	spring of thyme
5	black peppercorns
2	shallots, peeled and sliced
1 t	chopped garlic
16 oz	veal stock
4 oz	softened butter

Meat:

2	Filet Mignons

Roasted Fingerling Potatoes:

½ lb	fingerling potatoes
4	cloves of cleaned garlic
1 T	thyme, minced
¼ lb	golden chanterelles
2 oz	olive oil
1 t	shallots, minced
¼ t	garlic, minced
5	basil leaves, thinly sliced

Heirloom Tomato Carpaccio;

3	tomatoes, Heirloom varieties
¼ c	Parmigiano Reggiano, shaved
	Cypress black salt
	extra virgin olive oil

Method:
Render bacon in a saucepan over medium heat.
Add garlic and shallots and cook until soft.
Add the remaining ingredients.
Reduce to 8 ounces and strain. Continue to reduce until 4 ounces remain.
Lower heat and whisk in the butter.
Season with salt and pepper.

Grilled Filet Mignon:
Start grill using oak logs or staves.
Brush the steaks with oil. Season with salt and pepper.
Grill to desired temperature.

Roasted Fingerling Potatoes:
Preheat the oven to 425 ° F.
Slice one half pound of potatoes into one-half inch slices.
Toss with salt and pepper, 1 tablespoon chopped fresh thyme, 4 cloves of garlic and 1 ounce olive oil.
Place baking sheet to heat. Add potatoes and cook for twenty minutes.
Remove and discard the garlic cloves.
Heat a sauté pan on high heat, add 1 ounce of olive oil..
To the pan add ¼ pound cleaned chanterelles, one teaspoon of minced shallots and one minced clove of garlic. Season and toss with the potatoes and the basil.

Heirloom Tomato Carpaccio:
Slice the tomatoes as thin as possible and arrange on a plate alternating varieties.
Add the potatoes in the center of the plate and top with the grilled filet mignon.
Spoon syrup on the steaks.
Season the tomatoes with the black salt and shards of Parmigiano.
Drizzle with the extra virgin olive oil. 2 servings

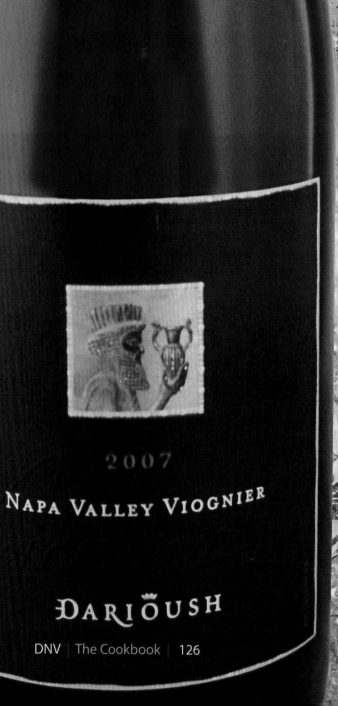

2007

Napa Valley Viognier

Darioush

DARIOUSH VIOGNIER
CARAMELIZED DIVER SCALLOPS, CAULIFLOWER PURÉE, TOASTED ALMONDS, BALSAMIC REDUCTION
WINEMAKER STEVE DEVITT, CHEF/OWNER RICHARD REDDINGTON ~ REDD RESTAURANT

Wine Making Facts :
Encépagement : 100% Viognier
Appellation : Darioush Estate Vineyards, Oak Knoll
Vineyard : Ashley
Total Production : 1340 cases
Harvest Details : Meticulous attention to detail
and minimal handling hand-harvested into small 28 lb.
baskets hand-sorted and whole cluster pressed
barrel lots racked prior to bottling
Facility : Darioush
Fermentation : Barrel fermented and aged 7
months sur-lie with bi-monthly batonage.
Coopers : Aged 7 months sur-lies in 15% new
French oak, Burgundy cooperage

DARIOUSH
4240 SILVERADO TRAIL
NAPA, CA 94558
707-257-2345
DARIOUSH.COM

"Honeysuckle, jasmine and citrus fruit aromas leap from the glass, introducing a vibrant and succulent mouthfeel of juicy peach and cantaloupe balanced by the bright acidity of Fuji apple and lemon zest. The 2007 Viognier finishes with lingering notes of dried apricot, nutmeg and vanilla bean." SD

VITIS, SAUVIGNON BLANC GLASS

It's unlike any other winery you will visit in the Napa Valley. Or, for that matter, the world. This fact is obvious the moment you spot Darioush. Inside you'll find a vibrant environment where it feels like the high-energy lobby of a luxury hotel, but it's actually the vision of a single man. Persia-born Darioush Khaledi came to California in 1975 seeking personal freedom and the American dream, which he realized by developing the state's largest independent grocery business. His success enabled him to pursue his lifelong goal of building an exquisite wine estate inspired by the châteaux of Bordeaux. Contrary to conventional wisdom, he chose to plant Cabernet Sauvignon grapes in the cooler regions of Napa. The resulting Cabernets emphasize his personal appreciation for complexity, character and style.

DARIOUSH CABERNET SAUVIGNON AND DARIOUSH SIGNATURE SHIRAZ
HORSERADISH CRUSTED BRAISED SHORTRIBS
WINEMAKER STEVE DEVITT, CHEF/OWNER RICHARD REDDINGTON ~ REDD RESTAURANT

DARIOUSH
4240 SILVERADO TRAIL
NAPA, CA 94558
707-257-2345
DARIOUSH.COM

Wine Making Facts :
Darioush Cabernet Sauvignon
Encépagement : 85% Cabernet
Sauvignon, 9% Merlot, 3% Cabernet
Franc, 3% Malbec
Appellation : Darioush Estate Vineyards
in Mt. Veeder, Oak Knoll, Napa Valley
Total Production : 9910 cases
Facility : Darioush
Fermentation : Fermentation includes
cold soaking for 4 days in a combination
of opened top and traditional
fermenters, with gentle pump-overs
and extended maceration for optimal color
extraction and tannin management
Harvest Details : Hand-harvested into
small 28 lb. baskets. Hand-sorted twice,
before and after de-stemming
Wood Origin : France

Wine Making Facts :
Darioush Signature Shiraz
Encépagement : 100% Shiraz
Appellation : Darioush Estate Vineyards
in Napa Valley and Oak Knoll
Total Production : 1160 cases
Harvest Details : Meticulous attention to
detail in vineyard and cellar, hand-harvested
into small 28 lb. baskets, hand-sorted
twice, before and after de-stemming
Facility : Darioush
Fermentation : Includes cold soaking for 4
days in a combination of opened top and
traditional fermenters, with gentle pump-
overs and extended maceration for optimal
color extraction and tannin management
Wood Origin : France
Barrels: Aged 18 months in new
French oak

"Enticing aromas of ripe black currant, blueberry and cacao introduce this bold, yet harmonious wine. A supple and focused palate reveals round flavors of juicy blackberry, cherry and espresso. Finely knit tannins prolong the elegant, poised finish that is accented by hints of cinnamon, cedar and nutmeg." SD

"Alluring fragrances of blackberry, orange zest and white pepper, the 2006 Signature Shiraz shows remarkable ripeness and concentration. Layers of black licorice, bittersweet chocolate and aged tobacco are intricately woven together with well integrated tannins, endless dark fruits and a long finish of espresso." SD

SOMMELIERS BLACK TIE, HERMITAGE SYRAH
SOMMELIERS BLACK TIE, BORDEAUX GRAND CRU

Darioush Viognier
Caramelized Diver Scallops, Cauliflower Purée, Toasted Almonds, Balsamic Reduction
Winemaker Steve Devitt, Chef/Owner Richard Reddington ~ Redd Restaurant

4	2 ½ oz. each scallops, Diver or Day Boat		2 T	almonds, slivered, toasted
2 c	cauliflower, one head cut into florets		2 T	golden raisins
			1 T	parsley, chopped
¼ c	cream		½ c	balsamic vinegar, reduced
1 ½ T	butter, unsalted		1 T	extra virgin olive oil
2 T	capers			

Method:

Bring balsamic vinegar to a boil, reduce by half, reserve.

Cut cauliflower into florets, reserving 1 cup for garnish.
Bring 2 quarts of water to a boil and season with salt.
Blanch garnish florets, until tender (about 60 seconds), shock in an ice bath.
Reserve for garnish.
Cook the remaining cauliflower until tender, strain and shock in ice water.
Cover with the cream and cook for 8 minutes.
Purée and put through a fine mesh strainer.

Season the scallops with salt and pepper.
Sauté scallops in olive oil to golden brown; cook about 1 minute on each side.
Remove and let rest.

In a sauté pan add butter and heat reserved cauliflower florets about 1 minute.
Add capers, almonds, raisins and parsley.
Season with salt and pepper.

Serving:
Put a small circle of cauliflower purée in the middle.
Add the caper raisin ragout to the middle and top with the scallops.
Drizzle balsamic reduction around plate and extra virgin olive oil to garnish. 4 servings

Darioush
4240 Silverado Trail
Napa, CA 94558
707-257-2345
darioush.com

DARIOUSH SIGNATURE SHIRAZ AND DARIOUSH CABERNET SAUVIGNON
HORSERADISH CRUSTED BRAISED SHORTRIBS
WINEMAKER STEVE DEVITT, CHEF/OWNER RICHARD REDDINGTON ~ REDD RESTAURANT

Short ribs:

6	beef short ribs, bone in, 1½ - 2 inch lengths
1 btl	dry red wine, 750 ml
1 lb	onions, large dice
½ lb	carrots, large dice
½ lb	celery, large dice
6	thyme sprigs
1 T	black peppercorns, toasted, freshly cracked
2 qt	beef or veal stock

Horseradish crust:

3 parts	bread crumbs
2 parts	butter
1 part	horseradish, prepared or fresh

Method:

Short ribs:
Marinade short ribs in wine, vegetables, peppercorns, and thyme overnight.
Remove short ribs, pat dry (reserve soaking liquid) and season with salt and pepper.
Sear short ribs, on all sides, in large braising pan.
Remove short ribs from pan and deglaze with the reserved soaking liquid.
Reduce liquid by 1/3 and then add stock.
Add back short ribs to pan and bring to a simmer.
Cover and cook in a 300º F oven for about 3 – 4 hours.
Cook until meat is tender and easily pulls away from the bone.
Strain vegetables from liquid and reduce liquid by 2/3 to a sauce consistency, (should lightly coat the back of a metal spoon).

Horseradish crust:
Mix all ingredients together and freeze.
Place about ¼ inch onto each short rib and broil. 2 servings

REDD
6480 WASHINGTON STREET
YOUNTVILLE, CA 94599
707-944-2222
REDDNAPAVALLEY.COM

DAVID ARTHUR
BRAISED WILD BOAR WITH POTATO GNOCCHI
WINEMAKER NILE ZACHERLE, CHEF DE CUISINE CRAIG DIFONZO ~ CANTINETTA PIERO

Wine Making Facts :
Encépagement : 100% Cabernet Sauvignon
Appellation : Napa Valley
Soils: Akin, Sobrante and hambright Yield : 1.5-2 tons/Acre
Alcohol Level : 15.0%
Philosophy : Vineyard fruit expression is our goal with refined tannins and rich density. French oak barrels are used exclusively and winemaking is delicate yet modern in style.
Harvest Details : Harvested on October 12th 2006, sorted pre- destemmer and pumped to tanks.
Facility : David Arthur Vineyards
Fermentation : The Cabernet Sauvignon fruit is cold soaked for 5 days in tank at 55° F warmed to 85 to 88 F during fermentation with a total maceration time of 22 days. Malolactic fermentation occurred in oak barrels.
Maceration : 15 to 22 days
Wood Origin : 100% French Tight grain
Percentage of New Barrels : 90%
Bottling Format : 6 packs 750ml, 6 packs 1.5L, 3L, 6L and 9L

DAVID ARTHUR VINEYARDS
200 LONG RANCH ROAD
RUTHERFORD, CA 94573
707-963-5190
DAVIDARTHUR.COM

VITIS, CABERNET SAUVIGNON GLASS

" The color is a dark ruby red nearly opaque with a deep core. Aromas of vanilla, roasted coffee beans and toasted oak spice back dense fruit aromas of blackberry, blueberry, dark cherry and cassis. Hints of earth and forest floor complex the nose. The palate is sweet, rich and broad. Its concentration is truly full palate and has a round, plush and firm styling that carries the dark fruits to a long finish." NZ

David Arthur began in the 1950's when butcher, businessman and father, Donald Long, acquired land by planting a grapevine and a dream. His commitment led to the acquisition of 1,000 acres on Pritchard Hill, but it was his intuition to purchase hillside terrior, — on what is now deemed the famous Rutherford benchmark soil — that was ingenious. Donald, as the name goes, was also long on patience and the land sat dormant for nearly two decades. It was then, in the late seventies, that Napa Valley was re-invented by a handful of vintners who have become the iconic families of the region. It was also when Donald's son David, began learning grape growing at UC Davis, and working for Joseph Phelps, and the Chappellet's, all of which were learning the trade through hands-on experience in the vineyard and in the cellar. In 1985, David with his brother Bob, founded David Arthur Vineyards. From the start, they utilized estate grown fruit to produce wines with complexity, structure and varietal character. With winemaker Nile Zacherle, David Arthur now produces select, hand-crafted varietals, including their flagship wine Elevation 1147. Today, David can be found touring the country in his famous wine bus, playing rock and introducing his wines to the people. Simply put, the Long family has as much character in person, as the wines they produce.

DAVID ARTHUR
BRAISED WILD BOAR WITH POTATO GNOCCHI
WINEMAKER NILE ZACHERLE, CHEF DE CUISINE CRAIG DIFONZO ~ CANTINETTA PIERO

1	boar shoulder, boneless	12	juniper berries
1	carrot, cut onto 3- inch pieces	4	star anise
2	celery, stalks, cut onto 3- inch pieces	1/8	coriander seed, toasted
1	onion, quartered	2	thyme sprigs, fresh
5 oz	Cabernet	3	parsley sprigs, fresh
2	thyme sprigs	4	garlic cloves
3	bay leaves	4	Idaho potatoes
I gl	chicken stock, or enough to cover	1 lb	AP flour
28 oz	San Marzano tomatoes, or one large can		

Preheat Oven to 350° F.
Poke holes in the potatoes with a fork and then roast them in the oven for about 45 minutes or until tender.

Boar:
Lay the boar meat out and cut into 3 pieces that will be easy to handle when searing.
Heat a sauté pan with oil, when hot place the seasoned meat in the pan and allow the meat to brown (about 4 to 5 minutes per side). Once the meat is caramelized, remove from the pan and place it into stock pot or deep baking dish. In the sauté pan add the celery, carrots, onions, tomatoes (with juice), herbs and bay leaf. Cook until tender, add one glass red wine (approximately 5 ounces) to deglaze the pan. Pour over the boar meat; add the stock (enough to cover), bring to a boil, cover and place in the 350° degree oven, along side the baking potatoes. Let boar braise for about 3 to 4 hours, or until the meat starts to fall apart.

Potato Gnocchi:
Once the potatoes are tender, remove from the oven. When cool enough to work with; halve and remove potato from skins and then run through a ricer or coarse sieve. Place potatoes in a mound and create a well in the center. Add most of the flour, pinch of salt, and egg yolk. Incorporate ingredients, adding more flour if necessary, and knead the dough until it comes together into a nice ball.
Cut the dough ball into quarters and roll each piece and into individual ropes. With a sharp knife cut individual pieces about 2 inches in size. Boil salted water. Poach potato gnocchi until they float on the top - they cook very quickly. Remove, strain and place in an ice bath to chill them down. Toss them in oil and set aside.

Plating:
Once the boar is cooked remove from the liquid and shred into large pieces. Strain the liquid thru a chinoise or sieve. Add gnocchi to the ragu a few minutes before serving so as to absorb the flavor. Place meat in the center of bowl, pour ragu on top of gnocchi and serve. Serves 4

CANTINETTA PIERO
HOTEL LUCA
6774 WASHINGTON STREET
YOUNTVILLE, CA 94599
707-944-8080
HOTELLUCANAPA.COM

DEL DOTTO VINEYARDS CABERNET SAUVIGNON
INVOLTINI OF VEAL STUFFED WITH PORCINI AND SPINACH, BLACK TRUFFLE CREAM, FETTUCCINE
WINEMAKER GERARD ZANZONICO ~ EXECUTIVE WINERY CHEF JOSHUA SCHWARTZ

Appellation : Rutherford Bench
Vineyard : Rutherford Estate
Soils : Valley floor
Average Vine Age : 16 years
Yield : 2 ½ tons per acre
Alcohol Level : 14.9%
Total Production : 800 Cases
Winemaking : Hand-sorted and free run juice only
Wood Origin : French oak
Percentage of New Barrels : 80%

DEL DOTTO ESTATE WINERY & CAVES
1445 ST. HELENA HWY SOUTH
ST. HELENA, CA 94574
707-963-2134
DELDOTTOVINEYARDS.COM

"The bouquet has dark chocolate, with red and black fruits. The mouth-feel is earthy, with elegant flavors of wet stone, match stick and flint, and licorice. The finish is long and rich; fruity, silky tannins, touch of vanilla, oak, black currant and cinnamon." GZ

SOMMELIERS BORDEAUX GRAND CRU WINE

In 1150 A.D., when Venice controlled the world, it was the Del Dotto family signature that influenced the Venetian government. Wine historians are able to authenticate Del Dotto's winemaking inheritance to Tuscany, Italy in 1450. Yes, even before Columbus sailed, there was a Del Dotto making wine. And so it makes perfect sense that David Del Dotto, the infomercial guru, built both his opulent winery and "Sacred Caves" in the center of Napa Valley. The winery is inspired by the splendor of Venetian architecture; custom marble columns, mosaic floors and hand-blown Murano glass chandeliers. Del Dotto wines are equally as opulent, bestowing extraordinary wine reviews and appraisals. "Wine is liquid art. We wanted to build a gallery of marble to house the sacred juice. Our family is dedicated to show respect to the history of a gift to mankind from God, sacred wine" says David Del Dotto. It remains a family business with the next generation of children, Desiree and Giovanni ready to carry on the Del Dotto tradition. With all this history, or perhaps because of it, Del Dotto is a Napa Valley personality with five hundred years of winemaking experience behind him.

DEL DOTTO CINGHIALE VINEYARD PINOT NOIR
DUCK BREAST WITH CONFIT CRESPELLES, CARAMELIZED BRUSSELS SPROUTS AND SOUR CHERRY JUS
WINEMAKER ROBBIE MEYER, EXECUTIVE CHEF JOSHUA SCHWARTZ

Encépagement : 100% Pinot Noir Cinghiale Vineyard

Micro-Climate : Coastal

Average Vine Age : 8 years

Yield : 2 Tons

Alcohol Level : 14.9%

Total Production : 950 Cases

Philosophy : Producing wines reflective of the site and indicative of the varietal character. In this case, achieving maturity that provides excellent fruit expression of fresh, wild, berries yet preserving the intriguing elements of fresh earth, forest floor, and tea, while harnessing the intensity and power that are achievable on these rocky hilltops so close to the Pacific Ocean.

Harvest Details : September 1st through 7th, 2007

Winemaking : All grapes are hand harvested and hand sorted and destemmed before beginning a 5 day cold soak in our fermentation tanks. The fermentations begin with some tanks fermenting with indigenous yeasts, while some are inoculated. Each tank is evaluated individually; harvest to harvest, to establish the proper treatments in terms of frequency of pump overs and punch downs, the amount of time on the skins, delestage treatments, and fermentation temperatures.

Maceration : 5 days Cold, 10 additional days on the skins

Wood Origin : French Oak for 17 months

DEL DOTTO ESTATE WINERY & CAVES
1445 ST. HELENA HWY SOUTH
ST. HELENA, CA 94574
707-963-2134
DELDOTTOVINEYARDS.COM

VITIS, PINOT NOIR WINE GLASS

"THE PINOT WAS CROPPED AT 1.9 TONS OF FRUIT PER ACRE, DISPLAYS A CLASSIC VOSNE-ROMANEE BOUQUET OF SPRING FLOWERS, FOREST FLOOR, BLACK RASPBERRIES, AND SWEET CHERRIES. THE WINE EXHIBITS ROUND, GENEROUS, FULL BODIED FLAVORS, EXCELLENT PURITY, AND FINE OVERALL BALANCE."

WINEMAKER ROBBIE MEYER

Del Dotto Cinghiale Vineyard Pinot Noir
Duck Breast with Confit Crespelles, Caramelized Brussels Sprouts and Sour Cherry Jus
Winemaker Robbie Meyer, Executive Chef Joshua Schwartz

3	duck breasts		2 T	olive oil
2	duck legs		4 T	sweet butter
4 c	duck fat		½ lb	dried sour cherries
1 c	kosher salt, plus a pinch		1 c	Pinot Noir
1 c	whole milk		½ c	Ruby Port
¾ c	AP flour		4 T	honey
2	eggs, lightly beaten		2T	sugar
2 T	olive oil		1	bay leaf, fresh
¼ c	ricotta cheese		2 c	dark chicken stock
1 t	garlic, minced		¼ c	demi-glacé
pinch	Espilette pepper (or crushed red pepper)			
2 t	chopped parsley		Materials:	
2 lb	brussels sprouts			bacon weight

Confit:
Cover duck legs in kosher salt 12 hours. Wash off salt well and place legs in shallow pot. Add duck fat and place on low heat. Preheat oven to 300º F. Once fat is melted cover with parchment round and place in oven for 2 ½ - 3 hours or until meat is tender. Once duck legs are cooked; cool, separate meat from bone, remove skin, shred meat and place in bowl. Add ricotta, garlic, parsley, Espilette pepper, and mix to consistency of tuna salad.

Crespelle:
Crespelle are Italian crepes. Wisk together milk, flour, eggs, olive oil, and pinch of kosher salt. Let sit for 1 hour and strain through fine mesh then refrigerate. Heat a nonstick 10 inch sauté pan. Spray with nonstick vegetable spray. Fill a 2 ounce ladle, then pour in batter and rotate pan in a circular motion to coat bottom. Cook crespelle until light brown and turn over. Cook for 30 additional seconds and remove, repeating to make six crespelles.

Assembly:
Separate confit mixture into six servings and place each in the center of one crespelle. Fold into an envelope shape and finish by browning crespelle packages in a sauté pan on low heat in butter until golden brown on both sides.

Brussels Sprouts:
Trim the ends off the sprouts and split in half. Heat olive oil in a large sauté pan. Place brussels sprouts cut side down to caramelize and then turn. Add one tablespoon of butter, season with salt and pepper and toss. Cover with lid and turn heat off until any noise stops. They will be tender. Check seasoning.

Cherry Sauce:
Place cherries in sauce pot. Cover with wine, port, honey, sugar and bay leaf and bring to simmer. Let sit for twenty minutes then strain reserving cherries. Add liquid back to pot, add chicken stock and demi-glacé. Bring to simmer. Reduce to sauce consistency and add cherries.

Duck Breast:
Remove silver skin and tenders from breasts. Score skin with sharp knife in cross hatch pattern. Season with salt and pepper. Heat heavy sauté pan, add oil and then duck breasts with the skin side down. Reduce heat to medium-high. Press each breast with bacon weight to stop from curling. Slowly render (melt) fat from each breast removing excess fat from pan as it accumulates. Once skin is a deep brown color, turn each breast over and continue to cook for one additional minute for medium rare. Let duck rest and slice.

Plating:
Place browned crespelle on plate lean sliced duck breast and garnish with brussels sprouts.
Finish with cherries and sauce. Serves 6

Del Dotto Estate Winery & Caves
1445 St. Helena Hwy South
St. Helena, CA 94574
707-963-2134
DELDOTTOVINEYARDS.COM

Involtini:

12	veal cutlet pieces, cut ¼ inch
1 lb	porcini mushrooms, fresh
9 oz	baby spinach, (one bag)
1	red onion, large
¼ c	olive oil
3 t	minced garlic
¼ c	bread crumbs
¼ c	Parmesan Reggiano, grated
2 T	parsley, chopped
1	egg yolk
2 c	AP flour

Truffle Cream:

3 oz	butter, unsalted
2 oz	AP flour
2 pt	heavy cream
4 T	minced black truffle
4 T	porcini mushroom oil

Pasta:

3 ½ c	AP flour
2 t	kosher salt
1 T	olive oil
4	eggs, large
2 T	cold water, if necessary

Involtini:

Pound each piece of veal with mallet to half the thickness. Medium dice porcini mushrooms and sauté in olive oil. Add Garlic and lightly toast. Add spinach and cook until well wilted. Remove from pan and drain well in colander. Slice red onion into ½ inch pieces. Grill dry until partially charred. Add to mushrooms and spinach in colander. Let cool. Once cool rough chop mushrooms onions and spinach. Place in mixing bowl, add parmesan cheese, bread crumbs, egg yolk, and parsley. Check and adjust seasoning with salt and pepper. Divide filling into 12 portions, placing each portion on a piece of veal and roll nice and tight. Pinch closed with toothpicks. Repeat then season all with salt and pepper and dust with flour. In heavy bottom sauté pan brown involtini in olive oil turning to get and even golden brown. Drain on paper towel, and remove toothpicks after resting 10 minutes. Place involtini in appropriate size casserole dish while you make the sauce.

Truffle Cream:

Melt butter in sauce pot. Wisk in flour to create roux. Be sure that your cream is cold to avoid lumps, wisk constantly, and slowly add your cream. Bring sauce to a simmer for 15 minutes. Incorporate truffle and porcini oil. Taste and season with salt and pepper. Pour sauce over veal in casserole dish. Reserve a cup of sauce to coat pasta. Sprinkle some grated parmesan cheese over veal. This is ready for the oven or can be held overnight in the refrigerator. Once ready to serve, preheat oven to 350º, place casserole in oven for 15- 20 minutes or until heated through and golden brown.

Pasta:

On wooden board or marble slab place 2 cups flour and hollow center to create a "well". Crack eggs into the well then add olive oil. With a fork slowly start incorporating flour with eggs. Add salt and continue to add ½ cup of remaining flour. If the dough does not come together easily, add cold water. Once dough is formed, knead well for 10 minutes until supple, it should feel moist, but not sticky. Wrap dough in plastic wrap and let sit for at least one hour before rolling out. You can roll this dough out by hand or use a pasta machine. When you roll it out make sure you can see your hand through the pasta sheets and use plenty of flour to keep it from sticking. Cut to your desired thickness. Wide strips for pappardelle or thin for tagliatelle. Boil a large pot of salted water and add your pasta. Homemade pasta cooks quickly, usually 2-3 minutes. Drain and mix with reserved sauce to create a bed for your involtini. Serves 6

Del Dotto Estate Winery & Caves
1445 St. Helena Hwy South
St. Helena, CA 94574
707-963-2134
DELDOTTOVINEYARDS.COM

DOLCE
APPLE TART WITH BLUE D'AUVERGNE CHEESE, MAUI ONION AND SMOKED BACON
WINEMAKER GREG ALLEN, WINERY CHEF ABI MARTINEZ

Wine Making Facts :
Philosophy: Dolce embraces a deceptively simple philosophy, the pursuit of perfection in the art of late harvest winemaking.
Varietals: 90% Semillon, 10% Sauvignon Blanc
Appellation: Napa Valley
Acreage: 20 acres
Alcohol Level: 13.8%
Harvest Dates: November 11–16, 2005
Oak Regimen: French oak barrels,
Percentage of New Barrels: 100%
Aging: 31 months
Fermentation: 3-20 weeks
Residual Sugar at Bottling: 12.0%
Bottling Format: 375mL

DOLCE WINERY
P.O. BOX 327
OAKVILLE, CA 94562
707-944-8868
DOLCEWINE.COM

SOMMELIERS, SAUTÉRNES WINE GLASS

"Aromas of stone and citrus fruits – pear, peach, and orange rind – are balanced by more subtle layers of honey and an earthy minerality. The 2005 Dolce will retain its youthful fruitiness for the first two or three years in bottle, after which its bottle bouquet will emerge as a complement to the ripe fruit. The texture is coating on the palate but the sweetness is held in balance by a mouth-watering oiliness. Flavors of concentrated and ripe citrus fruits dominate in the mouth and linger through the finish, which is both long and coating in texture. Given the opportunity to age, this wine will develop a perfume in the bottle that will add spice to the concentrated, fruit-driven aromas." GA

Onions:
1 c	chicken stock
2 T	balsamic vinegar
3 T	sugar
2 T	unsalted butter
1 T	Kosher salt
2	sweet onions, preferably Maui, thinly sliced
3	strips smoked bacon ¼" x ¾ "lardons

Tart Assembly:
10 each	puff pastry rounds 3 x ¼-inch thick
2 T	butter, clarified
3	apples, Golden Delicious, peeled, cored, sliced ¼-inch thick
2 oz	Blue d'Auvergne
1 T	rosemary, chopped

Preheat the oven to 375°F.
Onions: Reduce chicken stock, vinegar, sugar, butter and salt on medium high for 10 minutes.
Add the onions and simmer another 5 minutes. Place the mixture into a roasting pan and roast for 15 minutes or until golden brown. Remove and let cool. Brush the puff pastry rounds with the clarified butter.
Place a spoonful of onion mixture in the center of each round, top each with sliced apples and a pinch of rosemary. Bake for 10 minutes, top the tart with the blue cheese and bake an additional 4 minutes.
Remove from oven. Serve warm. 10 servings

DOMAINE CARNEROS LE RÊVE BLANC DE BLANCS
WARM MAINE LOBSTER AND ROASTED SWEET POTATO SALAD
WINEMAKER EILEEN CRANE, CHEF/OWNER KEN FRANK ~ LA TOQUE RESTAURANT

Wine Making Facts :
Wine : Le Rêve Blanc de Blancs
Encépagement : 98% Chardonnay, 2% Pinot Blanc
Winemaker : Sparkling, Eileen Crane
Appellation : 100% Carneros
Elevation : Average 100'
Aspect : Gently rolling hills
Micro-Climate : Cool region
Average Vine Age : 5-20 years
Yield : 2.5 - 3 tons
Alcohol Level : 12.5%
Total Production : 1,800 cases
Philosophy : To create a cuvée of great complexity
and finish in the classic blanc de blancs style. Vintage
dated, no oak cuvées, 7% malolactic fermentation
Harvest Details : Hand harvested into small bins, gently pressed
Fermentation : Cool 65° F
Bottling Format : 750 ml
Vineyards : Organic certified, CCOF

DOMAINE CARNEROS
1240 DUHIG ROAD
NAPA, CA 94559
707-257-0101
DOMAINECARNEROS.COM

SOMMELIERS BLACK TIE, CHAMPAGNE

" This sparkling wine is very expressive now and is destined to be a long-lived classic. Generous aromas of white flowers, baked pear, and lemon curd tempt the palate. Tastes of white fruit, ginger, crème brûlée and a grace note of toasted nuts from the long aging are followed by a remarkably long silky finish. " EC

If you visit, don't be intimidated by the grand façade of Domaine Carneros' French château overlooking coiffed gardens and vineyard covered hills. Inside, the winery's aristocratic lineage gives way to pure California warmth and charm. The esteemed French company Champagne Taittinger recognized early that the Carneros appellation had the potential to produce premier sparkling wines. Today, Domaine Carneros is creating handcrafted sparkling and Pinot Noir wines with all estate grown grapes coming from certified organic vineyards. With more than 30 years of winemaking experience founding winemaker at Domaine Carneros, Eileen Crane, eloquently says, "Our goal is simply to create the most memorable sparkling wine experience in the world."

DOMAINE CARNEROS ESTATE PINOT NOIR
SEARED SONOMA ARTISAN FOIE GRAS WITH FRESH CORN POLENTA AND CHANTERELLES
WINEMAKER TJ EVANS, CHEF/OWNER KEN FRANK ~ LA TOQUE RESTAURANT

Wine Making Facts :
Encépagement : 100% Pinot Noir
Appellation : 100% Carneros
Winemaker : Pinot Noir, TJ Evans
Elevation : Average 100'
Aspect : Gently rolling hills
Micro-Climate : Cool region
Yield : 3 - 3½ tons
Alcohol Level : 13.7%
Total Production : 5,000 cases
Philosophy : Classic Pinot Noir, velvety palate feel, long finish
Harvest Details : Hand harvested into small bins, gently pressed
Winemaking : Traditional open top fermenters
Facility : State-of-the-art lit by skylight, housing large solar collection system.
Maceration : 5 day cold soak
Wood Origin : 100% French, Allier and Vosges
Vineyards : Organic certified , CCOF

DOMAINE CARNEROS
1240 DUHIG ROAD
NAPA, CA 94559
707-257-0101
DOMAINECARNEROS.COM

VITIS, PINOT NOIR WINE GLASS

"THE GRAPES USED FOR OUR PINOT NOIR WERE CHOSEN FROM TWELVE CLONAL SELECTIONS FROM FOUR DIFFERENT CARNEROS ESTATE VINEYARDS. IT IS REDOLENT WITH AROMAS OF RASPBERRY AND BLACK CHERRY THAT ARE ENHANCED WITH HINTS OF SMOKE, ORANGE PEEL AND EXOTIC SPICE. THIS PINOT NOIR HAS A LUSCIOUS JUICINESS THAT INVITES CONTEMPLATION, AND A SECOND GLASS. "

WINEMAKER TJ EVANS

Domaine Carneros Le Rêve Blanc de Blancs
Warm Maine Lobster and Roasted Sweet Potato Salad
Winemaker Eileen Crane, Chef/Owner Ken Frank ~ La Toque Restaurant

1	Maine lobster, steamed, shelled, cut into small chunks
1/3 c	sweet potato, ½ inch dice
2/3 c	pumpkin, diced (or other hard squash)
1/3 c	onion, white diced
¼ c	crème fraîche
2 c	curly endive, chilled large, stems removed
1½ T	brown sugar
tt	sherry wine vinegar

tt	pumpkin seeds, toasted
tt	cardamom
tt	Vietnamese pepper
tt	cinnamon stick
tt	nutmeg
drizzle	canola oil

Materials:
   microplaner

Toss the diced sweet potato and pumpkin with a drizzle of canola oil and a little sea salt. Spread on a cookie sheet and roast in a 325° F oven for about 20 minutes until just tender.
Remove from oven, cool and reserve.

In a small bowl, season the crème fraîche with a little ground cinnamon, a little ground nutmeg, tablespoon brown sugar, a pinch of sea salt and a splash of sherry wine vinegar.
Reserve.

Put the diced white onion in a small saucepan with the remaining one teaspoon brown sugar. With a microplane shave a little Vietnamese pepper, cardamom and cinnamon stick into the pan.
Add just enough water to cover, and cook over moderate heat, uncovered, until the onions are tender and most of the liquid is cooked out.
Remove from heat, cool and reserve.

Plating:
Drizzle a ring of spiced crème fraîche around the rim of each plate.
Heat the roasted squash and remaining crème fraîche in a sauté pan.
Remove from heat and fold in lobster and half of the onion marmalade.
Cover and allow the vegetables to gently warm the lobster for a couple of minutes so it stays tender.
Spoon the lobster and sweet potato mixture into a ring mold in the center of each plate.
Toss the curly endive with the remaining half of the onion marmalade and a splash of sherry wine vinegar and arrange some on top of each salad.
Carefully lift the ring mold, sprinkle the plate with toasted pumpkin seeds and serve. 2 servings

DOMAINE CARNEROS
1240 DUHIG ROAD
NAPA, CA 94559
707-257-0101
DOMAINECARNEROS.COM

DOMAINE CARNEROS ESTATE PINOT NOIR
SEARED SONOMA ARTISAN FOIE GRAS WITH FRESH CORN POLENTA AND CHANTERELLES
WINEMAKER TJ EVANS, CHEF/OWNER KEN FRANK ~ LA TOQUE RESTAURANT

4 ears	corn, fresh, sweet white
4 T + 1 t	sweet butter (unsalted)
4	slices Foie Gras, "A" grade, preferably Sonoma Artisan, ½ inch thick
½ c	mushrooms, Chanterelle

Corn polenta:
Grate the kernels off the cob using the coarse side of a box grater.
Simmer the kernels, 2 tablespoons butter and a pinch of sea salt, over very low heat; about 5 minutes.
The mixture is ready when it just begins to thicken and set.
Adjust seasoning and keep warm.

Mushrooms:
Sauté the chanterelles in the remaining teaspoon of butter with a pinch of sea salt.
Keep warm.

Foie Gras:
Heat a heavy cast iron pan over medium heat; the pan needs to be very hot but not crazy hot.
Season the slices of foie gras generously with salt and black pepper.
Sear in the cast iron pan until they have a nice mahogany colored crust on each side; about 1½ minutes per side. There will be smoke.

Plating:
Divide the corn polenta between 4 wide rimmed bowls, top with a slice of seared foie gras and sprinkle with a few sautéed Chanterelles. 4 servings

La Toque
14 McKinstry Street
Napa, CA 94558
707-257-5157
latoque.com

ÈTOILE
Seared Day Boat Scallops, Braised Pork Belly, Uni Tangerine
Winemaker Tom Tiburzi, Chef de Cuisine Perry Hoffmann ~ Domaine Chandon ètoile

Wine Making Facts :

Vintage: Non-Vintage, Sur Lees

Encépagement : Chardonnay, Pinot Noir, Pinot Meunier

Appellation : Sonoma County and Napa County

Soils: Mixed sandy loam, clay loam and shallow rocky soils.

Elevation: 50 -1800 feet

Micro-Climate : Cool mediterranean

Yield : Average 4 tons/acre

Alcohol Level : 12.8%

Winemaking: Whole cluster press at .2 bar pressure, 24 hours juice settling, stainless steel tank primary fermentation with Saccharomyces bayanus yeast, no malolactic conversion, bottle secondary fermentation with proprietary blend of Saccharomyces bayanus and Saccharomyces cerevisiae yeast strains, 5 years sur lees aging in the bottle. Dosage liqueur sugar level at 10 grams/liter.

DOMAINE CHANDON
ONE CALIFORNIA DRIVE
YOUNTVILLE, CA 94599
707-944-2280
CHANDON.COM

VINUM XL, CHAMPAGNE GLASS

"Tiny bubbles elevate an attractive bouquet of ginger and brown spice-.baked apple, honey and cinnamon flavors meld with nutty caramel flavors gained from extended sur lees aging. The creamy structure with balanced acidity carries these flavors through the lingering finish. " TT

Founded in 1973, Domaine Chandon was the first American sparkling wine venture established by a french champagne house (Moët and Chandon). Chandon crafts a range of sparkling wines that reflect California's vibrant regional character yet remain true to the practices of méthode traditionnelle. Since 2002, the winery has also offered premium still wines from the champagne varietals. Domaine Chandon is at the forefront of sustainable farming practices and continues to replenish and restore the natural habitat. Visitors can enjoy a guided tour of the winemaking facilities, sip and snack on the scenic terrace, peruse local art exhibits, or savor an exquisite meal at ètoile, the only fine dining restaurant located within a Napa Valley winery. The blend of history and ingenuity makes Domaine Chandon truly sparkle.

ÈTOILE
Seared Day Boat Scallops, Braised Pork Belly, Uni Tangerine
Winemaker Tom Tiburzi, Chef de Cuisine Perry Hoffmann ~ Domaine Chandon ètoile

Pork belly:
1 lb.	pork belly or slab
	Applewood smoked bacon
1	onion, rough chop
1	carrot, rough chop
1	leek, rough chop
2	d'Anjou pears, rough chop
½ c	brandy
½ gl	chicken stock
½ gl	veal stock
5 oz	ginger root, peeled
3	pods star anise

Onion purée:
1	yellow onion, large, diced
5 T	butter
½ c	heavy cream
¼ c	vegetable stock
¼ c	sake

Sake vinaigrette:
1 T	sake
1 T	rice wine vinegar
1 t	Dijon mustard
1 T	mirin
3 T	light olive oil

Scallops:
10	scallops, Day Boat, 2 ½ oz., muscle removed
¼ c	butter, clarified
4 T	whole butter
5	Uni optional

Preheat oven to 325º F
Score the pork belly with ½ inch squares.
Over medium heat, render and brown, pork belly fat cap down (about 10 minutes).
Remove from pan and set aside in baking dish.
Pour out excess fat and sauté the spices, fruit and all the vegetables until translucent.
Deglaze with brandy and reduce to au sec (almost dry).
Add the chicken and veal stock and simmer for 30 minutes.
Pour liquid over pork belly, cover with foil and braise in oven for 2 hours or until belly is tender.
Once cooked, remove belly from liquid and place between two sheet pans with weight on top, and cool
(this will allow the belly to be uniform when ready to portion).
Strain the braising liquid, skim off fat and discard the vegetables.
Reduce braising liquid to sauce consistency.
When pork has cooled, portion into 2 by 1 inch rectangles and set aside.
Sear pork belly, all sides until caramelized; pour off rendered fat.
Add in reduced braising liquid and glaze belly. Set aside.

Onion purée: Sauté onions in butter until translucent, but do not brown.
Add in stock and cream and simmer for a few minutes.
Purée in blender until smooth adding the sake while blending.
Season with salt. Pass through a fine mesh strainer and reserve strained purée.

Sake Vinaigrette: Combine sake, vinegar, mustard, and mirin. Whisk in olive oil slowly to emulsify.

Scallion orange zest salad: Using a peeler, peel one orange making long strips of orange rind.
Remove the white, with a sharp knife to leave the rind.
Julienne the rind into thin strips, set aside. Peel and filet oranges to remove white pithy flesh.
Slice remaining oranges into rounds; reserve fruit. Toss scallions with Sake Vinaigrette and orange julienne.

Scallops: Season the scallops with salt and pepper.
Sauté scallops in butter to golden brown; cook about 1 minute on each side. Baste with butter while cooking.
Remove and let rest.

Serving: On each plate place 4 small onion purée circles. Onto two circles of onion purée, place pork belly, and
orange round, and uni atop. Onto the other two circles of onion purée, place scallops, and scallion salad. 5 servings

ÉTOILE AT DOMAINE CHANDON
1 CALIFORNIA DRIVE
YOUNTVILLE, CA 94599
707-204-7529
CHANDON.COM

ETUDE PINOT GRIS AND ETUDE PINOT NOIR
SOFTSHELL CRAB BLT CRISPY PORK BELLY, BRIOCHE, CALABRIAN CHILI AIOLI
WINEMAKER JON PRIEST, PROFESSIONAL CHEF GARY PENIR

ETUDE
1250 CUTTINGS WHARF ROAD
NAPA, CA 94559
707-257-5300
ETUDEWINES.COM

Wine Making Facts :
Etude Pinot Gris Carneros
Encépagement : 100% Pinot Gris
Appellation : Carneros
Vineyard : Grapes are grown in two
great vineyards—the Etude Estate
vineyard in Sonoma Carneros and Lee
Hudson's Napa Carneros vineyard.
Alcohol Level : 14.3%
Total Production : 2,600 cases
Philosophy : Our mission is to produce a
distinctive, highly enjoyable style of Pinot Gris
that is classically aromatic, supple and dry
Harvest Details : The fruit quality for Pinot Gris
was excellent, picked at optimum ripeness.
Fermentation : After gentle whole
cluster pressing, the juice is transferred
to small, 75-gallon stainless steel vats for
fermentation, then allowed to mature
undisturbed for five months before bottling.

Wine Making Facts :
Etude Pinot Noir Carneros ~ Estate
Encépagement : 100% Pinot Noir
Appellation : Carneros
Vineyard : Estate Grown
Average Vine Age : Vineyard planted in 2000
Alcohol Level : 14.4%
Philosophy : Our goal is to produce a distinctly
styled Pinot Noir of the highest quality, a
wine that can satisfy any "Burgundian" urge
and yet be proud of its California roots.
Harvest Details : August 29th to September 18th.
Facility : Étude Winery, Carneros
Wood Origin : 100% French Oak
Oak Regimen : Aged 12-14 months
Coopers : French Oak
Bottling Formats: 375ml and 750 ml

"This Etude Pinot Gris opens with inviting aromas of key lime, wet stone minerality, orange blossom and hints of white peach. The pure flavors carry over on the palate and mingle with subtle cardamom and jasmine notes. The wine is fresh with bright acidity and a richness that begs the next sip. Hints of clove spice linger on the satisfying finish." JP

"Deep garnet in color, the 2007 Pinot Noir bottling offers inviting aromas of black cherry and frambois strawberry with hints of cardamom and clove. The palate bursts with rich fruit, cherry liquor notes, toasted oak and a distinct minerality. The concentrated fruit combined with the fine grained tannins and lifted acidity creates a defined Pinot Noir with elegance and length." JP

O, PINOT NOIR AND RIESLING WINE GLASS

ETUDE PINOT GRIS AND ETUDE PINOT NOIR
SOFTSHELL CRAB BLT, CRISPY PORK BELLY, BRIOCHE, CALABRIAN CHILI AIOLI
WINEMAKER JON PRIEST, PROFESSIONAL CHEF GARY PENIR

Pork Belly and Cure:

12 oz	pork belly
1 ¼ c	salt
¾ c	brown sugar
1	bay leaf
10 ea	black peppercorns
3	thyme sprigs

Crispy Softshell Crab:

2 ea	softshell crabs, cleaned
4 ea	eggs, whisked with one ounce water
2 c	Wondra flour, separated
2	containers

Calabrian Chili Aioli

2	egg yolks
2 T	lemon juice
1 c	olive oil
3	Calabrian chilis, minced
tt	salt

Plating:

2 ea	softshell crabs, crispy, cut in half
8 oz	pork belly, cured and roasted
4 ea	Heirloom Cherry tomatoes, sliced thin
4 T	Calabrian chili aioli
4	Mâche bunches
4	Brioche bread slices , toasted, shaped like pork belly

Pork Belly Cure Method:
Mix herbs, pepper, salt, and brown sugar together in a bowl.
Place pork belly in bowl and cover completely with mixture, and cover for 12 hours in refrigeration.
After 12 hours remove from cure, wash excess cure off and dry with paper towels.

Pork Belly Method:
Place pork belly on a sheet tray with a rack tented with aluminum foil.
Cook at 375° F. until tender and skin is deep golden brown, around 2 hours.
A significant amount of fat should render out and you should be left with about 8 oz.
Cut into four equal pieces.

Calabrian Chili Aioli Method:
Put egg yolks, lemon juice, salt, and calabrian chilis in a blender and process for 10 seconds.
Slowly add olive oil until a smooth emulsion is achieved and the consistency is like mayonnaise.
Adjust seasoning.

Method:
Fill a large pot with canola oil to half the height of the pot. Heat to 375° ° F.
While the oil is heating, dredge the crab in flour, then egg, then into the flour again.
When the correct temperature is reached, gently lay the soft shell crabs away from you in the oil.
Fry until golden brown and crispy about 3 minutes. Place on paper towels and season with salt.

Plating Method:
Spread Calabrian Chili Aioli on toasted brioche
Set the pork belly on top of the brioche, and garnish with shingled tomatoes.
Place onto a plate with the soft shell crab so crab legs curl over the pork and brioche.
Dress the mâche with extra virgin olive oil and salt and place under the curl of the crab legs.
Garnish plate with cracked black pepper and extra virgin olive oil. 4 servings

FANTESCA CHARDONNAY
BACON WRAPPED PORK TENDERLOIN, FAVA BEANS AND ONIONS, CIDER JUS
WINEMAKER HEIDI BARRETT, CHEF/ CO-OWNER EDUARDO E. MARTINEZ ~ MARKET

Wine Making Facts :

Encépagement : Chardonnay

Appellation : Russian River

Alcohol Level : 14.4 %

Total Production : 700 cases

Philosophy: The goal was to make a wine that confidently places the fruit at center stage while complementing it with nuanced winemaking skill which adds depth, complexity and balance. The three separate vineyard lots were thoughtfully paired to individual oak and fermentation protocols to weave into a seamless blend.

Harvest Details : Late September and early October

Facility : Fantesca Estate

Wood Origin : French Oak

Oak Regimen : 9 months

Coopers : French

Bottling Format 750 ml

Other: The 2007 vintage is the first wine to benefit from Heidi Barrett's touch. She oversaw the barrel aging and final blend.

"This unique blend was selected for the classical characteristics embraced in the finest French White Burgundies: clean and crisp, bright acids, beautiful tropical notes and elegant structure." HB

FANTESCA ESTATE AND WINERY
2920 SPRING MOUNTAIN ROAD
ST HELENA, CA 94574
707-968-9229
FANTESCA.COM

SOMMELIERS, MONTRACHET WINE GLASS

Fantesca Estate and Winery is rich with history, having originally been in the dowry of Caroline Bale when she married Charles Krug in 1860. Even then, the property was recognized as prime mountain vineyard land and the perfect place for a Spring Mountain winery. In 1889, winemaker Hannah Weinberger, (one of the Valley's first female winemakers), won awards for her Cabernet Sauvignon. Over one hundred years later, owners Susan and Duane Hoff continually honor this commitment producing wines that Mrs. Weinberger would be proud of. Their estate vineyard, wine cave, and winery are considered the jewel of Napa Valley. In early 2008, this spirit came full circle as Fantesca welcomed veteran winemaker Heidi Barrett, whose stellar Napa Valley resume is as jeweled.

Fantesca
ESTATE & WINERY

2005
Napa Valley
CABERNET SAUVIGNON
Spring Mountain District

FANTESCA CABERNET
BRAISED BEEF CHEEKS RAVIOLI APERTO
WINEMAKER HEIDI BARRETT, PROFESSIONAL CHEF JOHN VLANDIS

Wine Making Facts :
Encépagement : Cabernet Sauvignon
Appellation : Napa Valley, Spring Mountain District
Vineyard : Fantesca Estate and Winery
Elevation: Fantesca's vineyard is located on the southeastern
side of Spring Mountain, with tremendous variations in slope
just under 10 acres of vines. The elevation and mountain
terrain offer superb sun exposure and a long growing season.
Alcohol Level : 14.5%
Total Production : 450 cases
Harvest Details : The grapes were harvested
the 2nd week of October.
Facility : Fantesca Estate and Winery
Wood Origin : French
Oak Regimen : 24 months
Bottling Format : 750ml, 1.5L, 3

FANTESCA ESTATE AND WINERY
2920 SPRING MOUNTAIN ROAD
ST HELENA, CA 94574
707-968-9229
FANTESCA.COM

SOMMELIERS, BORDEAUX GRAND CRU WINE

" The nose of this wine contains notes of black cherry and molasses. There are lively hints of rosemary and crushed herbs. As you take the wine in your mouth, you taste cherry, cedar, and lively acids. The wine finishes with beautiful, dusty tannins that will become more and more elegant as this mountain Cabernet ages. " HB

1 lb	beef cheeks	2T	olive oil
½ c	Spanish onions, chopped	2 c	red wine
¼ c	carrots, chopped	1 ½ qt	veal stock
1 rib	celery, chopped	5	peppercorns
10	garlic cloves, peeled	1	bay leaf
8	Cipollini onions, peeled	3	thyme sprigs
		8	ravioli circles or wonton wrappers

Preheat the oven to 225° F.
Season the cheeks with salt and pepper. Place the oil in a hot pan; sear the cheeks on each side until brown. Remove the cheeks and add the vegetables, cook until they are caramelized. Deglaze with the wine and add the stock and herbs. Cover the pan and cook in the oven for 3 ½ to 4 hours. Remove the cheeks and strain the liquid into a saucepan. Remove the Cipollini and save for garnish. Reduce the liquid by two-thirds, skimming occasionally. Season with salt and pepper. Shred the cheeks with a fork. Boil ravioli circles (or wonton wrappers) in salted water until el dente. Place a cooked warm pasta circle on the plate, add a tablespoon of shredded cheek, add sauce then remaining pasta circle, then Cipollini, repeat. 2 servings

FANTESCA CHARDONNAY
BACON WRAPPED PORK TENDERLOIN, FAVA BEANS, AND ONIONS, CIDER JUS
WINEMAKER HEIDI BARRETT, CHEF/PARTNER EDUARDO E. MARTINEZ ~ MARKET

1 lb	pork tenderloin, cleaned of silver skin
3 strips	Applewood smoked bacon
5	baby turnips, quartered and blanched
12	pearl onions, blanched
6 oz	fava beans, blanched and shelled
¼ c	parsley, chopped
tt	salt
tt	pepper
2 T	butter
2T	olive oil

Apple cider jus:

4 c	apple juice
¾ c	chicken stock
3	thyme sprigs
2 T	crushed garlic
3 T	apple cider vinegar
2 T	butter, cold

Apple jus method:
In a small pot reduce the apple juice to two cups, add chicken stock, thyme sprigs, crushed garlic and apple cider vinegar.
Strain sauce with a fine strainer.
Whisk in two tablespoons of cold butter. Keep warm.

Preheat oven to 350º F.

Tenderloin method:
Wrap the tenderloin in bacon and season.
In a oven proof skillet heat oil over medium-high heat.
Season and sear the pork tenderloin on all sides.
Place pork in preheated oven and finish cooking in the oven for about 25 minutes or until done.
Rest the pork tenderloin for 5 minutes at room temperature.

Vegetable method:
Melt butter in a sauté pan.
Add blanched vegetables and season with salt and pepper.
Place cooked vegetables on plate with sliced pork cut into one inch medallions.
Cover with several tablespoons of apple jus. 4 servings

MARKET
1347 MAIN STREET
ST. HELENA, CA 94574
707-963-3799
MARKETSTHELENA.COM

Far Niente Estate Chardonnay
Steamed Black Cod Rolls with Sweet Mango and Herbs
Winemakers Dirk Hampson and Nicole Marchesi, Winery Chef Abi Martinez

Wine Making Facts :

Philosophy: Since our first vintage of Chardonnay in 1979 and the introduction of Cabernet Sauvignon in 1982, Far Niente has held true to its philosophy of producing estate wines of complexity and elegance with a consistent house style.

Varietal: 94% Cabernet Sauvignon, 3% Cabernet Franc abd 3% Petite Verdot

Appellation: Oakville, Napa Valley

Acreage: 100 acres

Alcohol Level: 14.5%

Harvest Dates: October 20 – 31, 2006

Skin Contact: 12-29 days, 19% pressed for dryness

Wood Origin: 100% French oak

Oak Regimen: 16 months

Percentage of New Barrels: 73%

Far Niente Winery
PO Box 327
Oakville, CA 94562
707-944-2861
FARNIENTE.COM

" Full bodied and rich, creamy hints of minerality complement the sweet fruit throughout. The finish is very long, lingering and beautifully textured." DH & NM

Sommeliers Black Tie, Chardonnay

Mango:

1	mango, peeled, pitted, cut into a 1/8 inch dice
6	shallots, finely diced
¼ t	chili oil
2 T	scallions, minced
3 T	cilantro, minced
3 T	parsley, minced
½ T	mint, minced
	salt

Black Cod rolls:

10 oz	cod fillet, black, skin removed
¼ t	pepper, white, ground
2	cabbage leaves steaming
	salt

Dipping sauce:

1 T	soy sauce, sweet black
1 T	rice vinegar
1	yuzu juice (or lime juice)

Mango:
Combine diced mango, shallots, chili oil, onions, cilantro, parsley and peppermint.

Dipping sauce:
Combine all the ingredients in a bowl, mix well and set aside.

Black cod rolls:
Slice fish fillets horizontally into thin sheets about one-eighth inch thick.
Spoon some of the mango mixture on top of each slice and roll it up into a small log.
Repeat until all the slices are used, season each roll with salt and pepper.
Line a steamer with cabbage leaves, then place fish rolls on top and steam over high heat for about 3 minutes or until done. Serve hot with the dipping sauce. 4 servings

Far Niente Estate Cabernet Sauvignon
Whole Roasted Quail Stuffed with Hato Mugi, Sautéed Foie Gras, Porcini Mushrooms
Winemakers Dirk Hampson and Nicole Marchesi, Winery Chef Abi Martinez

Wine Making Facts :
Encépagement : Cabernet Sauvignon
Appellation : Oakville
Vineyard : Rock Cairn
Soils : Bale Clay Loam
Elevation: 200'
Aspect : Western with Eastern Exposure
Yield : 3.5 tons/ acre
Alcohol Level : 14.7%
Total Production : 3,000 cases (12 btl. 750ml)
Harvest Details : 25˚ - 26˚ Brix
Facility : Historic building with
state of the art equipment
Wood Origin : French
Oak Regimen : 18 – 24 months
Percentage of New Barrels : 60 - 80%

" Bright with ripe, purple fruits, this wine will impress with complex, layered aromas of black licorice and briar patch. The silky entry progresses along the palate and gives way to dense, velvety chocolate and toast. Full-bodied and concentrated through-out, the wine lingers on with a long, layered finish. " DH and NM

FAR NIENTE WINERY
PO BOX 327
OAKVILLE, CA 94562
707-944-2861
FARNIENTE.COM

SOMMELIERS BLACK TIE, BORDEAUX GRAND CRU

1 c	hato mugi, grain found in specialty stores		2 T	butter
8 oz	mushrooms, porcini, ¼ -inch dice		1	head cauliflower, rough chop
2 T	butter		4 oz	butter
2 T	olive oil		½ c	onion, yellow , ¼-inch dice
2	thyme sprigs		2 c	heavy cream
2	cloves garlic, crushed		4	quail, boneless
4 oz	foie gras, seared, rough chop			
2 oz	veal demi-glacé			

Quail: Hato mugi rinsed, cooked (about 45-50 minutes). Sauté mushrooms in butter; add garlic and thyme and cook two minutes. Mix the hato mugi, mushrooms, foie gras, veal demi-glacé and season. Stuff each bird and truss with string. Season exterior and sear quail breast side down in olive oil, turn them and roast in oven for about 13 minutes. Remove and baste birds in butter for 3-4 minutes. Remove from pan and let rest.
Cauliflower Puree: Sauté onions until translucent. Add cauliflower and sweat for additional 3 minutes. Add heavy cream and simmer, until the cauliflower is tender. Strain and reserve cream. Purée cauliflower until smooth with about 2 ounces of reserved cream. Season with salt and pepper. 4 servings

FAUST
CABERNET
SAUVIGNON
NAPA VALLEY
2005

Wine Making Facts :
Encépagement : 77% Cabernet
Sauvignon, 19% Merlot,
3% Malbec, 1% Cabernet Franc
Appellation: Napa Valley
Time in Oak: 18 months
Type of Oak: 100% French
Age of Oak: 30% New and
70% one-year old
Alcohol: 14.5%
Release date : February 2008
Average Vine Age : 6-20 years
Alcohol Level : 14.9
Philosophy : Great Napa Valley
Cabernet Sauvignon
Harvest Details : Hand harvested
and hand sorted
Winemaking: Gentle hands off
Oak Regimen : 18 months

" Ripe and concentrated aromas
and flavors of plum, blueberry and
dark cherry are accentuated by a
touch of fresh herbs, light cedar,
fresh tobacco leaves and a fine
spiciness. The fruit on the mid
palate is a laser beam of intense
pure, clean fruit which will broaden
over time. The finish is long with
finely-textured, ripe tannins. CT "

FAUST
P.O BOX 815
RUTHERFORD, CA 94573
707-286-2775
FAUSTWINE.COM

VINUM XL, CABERNET SAUVIGNON

Faust
Pan Seared Pheasant Breast, Ratatouille and Crispy Polenta Cake
Winemaker Charles Thomas Professional Chef John Vlandis

Pheasant Breast:
2	whole pheasant, (breasts removed)
2 c	pheasant stock
1 oz	clarified butter
8 oz	red wine
2	shallots, peeled and sliced
1	clove of garlic, minced
1	bay leaf
5	peppercorns
2	thyme, sprigs

For Ratatouille:
1	Japanese eggplant
1	small zucchini
1	small yellow squash
1	small red bell pepper

3T	olive oil
1	small onion, chopped fine
½ c	tomato sauce
2 t	minced garlic
1 T	Herbs de Provence
1 T	basil leaves, finely chopped
1 t	thyme, finely chopped

Polenta:
4 c	low-salt chicken broth
1 c	polenta (coarse cornmeal)
1/2 c	parmesan cheese, coarsely grated (packed)
2 T	butter

Method:
Season pheasant breasts with salt and pepper.
Heat a large sauté pan on high heat, add the clarified butter. Add the pheasant skin side down; continue to cook until nicely browned. Turn over and cook for two more minutes. Remove from the pan and keep warm. Add the shallots. Reduce the heat and cook for 2 more minutes. Add the garlic, bay leaf and peppercorns. Add the red wine and reduce by 2/3. Add the pheasant stock and simmer, occasionally skimming. Continue to simmer until sauce is of desired consistency. Strain and season.

For Ratatouille:
Cut eggplant, zucchini, yellow squash, onions and bell peppers into ¼-inch dice, keeping each separate. In a large heavy skillet cook the onions in oil over moderate heat, stirring, until tender. Add the garlic and eggplant. When the eggplant is cooked add the peppers herbs and squash. Add the tomato sauce cook 2 minutes. Season with salt and pepper.

For Polenta:
Generously butter 13 x 9 x 1 inch baking sheet. In a medium saucepan bring liquid to boil. Gradually add polenta, whisking constantly until smooth. Reduce heat to medium-low and cook until polenta is very thick, stirring frequently, about 10 minutes. Stir in Parmesan cheese and butter. Season to taste with salt and pepper. Transfer polenta to prepared baking sheet. Using wet hands, press polenta evenly over sheet to edges. Chill until firm, at least 3 hours. Cut polenta into circles.
Preheat oven to 425° F.
Place a sheet pan and 3 tablespoons olive oil in the oven. Heat for 3 minutes add the polenta and cook 10 minutes on each side. Remove from the oven and serve.

Plating:
Slice the pheasant and place on a plate, arrange a small circle of ratatouille in center and top with the polenta. Spoon sauce over the pheasant breast. 2 servings

Wine Making Facts :
Encépagement : 72% Cabernet Franc, 28% Cabernet Sauvignon
Appellation : Napa Valley
Vineyard : Coombsville area of Napa Valley
Soils : Coombsville Gravelly Loam, plus Aiken soils
Elevation : 300-1,200 feet
Aspect: Northeast facing
Micro-Climate : Warm Napa climate with cooling bay influence.
Average Vine Age : 30 years, old vines are athletically proportioned, balanced but muscular.
Yields : 2 - 2.5 tons/acre
Alcohol Level : 14.8%
Total Production : 180 cases
Fermentation : Whole berry fermentation using native yeasts
Aged : In French oak barrels for 22 months

" Lifted aromas of smoke, cassis, black licorice and espresso are immediately present. Broadly-textured, the fruit character spreads across the palate, bringing an array of flavors ranging from berries and cream to sage and gravel. AF &AE"

Favia
3091 Vichy Ave.
Napa, Ca 94558
www.faviawines.com

Sommeliers Bordeaux Grand Cru

FAVIA
WINEMAKERS ANNIE FAVIA AND ANDY ERICKSON, WINERY CHEF VINCENT NATTRESS
ROASTED PORK AND DUCK CONFIT CASSOULET

GROUP 1

1 c	fresh shelling beans, Cranberry or Rockwell
1 qt	water
2	bacon slices; cut into lardoons, blanched
½	yellow onion, finely chopped
1	bouquet garni, consisting of a bay leaf, 2 cloves, sprig thyme, 6 juniper berries, 10 pepper corns, 2 inches of cinnamon

GROUP 2

1 lb	pork short ribs, cut in to 2 ½" in length
8, 8 oz	pork sausage, cooked cut into ½" slices
1 lb	duck confit "drummies" - wing
1 T	olive oil

½	yellow onion, finely chopped
3 c	white wine
1 c	brown veal or duck stock
2	roma tomatoes, seeded and finely chopped
1	bouquet garni, minus the cinnamon.

GROUP 3

1	bacon slice, diced finely and frozen
1 c	bread crumbs
1 t	thyme leaves
1 t	rosemary

Marinated the ribs over night with white wine, sliced garlic, bay, thyme, juniper, pepper, olive oil and salt and refrigerate.

In a Dutch oven, heat the olive oil over medium high heat. Drain the ribs off of the marinade and dry them well. Brown the ribs on all sides then remove and reserve them. Next brown the gayettes lightly on all sides, and remove and reserve them as well. Finally, brown the confit wings on all sides and remove and reserve them.

Drain all but a tablespoon of the fat from the pan but do not scrape the pan clean; you want that caramelization on the bottom of the pan. Return the pan to medium high heat and add the onion, browning the onion thoroughly. Deglaze the pan with the wine, then add the stock and return to a simmer. Add the tomato and bouquet garni. Place the ribs on top, cover the pan tightly and simmer over low heat for 1 hour. After an hour, add the gayette and confit and simmer an additional 20 minutes. Remove from heat and allow to cool.

In a separate pan sweat the other half of the onion in olive oil, along with the blanched bacon. Add the bouquet garni, water and beans. Bring to a simmer and simmer about 10 to 20 minutes depending on the maturity of the beans, but just until the bean are starting to get tender. Do not overcook the beans, as they will be cooked again inside the assembled cassoulet. Remove the beans from heat and drain them, reserving the cooking liquid. Remove bouquet garni and discard.

Remove the cooled meat from its pan, using a strainer to separate the braising liquid from the solids. Reserve the meat braising liquid. Remove bouquet garni and discard. In a large bowl, mix the drained beans with the reserve liquid from the meat. Adjust seasoning with salt and pepper. Now cool both the meat and the beans thoroughly before the final assembly of the cassoulet.

In a ca sserole large enough to accommodate all the cooked ingredients, line the bottom of the pan with 1/3 of the beans. Add more of the reserved bean cooking liquid to the beans if necessary, as the beans will absorb more of the liquid while baking. At this point they should be of a very wet consistency.

Over this first layer of beans, place a layer ribs. Cover this layer with another 1/3 of the beans. Now place the gayette and confit on top of the beans. Cover the ribs with the remaining beans. Place the ingredients in group three, in a food processor and process thoroughly. Spread the ensuing crumbles liberally on the top of the cassoulet to form the crust once the dish is baked. Bake the cassoulet in a 375º F. oven on the center rack for between one hour and 90 minutes. If at this point the crust is not fully browned, place it briefly under the broiler to toast up the top. 4 servings

Girard
Artistry
2007
Napa Valley
Red Wine
Alc. 15% by vol.
Girard
Artistry
2007
Napa Valley
Red Wine
Girard

GIRARD ARTISTRY
MUSTARD GLAZED VEAL CHOP WITH BLACK-EYED PEA SUCCOTASH
WINEMAKERS MARCO DIGIULIO AND ZACH LONG, EXECUTIVE CHEF STEPHEN ROGERS ~ PRESS

Wine Making Facts :

Encépagement : 61% Cabernet Sauvignon, 13% Cabernet Franc, 11% Malbec, 9% Petit Verdot, 6% Merlot

Appellation : Napa Valley

Vineyard : A combination of hillside and valley floor vineyards

Average Vine Age : 35 years

Total Production : 4,600 cases (12/750ml)

Philosophy : Great wine always start in the vineyards. By working with the best vineyards we have access to the best fruit in Napa Valley to craft our award winning Artistry Bordeaux blend.

Winemaking : Hand picked in the cool early morning hours, hand sorted and gently crushed using a state-of-the-art Diemme destemmer/crusher.

Fermentation : Stainless Steel tanks

Maceration : Average 30 days. Native yeast fermentation is complemented by native malolactic fermentation in barrel resulting in complex fruit expression. The wine undergoes extended maceration to soften and fully integrate the tannins.

Wood Origin : 100% French

"Deep crimson in color with aromas of dark cherry, dark plum and blackberry. There are also nuances of leather, toasted nuts and baking spices. On the palate, this firmly-textured wine offers a full-mouth feel with flavors of mocha/cherry truffles, blackberry tart and dark currants. The firm tannins are very well integrated, making the wine approachable at an early age. There are multiple layers to this complex blend that reveal themselves through decanting or by giving the wine time to open up in the glass. " MD & ZL

GIRARD WINERY TASTING ROOM
6795 WASHINGTON STREET
YOUNTVILLE, CA 94599
707-968-9297
GIRARDWINERY.COM

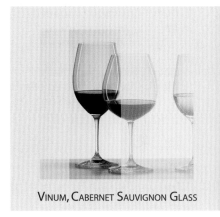

VINUM, CABERNET SAUVIGNON GLASS

When winemakers Marco DiGiulioand Zach Long playfully say they make wine in a "garagista," naturally, folks raise a few eyebrows. It's actually a 33,000 square foot, state-of-the-art, modern garage. Since its inception in 1975, Girard Winery has had a singular focus to produce world-class wines truly representing the unique terroir of Napa Valley. Through the combination of old world and modern winemaking techniques, and such a veteran winemaking team, they have succeeded. This environmentally friendly garagista is a winemakers dream; efficient, streamlined, and takes advantage of high technology. "Every wine should be an expression of the best that a vintage has to offer. I work with the kinds of high quality grapes that most winemakers can only dream of," says Marco seriously. Decades of commitment and research has allowed Girard to identify vineyards in which prized soil types and microclimates have combined to produce wines with distinctive character. By seeking out the best vineyards and matching them to the correct varietals, Girard has been able to handcraft stylistically diverse wines of elegance, balance, power and finesse. Girard Winery also has a modern tasting room in downtown Yountville. It's there— while sitting outside in their sidewalk garden—that you'll find, not eyebrows but wine glasses, being raised.

Veal Chops:
4	Bone-in Veal Chops, about 8-10 ounces each or 1 ½ inches thick
2 T	Dijon Mustard
1 T	honey
1 T	fresh lemon juice
1 t	lemon zest
1 t	rosemary, chopped
1 t	parsley, chopped
	salt and pepper

Black- Eyed Pea Succotash:
1 lb	fresh Black-eyed peas, shelled (substitute any fresh shelling bean of your choice)

1	onion, quartered
4	slices bacon
2	bay leaves
1	sprig thyme
3	cloves garlic, whole
5-6 c	vegetable stock (or water)
4 ears	fresh sweet corn, kernels cut off with a knife
1	fresh tomato, seeded and chopped
1 T	shallot, finely minced
2 T	butter
2 T	fresh Herbs, Chopped (any combination of parsley, chives, chervil, tarragon, basil, cilantro)
	squeeze of lemon

Method:
Pre-heat grill to medium-high.
Wrap the bone of each veal chop with a small piece of foil to protect while grilling. Allow veal chops to sit at room temperature for 20-30 minutes. Meanwhile, combine remaining ingredients for the glaze in a small bowl with a whisk. Season each veal chop with salt and pepper and brush with mustard glaze on both sides. Grill to desired temperature, about 12-15 minutes for medium rare chops. Remove veal chops to a carving board or serving platter. Rest for 4-5 minutes.

Black- Eyed Pea Succotash:
In a large pot, add black-eyed peas with enough water or vegetable stock to cover by about 1 inch. Add the quartered onion, bacon, bay leaves, thyme and garlic. Bring to a boil and reduce heat to a simmer. Cook until peas are just about tender, 20-30 minutes. Remove black-eyed peas from heat and discard onion, bacon, bay leaves, thyme and garlic, but reserve ½ cup of the broth. In a medium size saucepan, add the reserved broth and minced shallot and bring to a simmer. Add the black-eyed peas, corn kernels and diced tomato. Continue cooking 3-4 minutes. Add the butter, fresh herbs and a squeeze of lemon. Stir until butter has emulsified, and season to taste with salt and pepper. Serves 4.

Press
587 St. Helena Highway
St. Helena CA 94574
707-967-0550
PRESSSTHELENA.COM

GHOST BLOCK
2006
ESTATE
CABERNET SAUVIGNON
OAKVILLE - NAPA VALLEY

GHOST BLOCK
SPICED NEW ZEALAND LAMB LOIN FENNEL FRONDS, WHITE PEPPER FOAM, CAULIFLOWER PURÉE
WINEMAKER ROB LAWSON, PROFESSIONAL CHEF GARY PENIR

Wine Making Facts :
Encépagement : Cabernet Sauvignon
Appellation : Oakville
Vineyard : Rock Cairn
Soils : Bale Clay Loam
Elevation: 200'
Aspect : Western with Eastern Exposure
Average Vine Age : 25 years
Yield : 3.5 tons/ acre
Alcohol Level : 14.7%
Total Production : 3,000 cases (12 btl. 750ml)
Harvest Details : 25° - 26° Brix
Facility : Historic building with state of the art equipment
Fermentation : 88°F
Wood Origin : French
Oak Regimen : 18 – 24 months

" Bright floral aromas of roses, blueberries, and cassis lead into a ripe full bodied mouth feel loaded with flavors of blackberries, cherries and spice. The wine lingers on the palate with a nice citrus, chocolate and tobacco finish." RL

GHOST BLOCK
7830-40 ST. HELENA HWY.
OAKVILLE, CA 94562
707-945-1213
GHOSTBLOCK.NET

VITIS, CABERNET SAUVIGNON WINE GLASS

Nestled on a gently sloping knoll on the north edge of Yountville, Ghost Block vineyard is named in honor of the historic Pioneer Cemetery for which it borders. According to local lore, George C. Yount who was the first person to plant a grapevine in the Valley, and still wanders the hillside overseeing the vast spectrum of an industry he founded on this very land. In 1877, the 9th bonded winery in California was established and today the same winery is home to Ghost Block, Elizabeth Rose Syrah Rosé and Oakville Winery labels. Each brand is a reflection of the property, the heritage and the extraordinary quality that the Oakville and Yountville appellations provide.

GHOST BLOCK
SPICED NEW ZEALAND LAMB LOIN FENNEL FRONDS, WHITE PEPPER FOAM, CAULIFLOWER PURÉE
WINEMAKER ROB LAWSON, PROFESSIONAL CHEF GARY PENIR

Ingredients:

1	lamb loin, cleaned and tied
1	fennel bulb, shaved paper thin on a mandoline
½ c	fennel Fronds

Meyer Lemon Viniagrette:

⅛ c	Meyer lemon juice
¼ c	extra virgin olive oil
1	Meyer lemon zest
tt	salt and pepper

Spice Mix:

½ T	fennel seeds
4	bay leaf
½ T	coriander
1 T	salt

Smoked Paprika Oil:

2 T	smoked paprika
1 c	olive oil

Cauliflower Purée:

1	cauliflower, sliced ¼ inch
t	salt
tt	Meyer lemon juice
	cream to cover

White Pepper Foam:

1 ½ c	lamb stock or chicken stock
½ c	white pepper
1t	lecithin
tt	salt
tt	lemon juice

Method:
Preheat oven to 375° F.
Season Lamb with spice mix, sear in a pan, and roast until medium rare.
Place cauliflower purée in the bottom of a bowl.
Lay one piece of lamb on purée with the slice face up.
Dress fennel and fennel fronds with vinaigrette.
Gently place salad off-center on lamb so it looks like the salad is falling off the side of lamb.
Drizzle paprika oil around lamb.
Blend white pepper foam, scoop up foam and place on salad.

Spice Mix Method:
Blend all fennel, bay leaves, and coriander in a spice grinder until a powder is achieved.
Pass through a fine sieve then add salt and mix.

Cauliflower Purée Method:
Place cauliflower, cream, and salt in a saucepot and cook until extremely tender.
Put the cauliflower in a blender and add cream until proper consistency is achieved.
Season with salt and Meyer lemon juice.

Meyer Lemon Vinaigrette Method:
In a bowl mix Meyer lemon juice, zest, salt and pepper.
Slowly whisk in extra virgin olive oil.

Smoked Paprika Oil Method:
Cook smoked paprika in oil until fragrant and oil takes on a deep red color.
Strain through a coffee filter.

White Pepper Foam Method:
Cook stock and pepper for ½ hour in a saucepan to infuse intense pepper flavor.
Strain and add salt, lecithin and lemon juice and blend with an immersion blender until foam is achieved. 2 servings

GRGICH HILLS
ESTATE

Napa Valley
CHARDONNAY
ESTATE 2006 GROWN

GRGICH HILLS ESTATE CHARDONNAY
JASMINE AND WILD RICE WITH TOASTED ALMOND AND DRIED SUMMER FRUIT
WINEMAKER MIKE GRGICH, EXECUTIVE CHEF IGNACIO ALSARO ~ RUTHERFORD GRILL

Wine Making Facts :
Encépagement : 100% Chardonnay
Appellation : Napa Valley
Vineyard : This is the first vintage that our Chardonnay
vineyards were certified organic and Biodynamic®.
Micro-Climate : The Carneros region, bordering the San
Francisco Bay and straddling Napa and Sonoma counties,
has summer fog and constant cooling winds, which make it
arguably one of the finest regions to grow Chardonnay.
Average Vine Age : Mostly planted in 1998
Yield : Around two tons per acre
Alcohol Level : 14.3%
Philosophy : As always, we did not allow the Chardonnay
to undergo malolactic fermentation and our Biodynamic®
farming created a wine that is alive with delicious acidity.
Fermented and Aged: 10 months in French oak
Facility : We are estate grown and bottled.
Fermentation : Indigenous yeast

*"The relatively cool vintage yielded a beautifully balanced
Chardonnay with notes of lemon zest, flowers and honey with a
hint of crushed stones." MG*

GRGICH HILLS CELLARS
1829 SAINT HELENA HWY
RUTHERFORD, CA 94573
707-963-2784
GRGICH.COM

SOMMELIERS, CHARDONNAY WINE GLASS

1 c	wild rice, 6 ounces	½ c	green onion tops, finely chopped
4 c	water	2 T	celery, finely chopped
1 t	salt	2 T	red onion, finely chopped
½ c	dried Calmyrna figs, finely chopped	2 T	raspberry vinegar or red wine vinegar
½ c	pecans, toasted and chopped approximately 1 ounce	1 T	fresh lemon juice
		1	garlic clove, minced
½ c	cashews, unsalted, toasted and chopped (approximately 1½ ounces)	1 t	Dijon mustard
		1 t	sugar
		¼ c	vegetable oil
		¼ c	olive oil

Procedure:

Combine 4 cups of water and salt in a medium saucepan. Bring to a boil. Add rice. Reduce heat to
medium-low, cover and simmer until rice is tender, approximately 45 minutes. Drain well and cool.
Transfer to a large bowl. Mix in figs, pecans, cashews, green onion tops, celery and red onion.
This can be prepared 1 day in advance. Cover and refrigerate. Mix vinegar, lemon juice, garlic, mustard
and sugar in the blender. With the blender running, gradually mix in vegetable and olive oil.
Pour dressing over rice mixture and toss. Season salad with salt and pepper to taste. 6 servings

HARTWELL ESTATE CARNEROS DISTRICT SAUVIGNON BLANC
SEARED FENNEL CRUSTED AHI TUNA, SUMMER SQUASH CARPACCIO
WINEMAKER BENOIT TOUQUETTE, EXECUTIVE CHEF NASH COGNETTI ~ TRA VIGNE RESTAURANT

Wine Making Facts :

Encépagement : Sauvignon Blanc 100%

Appellation : Carneros

Vineyard/Micro-Climate : Our vineyard, in Napa Valley's cool southernmost appellation, is just one mile from San Francisco/San Pablo Bay

Average Vine Age : 5 years old vines

Yield : 4 tons per acre

Alcohol Level : 14.60

Total Production : 496 Cases

Harvest Details : Harvested September 12-18, 2007

Winemaking: Three distinct clones of Sauvignon Blanc provide individual characteristics in this layered, complex wine.

Wood Origin : French oak only

Oak Regimen : The wine was fermented in 60% small stainless steel barrels and 40% French oak 20 % château barrels.

New Barrels: 100% new oak

Aged : On the lees for eight months and stirred frequently, some barrels have accomplished the malolatic fermentation to give more complexity to the blend.

"The small stainless barrels bring a vibrant acidity to the wine and protect the lively varietal character of the Sauvignon Blanc which offers a bouquet of tropical notes, lime, grape fruit and citrus; on the other hand, the wine that was fermented and aged in oak contributes additional structure with a round mid-palate and long finish." BT

HARTWELL VINEYARDS
5795 SILVERADO TRAIL
NAPA, CA 94558
800-366-6516
HARTWELLVINEYARDS.COM

SOMMELIERS, LOIRE WINE GLASS

Beginning with a single acre Bob and his wife Blanca began construction on their Tuscan-style winery and caves in 1997. Long-haired Scottish Highland cattle now graze on the 90-acre property, which lies on the slope of a dormant volcano that last erupted four million years ago. Those who put Hartwell on their Napa itineraries experience an intimate, salon-style tasting in Hartwell's caves. Wine pairings with imported cheeses are followed by a barrel tasting of a future release accompanied by truffles with Hartwell's own cabernet mixed into the chocolate. All Hartwell's wines are estate-produced in the renowned Stags Leap appellation, with the hilly terrain, temperature fluctuations, and maximum exposure to sunlight which create the optimum growing conditions and define this esteemed microclimate.

HARTWELL ESTATE CARNEROS DISTRICT SAUVIGNON BLANC
SEARED FENNEL CRUSTED AHI TUNA, SUMMER SQUASH CARPACCIO
WINEMAKER BENOIT TOUQUETTE, EXECUTIVE CHEF NASH COGNETTI ~ TRA VIGNE RESTAURANT

Marinade:
½ c   champagne vinegar
7-8   mint leaves, chopped
½ t   chili flakes, crushed
1 c   olive oil, extra virgin

"Carpaccio":
1   zucchini, green
1   zucchini, yellow
2   tomatoes, roma

1½ T   mint, thinly sliced, packed
1½ T   basil, thinly sliced, packed

Tuna:
4 - 5 oz   Ahi Tuna steaks
½ c   fennel pollen or ground fennel seed

Marinade:
Combine and season to taste. The marinade should be quite acidic.

"Carpaccio":
Slice the zucchini tomatoes into rounds the thickness of a quarter with a mandolin or knife.
Marinade zucchini and tomatoes in the refrigerator for 1 hour.
Alternating, arrange slices of green zucchini, yellow zucchini, and tomatoes onto four plates in a pinwheel fashion.
Drizzle remaining marinade and olive oil over the squash and tomatoes.
Season with some coarse sea salt and the herbs.

Tuna:
Season the tuna liberally with salt and pepper.
Coat tuna steaks evenly with the fennel pollen.
Sear or grill the tuna on all sides until rare or medium rare, taking care not to burn the pollen.
Slice the tuna on a bias and place in the center of each carpaccio plate to serve. 4 servings

TRA VIGNE
1050 CHARTER OAK AVENUE
ST HELENA, CA 94574
707-963-4444
TRAVIGNERESTAURANT.COM

HILL FAMILY ESTATE ORIGIN
GRILLED JERK CHICKEN, ROASTED VEGETABLES, AND DRIED FRUIT INFUSED RICE
WINEMAKER ALISON DORAN, WINERY CHEF PETER L. JACOBSEN

Encépagement : Merlot 57%, Cabernet Sauvignon 43%

Appellation : Napa Valley

Vineyard : 12% Oak Knoll AVA; Valley Floor, 10% Atlas Peak

Appellation; 1500 ft elevation, 42% Napa Carneros; terrace, 30% St Helena; narrow sub valley and 6% Wooden Valley; east hillside

Soils: various – mostly gravelly terraces

Average Vine Age : 10

Yield : 2.8 tons per acre

Alcohol Level : 14.5%

Total Production : 728 cases

Philosophy : Determine the best lots from the vintage and find the blend with the most perfect balance

Harvest Details : Merlot did really well - in a year when tannin levels were difficult to manage

Winemaking : 3 days cold soak, nice warm fermentations, press at least 3 days past dryness

Fermentation: D254 and Pasteur red yeast, sprinklers at the beginning and tub and screen at the end

Wood Origin : 16 months in 85%French oak barrels, 10% American Oak, and 5% Hungarian Oak

Oak Regimen : in barrel sixteen months

HILL FAMILY ESTATE
6512 WASHINGTON STREET
YOUNTVILLE, CA 94599
707 944 9580
HILLFAMILYESTATE.COM

VITIS, BORDEAUX WINE GLASS

"Nose takes off with really pretty blackberry and violets, some toasty oak. On the palate; full, rich, and fruity with jammy berry and black licorice undertones and soft tannin, tasty and drinkable. Palate softens and lengthens as it sits out in the glass."AD

The Hill family has a passion for farming California soil that spans four generations. Patriarch Doug Hill, has spent the last thirty-four years in vineyard management; acquiring 100 acres which comprises 12 unique vineyards, a commanding knowledge of grape-growing, and a sincere appreciation for Napa Valley's soil and its magical ability to harvest exceptional fruit. In order to create a portfolio of wines rich in character and complexity it takes the entire Hill family alongside winemaker Alison Green Doran. "Each vineyard has its own distinctive qualities, the one common element shared across our vineyards is our commitment to unfailing exploration and experimentation," says son Ryan, enthusiastically. Hill Family Estate has a jewel of a tasting room in the center of Yountville, along with a 1.5 acre farm where they grow fruit and vegetables for the Bardessono Inn and Spa. Guests rave about the tasting experience, which is relaxed, informative and extremely entertaining. For the Hills, it's all about the passion, the pursuit for perfection and carrying on a family legacy.

Hill Family Estate Origin
Grilled Jerk Chicken, Roasted Vegetables, and Dried Fruit Infused Rice
Winemaker Alison Doran, Winery Chef Peter L. Jacobsen

Chicken:

1	Chicken, 3 to 4 pounds
4 T	Jamaican Jerk, homemade or if purchased I prefer Walkerswood
1/3 c	olive oil
1 t	salt
1	zucchini, large
1	onion, large

Dried Fruit Infused Rice:

1	garlic clove
2 c	basmati rice or any long grain rice
2 ½ c	water
1 T	butter or oil
1 T	cumin, dried
3 T	raisins
3 T	cherries, dried
3 T	ginger, candied

Method:
Stir the Jamaican Jerk, salt and olive oil together to make a spicy oil mixture.
Lift the skin up from the chicken and slide a spoonful of the spicy oil mixture under the skin and smear it around. Do a spoonful over each breast and leg and on the back over each thigh. Reserve the last 2 tablespoons of spicy oil to smear around inside the body cavity.
The idea is to deep marinate the chicken so the spicy mixture fully infuses the meat.
Put the chicken in a plastic bag and let it marinate in the refrigerator for at least 2 hours, 4 hours is better. Overnight can also work.

Prepare rotisserie, grill or preheat oven to 300º F:
The chicken should be slow roasted over a low fire. A rotisserie is best, because it does the turning for you. A grill is the traditional way, (Think about it, how many people in Jamaica have an electric rotisserie), and, of course, the recipe is an ancient one, said to have originated with the indigenous Arawak Indians of Jamaica. Skew the chicken, place in rotisserie. If cooking on the grill, cut the chicken in half and lay on the grill, but not directly over the coals (indirect heat is good) and turn it about every 15 minutes. Covering the chicken on the grill is good too, if possible. And, of course, you can cook it in the oven. Set the oven at 300º degrees F. No matter how you do it, it should take about 1½ hours to be fully cooked. When the internal temperature at the thickest/deepest part, reaches 170 º degrees , poultry is considered fully cooked.

Vegetables:
For the vegetables, the garlic should be finely chopped; the zucchini and onion should be coarsely cut up in about ½ - ¾ inch pieces. Place the vegetables under the chicken to catch the drippings as they fall into the vegetable pan. Once the chicken is done, put the vegetables in a frying pan and sauté it so that they are well cooked and soft. It is a perfect spicy topping for the fruity rice.

Fruit infused Rice:
While the chicken is cooking, put the dried fruit in a cup and cover with water. Heat it up in a microwave or sauce pan, until hot. Let sit 5-10 minutes to soften and swell the fruit. Pour off the water. Wash the rice, put in a pan with the water, fruit and cumin, bring to a boil, stir, cover and cook at lowest heat for about 15-20 minutes, until soft. Turn off, let sit covered for 10 minutes and then fluff the rice with a fork; it is ready to eat.

Plating:
Cut up the chicken and serve it all family style. I used to put it all onto a large platter and everyone would click their wine glasses in a toast to family, wine and the blessings we all have received in this lifetime and then we all dug in to a fun and hearty meal. We sincerely wish you, your family and friends, fun and the blessings of a life well lived. Serves 4

HILL FAMILY ESTATE WINES

ANTIQUE FAIR

HILL FAMILY ESTATE
6512 WASHINGTON STREET
YOUNTVILLE, CA 94599
707 944 9580
HILLFAMILYESTATE.COM

HOFFMANN, AUM WHITE WINE AND AUM CABERNET SAUVIGNON
GOAT CHEESE TARTLET, HERB SALAD, WHITE TRUFFLE OIL
WINEMAKER PETER HOFFMANN, PROFESSIONAL CHEF JOHN VLANDIS

**HOFFMANN WINES
330 FAIRVIEW DRIVE
NAPA, CA 94559
707-266-8803**
HOFFMANNFAMILYWINES.COM

Wine Making Facts :
Encépagement :   60% Viognier, 30%
Sauvignon Blanc 10% Symphony
Vineyard : Organic and
biodynamically farmed
Soils: Clay loam
Micro-Climate : Warm to hot
days and cool nights
Average Vine Age : Viognier planted in
1995, Sauvignon Blanc planted in 1986
Yield : 5 to 6 tons per acre
Alcohol Level : 12.8%
Total Production : 250 cases
Harvest Details : Viognier September 6th
and the Sauvignon Blanc on August 26th,
by hand into quarter ton micro bins
Winemaking: Native or natural process for
all aspects of winemaking. We also stir lees.
Fermentation : Native yeast 19 days
Oak Regimen : Medium plus
Burgundian toast
Bottling Formats: Bottled February 2009

Wine Making Facts :
Encépagement : 100% clone 7 Cabernet
Appellation : St. Helena, Napa
Vineyard : 100% Estate Owned
Soils: Clay loam
Elevation: 260 ft.
Aspect : North-South Row direction on
a slight south west facing slope
Micro-Climate : Warm to hot days /cool nights
Alcohol Level : 13.2%
Total Production : 200 cases
Harvest Details : Harvested September 13th
by hand into quarter ton micro bins
Fermentation : Native yeast 21 days
 Wood Origin : Center of France
Oak Regimen : Medium plus Burgundian toast
Percentage of New Barrels : 20% - 30%
Coopers : Tonnellerie Quintessence Bordeaux
Bottling Formats: Bottled March 2007

"The 2008 Aum Tres Joyas California white wine The perfumed nose shows layers of bright citrus fruit intermingled with scents of honeysuckle and tangerine creamsicle. The complex sweet scent continues on the palate with balance, acidity and a bright lingering finish." PH

"This wine was made to age yet is entirely drinkable now. Rich red cherry and chocolate dominate with a beautiful integration of tannic structure. Well rounded acidity and seamless tannins prevail in a long and complex finish." PH

TYROL, CABERNET WINE GLASS
TYROL, VIOGNIER - CHARDONNAY WINE GLASS

HOFFMANN, AUM WHITE WINE AND AUM CABERNET SAUVIGNON
GOAT CHEESE TARTLET, FRISÉE, HERB SALAD, WHITE TRUFFLE OIL
WINEMAKER PETER HOFFMANN, PROFESSIONAL CHEF JOHN VLANDIS

Pâté Brisée :
1 ½ c	AP flour
8 T	butter, frozen, cubed
½ t	salt
½ t	sugar
4 - 6 T	water, ice cold

Custard:
2 c	half and half
3 ea	eggs, large

1 ½ t	kosher salt
1/8 t	nutmeg
4 oz	goat cheese
1	chervil bunch, stems removed
1 t	tarragon, chopped
1 T	chives, chopped
1 c	frisée
tt	white truffle olive oil

Method:
Preheat oven to 375° F.

In a food processor place flour, sugar and salt. Pulse a few times to incorporate.
Add frozen butter cubes and pulse until dough forms pea size pieces. Do not overwork.
Pour in 2/3 of water and pulse just until a ball loosely forms. Add more water if necessary.

Roll out pâté brisée to 1/8 inch thick, cut out appropriate size for your tart molds.
When all the molds have been completed place in the freezer for 30 minutes.
Line with parchment paper and fill with pie weights. Place in oven and bake until they are light brown. Remove from the oven and remove the weights and paper. Let cool.
Reduce temperature to 325° F.

Heat the half and half with the salt and the nutmeg to a simmer. Let it cool 10 minutes.
Place the eggs in a blender and turn on low, slowly add the half and half.
Add goat cheese and mix until it is smooth.
Divide the remaining cheese evenly into the tart shells.
Pour the egg mixture into the shells and bake in a 325° F oven until set.
Remove from the oven, let cool slightly before serving. Refrigerate for later use.
Re-warm in a 325 ° F oven for 10-15 minutes. Remove from the molds and serve.

Top with an herb salad:
Frisée, chives, tarragon and chervil, toss with white truffle oil and seasoned rice vinegar. Sprinkle with sea salt. Garnish the plate with white truffle oil, basil oil and Cypress black salt. 6 servings

INDULGE THE PASSION.

2007
Pinot Noir

hope & grace

Santa Lucia Highlands

HOPE & GRACE PINOT NOIR
GRILLED WOLF FARMS QUAIL, SPRING MORELS AND GARDEN FAVA BEANS
WINEMAKER CHARLES HENDRICKS, PROFESSIONAL CHEF JOHN VLANDIS

Wine Making Facts :
Encépagement : 100% Pinot Noir
Alcohol Level : 14%
Vineyard designation: Doctor's Vineyard Hahn Estate
Appellation : Santa Lucia Highlands, Monterey County
Total Production : 38 barrels produced
Winemaking techniques: Sustainably grown
vineyards, light-touch winemaking
Winemaking: Produced in a traditional
Burgundian style, full of richness,
earthiness and velvety textures.
Barrel Aging: 16 Months
Barrels: Remond and Cadus French Oak Barrels
Winemaking: Sur Lie
Wood Origin : French Oak
Oak Regimen : 16 Months on Oak

HOPE AND GRACE
6540 WASHINGTON STREET
YOUNTVILLE, CA 94599
707-944-2500
HOPEANDGRACEWINES.COM

VITIS, PINOT NOIR WINE GLASS

" Deep aromas of wild berries, almonds, white pepper and a hint of rose. On the first taste, the wine tantalizes the tongue with vivacious cherry fruit swirling amidst subtle oak spice, and a slight hint of smoky bacon. A superbly balanced wine, drinking beautifully now, but will benefit with short term cellaring. " CH

Winemaker and owner, Charles Hendricks believes in gently coaxing wine from the grapes, rather than forcing or over-manipulation. Named for his two daughters, Hope and Grace, Charles has created a portfolio of limited production, single varietal wines. After twenty successful years as a consulting winemaker for such prestigious wineries as Barnett, Regusci, Bacio Divino and Viader, Charles launched his own label. The hope and grace tasting room is located in the heart of Yountville, and includes an elegant tasting salon, filled with contemporary art and antiques. Along with a passion for winemaking, Charles says that it is nature's job to conceal, and the artist's job to reveal.

INDULGE THE PA
hope & grace
2006
ST. HELENA
CABERNET SAUVIGNON
NAPA VALLEY
2006
Malbec
hope & grace
Napa Valley

HOPE AND GRACE CABERNET SAUVIGNON AND HOPE & GRACE MALBEC
PAVÉ OF BLACK ANGUS NEW YORK SHIITAKE MUSHROOM SALSA
WINEMAKER CHARLES HENDRICKS, PROFESSIONAL CHEF JOHN VLANDIS

HOPE AND GRACE
6540 WASHINGTON STREET
YOUNTVILLE, CA 94599
707-944-2500
HOPEANDGRACEWINES.COM

Wine Making Facts :
Encépagement : 100% Cabernet Sauvignon
Appellation : Napa Valley Appellation
Designated Vineyards: Renowned
Lewelling Vineyards in St. Helena
Alcohol Level : 14%
Production: 32 barrels produced
Barrel Aging: 24 Months
Wood Origin : Center of France
Coopers : Chateau Feré French Oak Barrels
Harvest Details : Bountiful harvest that
produced vibrant, fruit rich wines.
Release: sixth vintage release

Wine Making Facts :
Encépagement : 100% Malbec
Winery : hope & grace Winery
Appellation : Oakville, Napa Valley
Vineyard : Hoxsey Vineyard
Alcohol Level : 14%
Total Production : 300 cases
Wood Origin : French Oak
Oak Regiment : 24 Months on Oak
Wood Origin : Never & Allier
History: Malbec was brought to the new world,
ripens in warmer sun, and exudes the rich
colors and flavors of a variety unbound. The
2006 vintage marks the third release of Malbec
for hope & grace wines, and has become a
permanent member of our portfolio.

"Intense aromas of cocoa powder, dark berries and black licorice come forward with the first swirl, followed by undertones of spicy plum, marjoram and lead pencil. Fully textured, the plum and cherry flavors broaden with the sumptuous weight of the wine across the palate. The wine leaves the mouth with the vibrant fruit of the vintage." CH

"Intriguing aromas of raspberry, black pepper, anise, and bergamot tea with subtle notes of fig leaf and sweet oak. Red fruit gushes across the palate from start to finish, with a silky full bodied texture; lively acidity keeps the fruit and spice lingering long after the sip is gone." CH

VITIS, CABERNET SAUVIGNON WINE GLASS

HOPE & GRACE PINOT NOIR
GRILLED WOLF FARMS QUAIL, SPRING MORELS AND GARDEN FAVA BEANS
WINEMAKER CHARLES HENDRICKS, PROFESSIONAL CHEF JOHN VLANDIS

Quail:
4   quail, semi-boneless

Ingredients:
1 t   shallots, minced
1   thyme sprig, leaves removed
       and minced
1 t   soy sauce
¼ c   grape seed oil
tt   salt and pepper
20   small morels

1 lb   fresh fava beans.
20   cherry tomatoes, sliced in half
1 c   pea shoots
2 T   extra virgin olive oil
2 T   butter, softened
½ t   shallots, minced
1 t   thyme, minced
1 T   seasoned rice vinegar
tt   salt and pepper

Preheat grill.

Place quail on grill skin side down, cook two minutes and turn. Grill quail to desired temperature. Keep warm. Heat a large sauté, add butter and olive oil.
Heat until butter has melted, add morels and sauté for 3 minutes add fava beans, thyme and shallots and continue to cook until the fava beans are warm. Remove from the heat. Place the pea shoots and tomatoes in a mixing bowl; add the morels and the seasoned rice wine vinegar. Season with salt and pepper.
Divide the morel and pea shoot salad between 4 plates. Top with the quail. 4 servings

HOPE & GRACE CABERNET SAUVIGNON AND HOPE & GRACE MALBEC
PAVÉ OF BLACK ANGUS NEW YORK, SHIITAKE MUSHROOM SALSA
WINEMAKER CHARLES HENDRICKS, PROFESSIONAL CHEF JOHN VLANDIS

Shiitake Mushroom Salsa:

1 lb	shiitakes, diced
1 t	garlic, minced
1 piece	ginger, sliced ¼ inch thick
2 oz	soy sauce, low sodium
1 t	sesame oil
3 T	kecap manis
¼ c	scallions, sliced
2 T	cilantro, minced
10	Thai basil leaves, minced
½	red pepper, diced
3 oz	olive oil

Pavé of Black Angus New York:

2 lb	New York Steak cut into 2 x 3- inch rectangles
2 oz	olive oil
	salt and fresh ground pepper

Method:
Heat olive oil and sesame oil in a large pot, add the ginger and cook 2-3 minutes.
Remove the ginger.
Add the garlic and cook 10 seconds, do not brown, add the mushrooms and cook until tender.
Remove from the heat, place on a sheet pan to cool.
Add the remaining ingredients.
Serve room temperature.

Pavé of Black Angus New York:
Season the beef with salt and pepper.
Heat oil in a large sauté pan.
Sear on high heat, turning to brown on all sides.
Cook to desired temperature.
Let rest for 15 minutes.
Slice and place on top of shiitake mushroom salsa. 2 servings

HOPE AND GRACE
6540 WASHINGTON STREET
YOUNTVILLE, CA 94599
707-944-2500
HOPEANDGRACEWINES.COM

JOSEPH PHELPS
VINEYARDS
Viognier
NAPA VALLEY
VINTAGE 2007

JOSEPH PHELPS VINEYARDS VIOGNIER
CATALAN SEARED GARLIC SHRIMP
WINEMAKER ASHLEY HEPWORTH, WINERY CHEF STEPHEN PAVY

Wine Making Facts :
Appellation : Napa Valley 100% estate-grown
Harvested : Grapes were harvested
at an average 23.7° Brix
Fermentation : Stainless steel tanks with the
lees stirred during and after fermentation.
Aged : 10 months
Barrels : 100% French
Bottled : June, 2008
Winemaking: We picked the Viognier
at the height of ripeness, capturing its
beautiful aromatics while preserving
the acidity in the grapes.

JOSEPH PHELPS VINEYARDS
200 TAPLIN ROAD
ST. HELENA, CA 94574
707-967-9153
JPVWINES.COM

SOMMELIERS, VIOGNIER WINE GLASS

"The wine exudes a bouquet of jasmine, crushed rock and freshly peeled tangerine intertwined with honey, pastry cream and orange blossom. The bright acidity is a result of partial malolactic fermentation and seamlessly balances the sweet fruit characteristics."AH

This is one of the oldest and most respected wineries in the Napa Valley. "Joe Phelps is truly a pioneer," says Damian Parker, Director of Winemaking at Joseph Phelps Vineyards. "The 1974 Insignia was the first Bordeaux-style blend produced in California under a proprietary label. That same year, our Syrah revived a French varietal whose plantings here had disappeared for more than 50 years. And in 1990 we introduced a whole new family of Rhône-style wines." This year, beginning with the 2009 harvest, Joseph Phelps Vineyards will own and control virtually all of its grape sources, becoming 100 percent estate-produced except for its limited production of Syrah.

JOSEPH PHELPS VINEYARDS INSIGNIA
HORSERADISH AND GARLIC PRIME RIB
WINEMAKER ASHLEY HEPWORTH, RESTAURATEUR TYLER FLORENCE

Wine Making Facts :
Encépagement : Cabernet Sauvignon, Petit Verdot and Merlot
Appellation : Napa Valley
Vineyard : 100% estate-owned Napa Valley vineyards which
break down as follows: South Napa, 39% (Suscol Vineyard),
Stags Leap District, 30% (15% Barboza Vineyard and 15% Las
Rocas Vineyard), Oak Knoll District, 16% (Yountville Vineyard),
Rutherford, 11% (Banca Dorada Vineyard), St. Helena, 4% (Spring
Valley Ranch Vineyards)
Philosophy : With the release of the 1974 vintage in 1978,
Insignia was America's first Bordeaux-style blend produced
under a proprietary label.
Harvest Details : Harvested between Sept. 4th through Oct. 15th
Facility : Joseph Phelps Vineyards
Wood Origin : France
Barrels : Taransaud, Dargaud Jaegle, Nadalie, Demptos, Marcel
Cadet and Sylvain.
Aged : 24 months in French oak
Percentage of New Barrels : 100%

JOSEPH PHELPS VINEYARDS
200 TAPLIN ROAD
ST. HELENA, CA 94574
707-967-9153
JPVWINES.COM

SOMMELIERS BLACK TIE, BORDEAUX MATURE

"RICH AROMATICS OF MINERAL, BAKING SPICES, DARK CHOCOLATE, GRAPHITE, AND OPULENT PLUM AND BLACKBERRY LEAD TO THE CONCENTRATED AND BALANCED MOUTHFEEL. SILKY, WELL STRUCTURED TANNINS, CORE BLACK FRUIT AND SWEET OAK NOTES FROM OUR ESTATE VINEYARDS CREATE LENGTH AND WEIGHT THAT WILL ALLOW THIS BEAUTIFUL WINE TO AGE, AS WELL AS REMAIN APPROACHABLE IN ITS YOUTH."

WINEMAKER ASHLEY HEPWORTH

Joseph Phelps Vineyards Viognier
Catalan Seared Garlic Shrimp
Winemaker Ashley Hepworth, Winery Chef Stephen Pavy

¾ lb	medium shrimp, shelled and de-veined
5 T	extra virgin olive oil
3 T	minced garlic
¼ t	red pepper flakes
2 T	chopped Italian parsley
2 c	Amontillado Sherry
	sea salt

Method:

Sprinkle shrimp with salt and let sit for 10 minutes.

In a skillet (or flame proof shallow casserole – I used cast iron, it is nice to have something you can take right to the table), heat oil over medium to medium-high flame.

When oil is hot, add garlic and pepper flakes, stirring for 20-30 seconds so garlic does not burn. Add shrimp and stir until they have turned pink.

Add sherry, parsley, and salt to taste; continue cooking until the sherry evaporates and the sauce thickens slightly.

Take from stove immediately to table. 3 servings

JOSEPH PHELPS VINEYARDS INSIGNIA
HORSERADISH AND GARLIC PRIME RIB
WINEMAKER ASHLEY HEPWORTH, RESTAURATEUR TYLER FLORENCE

Beef:

1	prime rib beef roast, (3 rib) about 6 lb
5	garlic cloves, smashed
2	garlic heads, halved
½ c	horseradish, grated fresh or prepared
½ c	sea salt, course granules
¼ c	freshly ground black pepper
½ c	extra-virgin olive oil
2	carrots, peeled and chopped
2	parsnips
1	red onion, halved

Wild Mushrooms:

1 T	unsalted butter
2 lb	mushrooms, assorted such as cremini, oyster, shiitake, chanterelle, or white, trimmed and sliced
2	thyme sprigs, fresh and only leaves
tt	sea salt
tt	freshly ground black pepper
½ c	Cabernet Sauvignon
¼ c	reserved beef broth (drippings from roast) or low-sodium canned broth
¼ c	heavy cream
1 T	chives, minced
	Extra-virgin olive oil

Method:
1. Preheat the oven to 350° F.
2. Lay the beef in a large roasting pan with the bone side down. (The ribs act as a natural roasting rack.)
3. In a small bowl mash together the garlic, horseradish, salt, pepper, and olive oil to make a paste.
4. Massage the paste generously over the entire roast.
5. Scatter the vegetables and halved garlic around the meat and drizzle them with a 2-count of oil.
6. Put the pan in the oven and roast the beef for about 1½ to 2 hours for medium-rare (or approximately twenty minutes per pound). Check the internal temperature of the roast in several places with an instant-read thermometer; it should register 125° degrees F. for medium-rare.
7. Remove the beef to a carving board and let it rest for 20 minutes. The internal temperature of the meat will continue to rise by about 10 degrees.
8. Remove the vegetables and set aside. Pour the pan juices into a fat separator or small bowl and set aside to allow the fat and beef juices to separate.
9. Pour off and discard the fat. You will use the tasty beef juices for the mushrooms.
10. Place a clean skillet over medium heat.
11. Add the butter and a 2-count drizzle of oil.
12. When the butter starts to foam, add the mushrooms and thyme; and season with salt and pepper.
13. Stir everything together for a few minutes.
14. Add the red wine, stirring to scrape up any stuck bits; then cook and stir to evaporate the alcohol.
15. When the wine is almost all gone, add the reserved beef juices.
16. Let the liquid cook down and then take it off the heat.
17. Stir in the cream and chives, and season with salt and pepper. Serves 6 - 8.

JOSEPH PHELPS VINEYARDS
200 TAPLIN ROAD
ST. HELENA, CA 94574
707-967-9153
JPVWINES.COM

KEEVER VINEYARDS SAUVIGNON BLANC
HEIRLOOM MELON SALAD, PORCINI MUSHROOM, IBERICO HAM, VANILLA-SHERRY VINAIGRETTE
WINEMAKER CELIA WELCH, EXECUTIVE CHEF SEAN O'TOOLE ~ BARDESSONO

Wine Making Facts :
Encépagement : Sauvignon Blanc
Appellation : Napa Valley
Alcohol Level : 14.2 %
Total Production : 237 Cases
Winemaker : Celia Welch
Facility : Keever Vineyards and Winery
Fermentation : Barrel fermentation
Coopers : 50% stainless steel and
50% French oak
Fining/Filtering : Filtered three
days before bottling
Bottling Formats: 750 mL
Bottled : February 23, 2009

KEEVER VINEYARDS
P.O. BOX 2906
YOUNTVILLE, CA 94599
707-944-0910
KEEVERVINEYARDS.COM

VITIS, SAUVIGNON BLANC WINE GLASS

" Delicate floral aromas and lively citrus notes swirl around deeper tropical tones of fresh pineapple, guava, and mango in this intensely aromatic Sauvignon Blanc. Orange peel, bright, juicy fresh pineapple and a touch of vanilla add a crisp, fresh sensation to the palate flavors, while texturally the wine is rich and broad, finishing to a soft, silky sensation. " CW

Olga Keever has just one word to describe the past year at Keever Vineyards: Excitement. Their rising-star winemaker, Celia Welch, was named Winemaker of the Year by Food and Wine magazine. Built on the site of an old horse ranch in the hills overlooking Yountville, the winery makes 100% estate-produced wines that truly reflect the Keever family. Keever limits production of its Estate Cabernet to just three tons or less per acre and uses some of the smallest tanks in the Napa Valley to ferment in smaller lots and specific clones and vineyard blocks. Gravity-flow and hand-sorting ensure the gentlest possible handling of fruit.

KEEVER

V I N E Y A R D S

ESTATE GROWN

2006

Yountville ✦ *Napa Valley*

Cabernet Sauvignon

ALC. 14.9% BY VOL.

KEEVER VINEYARDS CABERNET SAUVIGNON
ROASTED CALIFORNIA WHITE BASS, PORCINI, SPICED BLACK MISSION FIG, WATERCRESS
WINEMAKER CELIA WELCH, EXECUTIVE CHEF SEAN O'TOOLE ~ BARDESSONO

Wine Making Facts :
Encépagement : 100% Cabernet Sauvignon
Appellation : Yountville, Napa Valley
Vineyard : Keever Vineyards Estate, Yountville
Soils : Cortina Series Soil, a gravelly clay loam
Aspect : Hillside vineyard with an eastern exposure
Alcohol Level : 14.9%
Total Production : 511 Cases
Facility : Keever Vineyards and Winery
Percentage of New Barrels : 90%
Time in Oak: 20 months
Fining/Filtering : Unfined and unfiltered
Bottling Formats: 750mL, 1.5 L, 3 L
Bottled : July 18, 2008

KEEVER VINEYARDS
P.O. BOX 2906
YOUNTVILLE, CA 94599
707-944-0910
KEEVERVINEYARDS.COM

VINUM XL, CABERNET SAUVIGNON GLASS

"AROMAS ARE FORWARD, BRIGHT FRUIT: BLACKBERRY, BOYSENBERRY, AND CASSIS WITH VANILLA, ALLSPICE, CINNAMON STICK, AND A TOUCH OF CEDAR. THE PALATE IS VERY FULL, SOFT, AND RIPE, WITH LOTS OF JUICY BERRY AND VANILLA FLAVORS. THE TEXTURE IS DENSE, SOFT, AND FRUIT-FOCUSED, WITH DARK BERRY FLAVORS LINGERING."

WINEMAKER CELIA WELCH

KEEVER VINEYARDS SAUVIGNON BLANC
HEIRLOOM MELON SALAD, PORCINI MUSHROOM, IBERICO HAM, VANILLA-SHERRY VINAIGRETTE
WINEMAKER CELIA WELCH, EXECUTIVE CHEF SEAN O'TOOLE ~ BARDESSONO

Melon:
1 melon, small, cavaillon or charente,
  (substitute a cantaloupe)

Mushrooms:
½ lb mushrooms, porcini, fresh,
  sliced ½" thick

Vinaigrette:
1 vanilla bean, scrape seeds
½ c olive oil, extra virgin
3 T sherry vinegar

1 T pure maple syrup
1 lime

Plating:
 1 bunch spearmint
¼ lb ham, Iberico thinly sliced from
  the deli (substitute San Danielle)

Melon:
Peel the skin from the melon.
Slice each half into 9 pieces and remove the seeds with a spoon.
Chill.

Mushrooms:
Sauté the porcini slices in olive oil.
Remove from the pan and cool at room temperature.

Vinaigrette:
Simmer the fresh vanilla bean and seeds, sherry vinegar, and maple syrup.
Cook for 3 minutes to blend the flavors.
Remove the vanilla pod, whisk in some olive oil to make the vinaigrette, and adjust with fresh
lime juice to balance the acid.

Serving:
Arrange three slices of melon on each plate with a porcini between each.
Pick and place some mint leaves whole on top of the melon.
Drizzle with the vanilla sherry vinaigrette.
Season with fresh black pepper and sprinkle with some coarse sea salt.
Finish with the sliced ham and serve room temperature. 4 servings

BARDESSONO INN AND SPA
6526 YOUNT STREET
YOUNTVILLE, CA 94599
707-204-6000
BARDESSONO.COM

Keever Vineyards Cabernet Sauvignon
Roasted California White Bass, Porcini, Spiced Black Mission Fig, Watercress
Winemaker Celia Welch, Executive Chef Sean O'Toole ~ Bardessono

2 lb	California white bass		1 piece	fresh vanilla bean
2 lb	porcini mushrooms		1 bunch	watercress
1 pt	black mission figs			olive oil
2 c	ruby port wine			
1 stick	cinnamon			
1 t	black peppercorns			

Method:

Preheat oven to 400º F.
Remove the bones from the white bass fillet.
Cut the fillet into four 6 ounce portions.
Season with salt and pepper.
Sauté the fish skin side down until crispy.
Place the pan in a 400 ˚F oven for 4 minutes, serve medium.

Scrape the stems of the porcini to remove any dirt and slice ¼ inch thick.
Sauté mushrooms in olive oil until tender.
Season with salt and pepper.

Simmer the ruby port wine to a boil with the cinnamon, black pepper, and vanilla.
Add the figs and cook until tender.
Remove the figs and reduce the port to a glaze.
Place the watercress sprigs into some ice water, remove, pat dry, and reserve.

To serve, place some sautéed mushroom on a plate with the fish atop.
Garnish with two glazed figs and drizzle some sauce around.
Finish with the raw watercress and serve. 4 servings

KEEVER VINEYARDS
P.O. BOX 2906
YOUNTVILLE, CA 94599
707-944-0910
KEEVERVINEYARDS.COM

Wine Making Facts :
Encépagement : Syrah (clones 174, 383, 470, 525, 877 and Durrell)
Appellation : Mount Veeder
Vineyard : Lagier Meredith Vineyard
Soils : fractured shale and sandstone
Elevation: 1,300 feet
Aspect : mostly east facing
Average Vine Age : 10 years
Yield : 2 to 3 tons per acre
Alcohol Level : 14.8%
Total Production : 940 cases
Philosophy : Our role is to shepherd the wine from vineyard to bottle and protect it from too much winemaking.
Harvest Details : Picked October 1st and 6,th in 2005
Fermentation : Fermented in open-topped T-bins. Punched down 2 to 3 times daily.
Wood Origin : France
Oak Regimen : 20 months
Coopers : François Frères
Bottling Format : 750 ml and 1.5 liter bottles

"Deep dark color, brilliant at the edge. Aromas of flowers and dark fruit with a hint of mint. White pepper on the nose. A bit earthy, with a note of bacon. Long finish and seamlessly integrated flavors -- whole wine." SL

LAGIER MEREDITH
4967 DRY CREEK ROAD
NAPA, CA 94558
707-253-0653
LAGIERMEREDITH.COM

O SERIES SYRAH WINE GLASS

LAGIER MEREDITH SYRAH
SYRAH GRAPE VINE TEA SMOKED DUCK SALAD
WINEMAKER STEPHEN LAGIER, PROFESSIONAL CHEF NAIKANG KUAN

Duck:
4	breasts, 2.5 pounds each, cleaned and scored
1½ T	salt
1 t	pink salt
1 T	black pepper
1 T	granulated sugar

Smoking:
2 c	dried vine clippings or other smoking wood chips; hickory, cherry, apple wood
½ c	black tea leaves
1	orange, zest, peeled

Pickling:
24	red pearl onions
8	Tokyo turnips
1½ c	water
1½ c	sugar
1½	rice wine vinegar

Serving:
1	apple, peeled, wedged
2 c	micro-greens

Duck:
Combine salt, pink salt, black pepper, and sugar in a small mixing bowl, mix well.
Rub the salt mixture onto breast and marinate in the refrigerator two to four hours.
Rinse duck well. Pat dry well.

Smoking:
Heat cast iron pan with a rack attachment at medium heat.
Place skin down. Place the smoke mixture on bottom of the pan; rack then place cover on top. At this point there should be quite a bit of smoke coming out. Allow the tea and vine clippings to smoke, but not burn. Smoke the duck about ten minutes, the duck should take on a brownish color and be partly cooked. Remove the duck breast and place skin side down onto a cool sauté pan. Place the sauté pan on medium-low heat and allow the duck skin to render. Press down occasionally to even out the skin and press out the rendered fat. Pour out excess duck fat from the sauté pan as the duck fat is rendered. Take care not to cook the duck too fast as this will leave a great deal of fat under the skin and scorch the skin with the sugar cure on it. When the duck skin starts to crisp, and most of the fat has rendered away, flip the duck breast over to skin side up and turn off the stove. Allow the duck breast to sit in the sauté pan for about five minutes. This residual heat will complete the cooking.

Pickling:
Peel the red pearl onion, cut each in half and separate into petals. Peel and quarter the Tokyo turnip, blanch in salted boiling hot water until tender.
Combine and simmer in the water, sugar and rice wine vinegar. Pour half of the liquid into another sauce pot. Place the Tokyo turnip wedges into one of the sauce pots containing pickling liquid and place the red pearl onion petals into the other sauce pot containing the remaining pickling liquid. Bring the two pickling solutions with the vegetables up to a simmer briefly and keep in a warm location.

Serving:
Assemble the duck salad by dressing the greens lightly with the pickling solution and placing the greens, turnip, and pearl petals in four shallow soup bowls.
Slice the duck breast lengthwise thinly, fold each slice, drape them on the greens, and serve. 6 small servings

LAIL VINEYARDS SAUVIGNON BLANC
SALT-ROASTED SALMON TOSTADAS, TOMATILLO-AVOCADO SALSA
WINEMAKER PHILIPPE MELKA, CHEF/OWNER CINDY PAWLCYN ~ MUSTARDS GRILL

Wine Making Facts :
Encépagement : Sauvignon Blanc
Appellation : Napa Valley
Vineyard : A blend from several vineyards
Micro Climate : Howell Mountain, Coombsville, Dutch Henry Canyon, Oakville
Average Vine Age : 14 years
Yield : 3 - 4 tons per acre
Alcohol : 14.6%
Total Production : 1000 cases
Philosophy : Lail Vineyards brings its legacy from four generations of Napa Valley vintners to the 21st Century with its continuing quest to produce wines of the highest excellence
Harvest Details : Multiple

LAIL VINEYARDS
P.O. BOX 249
RUTHERFORD, CA 94573
707-968-9900
LAILVINEYARDS.COM

VINUM, SAUVIGNON BLANC GLASS

"Very fine Sauvignon Blanc in a supple, complex, refined style. It is full bodied, finely flavored (apple, lemon peel, vanilla, roasted nut, pineapple and pink grapefruit), and very long on the finish." PM

Founded in 1995, and led by its Managing Partner, Robin Daniel Lail, sits atop a foundation of 130 years of Napa Valley winemaking history and tradition. The company traces its roots back five generations to the founding of Inglenook Vine-yards, by Robin's great grand-uncle Captain Gustav Niebaum in 1879. Following the sale of Inglenook in 1964 Robin apprenticed with Robert Mondavi and subsequently co-founded Dominus and Merryvale in the early 1980's. Robin and her daughters Erin and Shannon carry forward the baton into the 21st Century, and have reached into the sixth generation naming their Grave style Sauvignon Blanc "Georgia" for Erin's first daughter. His children and grandchildren revel in the opportunity to carry the family tradition of seeking perfection in their wines into the 21st Century."

Blueprint

Lail Vineyards

2006
CABERNET SAUVIGNON
NAPA VALLEY

Lail Vineyards Cabernet Sauvignon
Oak Wood Grilled Pork Chop, Flageolet and Wild Mushroom Ragout
Winemaker Philippe Melka, Professional Chef John Vlandis

Wine Making Facts :
Encépagement : Cabernet Sauvignon 85%
and Merlot 15%
Appellation : Napa Valley
Vineyard : A blend from several vineyards
Micro Climate : Howell Mountain, Coombsville,
Dutch Henry Canyon, Oakville
Average Vine Age : 14 years
Yield : 3-4 tons per acre
Alcohol : 14.6%
Total Production : 2000 cases
Philosophy : Lail Vineyards brings its
legacy from four generations of Napa
Valley vintners to the 21st Century
with its continuing quest to produce
wines of the highest excellence
Harvest Details : Multiple

Lail Vineyards
P.O. Box 249
Rutherford, CA 94573
707-968-9900
LAILVINEYARDS.COM

Vinum, Cabernet Sauvignon Glass

"This 85% cabernet sauvignon and 15% merlot wine shows finesse, harmony and seduction. The mouthfeel is round with soft texture and beautiful aromatics of chocolate, black currants, loam and licorice finishing with a sense of delicate power."

Winemaker Philippe Melka

LAIL VINEYARDS SAUVIGNON BLANC
SALT-ROASTED SALMON TOSTADAS, TOMATILLO-AVOCADO SALSA
WINEMAKER PHILIPPE MELKA, CHEF/OWNER CINDY PAWLCYN ~ MUSTARDS GRILL

Salmon:

3, 3oz	wild king salmon fillets, cleaned of pin bones
1½ T	olive oil

Cumin-Scented Black Beans:

8 oz	black beans, soaked overnight
1	guajillo chile, small dried or
2	dried chiles de árbol, seeded
1	bay leaf
4 - 5 c	vegetable or chicken stock

Tomatillo-Avocado Salsa:

8 oz	tomatillos, husk removed, cut into ¼" dice
1½	avocados, peeled, ¼" dice
3	scallions, light colored parts, minced
1	jalapeño chile, seeded, minced
3 T	cilantro leaves, minced
½ t	sea salt
¼ t	black pepper, freshly ground
½ t	cumin seeds, toasted, ground
1 T	rice vinegar
3 T	olive oil

Tostada Greens:

3 c	arugula, loosely packed
1 c	red radishes, very thinly sliced
1 c	watercress, washed, coarsely chopped, no stems
1 T	rice vinegar
3 T	olive oil

Salmon:
Preheat a grill pan over medium heat or prepare the BBQ.
Slice the fillets into 6 even pieces, about 3 ounces per serving.
Brush fillets with olive oil and season with sea salt and fresh ground pepper.
Grill both sides of fillets.

Tostada Greens:
Combine the arugula, radishes, and watercress in a large bowl. Cover and refrigerate.
Emulsifiy oil and vinegar (reserve some if necessary for finishing salsa), dress greens lightly.

Tomatillo-Avocado Salsa:
Gently combine all the ingredients except the vinegar and oil.
Emulsifiy oil and vinegar, add just enough to moisten salsa.

Cumin-Scented Black Beans:
Sauté onion and garlic until translucent ; add mixture to beans.
Add just enough of the reserved liquid to make the beans saucy.
Simmer for 15 to 20 minutes, adding more liquid if needed.
Purée 1/3 of beans, in a food processor with just enough of the reserved liquid to make a thick paste.
Add back to whole beans; add more liquid if needed. Season with salt and pepper.
Add the toasted chiles, bay leaf, sautéed onions, garlic and ground cumin.
Add enough stock to moisten, and simmer 15 to 20 minutes. Stir in the cilantro, just before serving.

Serving:
To serve, place a crisp tortilla on each plate and top each with the beans.
Layer on some salmon, then a small mound of greens.
Top with a couple tablespoons of the salsa and a sprinkling of cheese.
Finish each plate with a wedge of lime. 6 servings

MUSTARDS GRILL
7399 St. Helena Highway
Yountville, CA 94558
707-944-2424
MUSTARDGRILL.COM

Lail Vineyards Cabernet Sauvignon
Oak Wood Grilled Pork Chop, Flageolet and Wild Mushroom Ragout
Winemaker Philippe Melka, Professional Chef John Vlandis

1 lb	flageolets covered in cold water overnight (preferably Rancho Gordo beans)	4, 14 oz	pork chops
1	leek, white part, small diced	1 sachet	sprig of thyme, 10 peppercorns, 2 bay leaves, 1 sprig rosemary
1	carrot, small diced	1 pint	white pearl onions, peeled
1	celery rib, small diced	2 T	minced garlic
1lb	mixed wild mushrooms, (chanterelle, shiitake, or portobello), medium dice	2 oz	olive oil
		1 qt	chicken (rich brown) or veal stock
¼ lb	applewood smoked bacon, medium dice	12 oz	dry red wine

Garnish:
Rosemary sprig and sautéed brussels sprouts leaves.

Method:
Place flageolets in large pot and cover with cold water, bring to a simmer and cook until tender. (May be done a day ahead).
Drain water and keep warm.
Heat oil in a large pot, add bacon and cook until crispy, add pearl onions and cook until golden brown.
Add garlic and cook for thirty seconds, add carrots, leek and celery, continue to cook for 3 minutes.
Add mushrooms and sauté until soft.
Add wine and reduce by half.
Add stock and sachet, bring to a boil, then add the flageolets and simmer for 15 minutes.
Remove sachet and season with salt and pepper.
Brush pork chops with olive oil, season with salt and pepper and grill until done.
Place flageolets on plate and place pork chop on top.
Garnish with a rosemary sprig and sautéed brussels sprouts leaves. 4 servings

las BONITAS

2008 CHARDONNAY

NAPA VALLEY

ALC 14.6 % BY VOL.

Las Bonitas Chardonnay
An Expression of Squash : Aerated, Roasted and Escabeche
Consultant Garret Murphy, Executive Chef Aaron London ~ Ubuntu

Clonal Selection : primarily consisting of
Hermann Wiemer selection, and of Clones 4, 15,
Dijon 76 and Dijon 96.
Appellation: Atlas Peak District
Alcohol Level: 14.2%
Total Production: 190 cases
Philosophy: We cooperate with wonderfully
talented Napa Valley winemakers who
source from the best vineyards.
Winemaking: No malo-lactic fermentation, allowing
the wine to retain all of its natural acidity.
Oak Regiment: 70% French & American oak,
and 30% small stainless steel barrels

*"The 2008 displays sweet floral aromas of pear blossoms,
apricot, jasmine. On the palate, the texture is rich, soft, and
fully ripe. Soft yeasty notes and sweet fruit flavors fill the
mouth with a finish of lush tropical fruit and just a touch of
lemon zest." GM*

Las Bonitas
1245 Main Street
Napa, CA 94559
707-255-7150
VINTNERSCOLLECTIVE.COM

Sommeliers, Montrachet Wine Glass

What happens when Napa Valley's most explorative winemakers let go and just have some fun? They talk about small side projects and great fruit sources. And Las Bonitas Chardonnay is the lucky bottle that receives the grapes and winemaking magic from such "barrel talk". Vintner's Collective, a multi-winery tasting room in the center of Napa town, is the perfect gathering spot for such collaboration. Owners Garret and Kim Murphy produce the wine – with a little help from the renowned winemakers that are their friends and colleagues– with most credit going to vintners like Vinoce Vineyard's Brian Nuss, Mi Sueño Winery's Rolando Herrera and Ancien Wines' Ken Bernards. But don't let the fun fool you, these winemakers have palettes so perfected that they can tell exactly where the grapes were grown, in what soil composite, and now they are dissecting the flavor profiles of actual clones in the wine. "Each specific type of Chardonnay vine add its own unique flavor to the finished wine" says Garret. The Murphys' have heart too, naming the wine Las Bonitas after their girls, which translates loosely in Spanish to "the pretty ones". Their label features locks of blonde hair with vine tendrils.

LAS BONITAS CHARDONNAY
AN EXPRESSION OF SQUASH: AERATED, ROASTED AND ESCABECHE
CONSULTANT GARRET MURPHY, EXECUTIVE CHEF AARON LONDON ~ UBUNTU

½ c	vadouvan spice	12	Pattypan squash, medium
1 c	Grapeseed (or other neutral oil)	1	peel of one orange
5	zucchini, medium	12	squash blossoms
3 T	lemon juice	½	preserved lemon, diced (substitute with extra lemon zest and juice)
1	garlic head, cut in half		
1	shallot, sliced		
1	lemon, sliced		Garnish:
2	Eisley wax peppers, or 1 hot banana pepper		sweet herbs (we use micro cilantro, Delfino cilantro and banana mint, but if these cannot be found, substitute with any mix of mint, cilantro and basil)
½	basil, bunch		
½	thyme, bunch		
1	mint, bunch		
2 T	honey		Resources:
16	baby squash		LeSanctuaire.com for vadouvan spice and xanthan gum
1 T	AP flour		

Method:

1. Add the vadouvan spice to the grapeseed oil in a saucepan and bring it up to 140° F , turn it off and let it steep for half an hour, creating vadouvan oil.
2. Slice the peel off the zucchini, about ¼ inch thick, and stack it on your cutting board, reserve the insides of the squash for the Escabeche. Slice the peel crossways so you create short strips that are about 1/8 of an inch wide.
3. Heat a pan over high heat until just smoking and add 2 tablespoons of vadouvan oil, the sliced squash and a pinch of salt and stir until completely coated with oil. Continue to stir over high heat until the skin becomes bright green and the flesh is lightly cooked. Chill immediately.
4. Once the zucchini is fully chilled, place it in a blender with 1 tablespoon lemon juice, and blend until a smooth purée is created, then pass it threw a chinoise or fine sieve. We finish ours with a pinch of xanthan gum and put it in a siphon with two chargers of nitrous to change the texture on the plate, but it's still good either way.
5. Dice the zucchini cores and place them in a pot with the garlic, shallot, sliced lemon, sliced peppers, basil, and ¼ bunch of thyme, cover with water and simmer for about 45 minutes until flavor is absorbed.
6. Turn off the heat and add ½ bunch of mint to the pot and allow it to steep for 3 minutes until infused but still bright in flavor, then strain immediately.
7. Whisk in the honey and 2 tablespoons of lemon juice and adjust salt. Set aside (this is the Escabeche).
8. Cut 12 of the baby squash in half and salt and toss with the flour in a mixing bowl.
9. Heat a large pan over high heat, add 1 tablespoon vadouvan oil and sear quickly on both sides, trying to keep the squash raw in the middle.
10. Your Escabeche should by now have dropped to about body temperature. Lay your seared baby squash in a single layer in a shallow dish and pour the Escabeche liquid over them, allowing it to sit at room temperature for at least half an hour.
11. Score the Pattypan squash in one concentric line around the middle, then use a paring knife to peel the skin off smoothly all the way to the line, leaving you with squash that is peeled on the bottom and not the top, reserve the peels for the Condimento (instructions below). Cut the squash in half from stem to blossom end, and score the cut sides with the tip of a knife 1/8 inch deep, and ¼ of an inch apart.
12. Heat a large pan over high heat, and add 1 tablespoon of vadouvan oil and cook the squash with ¼ bunch of thyme and the chopped peel of one orange until golden brown on both sides. At this point, they should be tender, but not mushy.
13. Clean the squash blossoms by separating the petals and the stamen from the base.
14. Heat a pan with 1 tablespoon vadouvan oil over high heat and add in your reserved squash peels and sauté for one minute, then add the blossom pedals and sauté for 1 more minute until just wilted, chill immediately.
15. Once chilled, chop the sautéed petals and peels, then mix in a bowl with a pinch of salt, half-bunch of mint chiffonade and the preserved lemon.
16. With the remaining 4 baby squash, simply slice them thinly or shave them on a mandolin and season lightly with salt.
17. Spoon or siphon the squash purée artistically onto four plates and pop them into a 350° F degree oven for 2 minutes to heat, then place a quenelle or spoonful of the condimiento onto each plate.
18. Divide the roast squash and Escabeche between each plate.
19. Drizzle some of the Escabeche liquid around each plate, but not directly into the puree.
20. Heat the remaining vadouvan oil and solids and drizzle some around the edge of the plate, directly into the Escabeche to create a sort of a broken sauce.
21. Toss the blossom bases and roe in a little of Escabeche liquid and divide them between each of the plates. Garnish with the sweet herbs and serve. Serves 4

UBUNTU
1140 MAIN STREET
NAPA, CA 94559
707-251-5656
UBUNTUNAPA.COM

MARTIN ESTATE CABERNET SAUVIGNON AND ROSÉ OF CABERNET SAUVIGNON
SLOW ROASTED KOBE BEEF ROULADE
WINEMAKER FREDERIC DELIVERT, CHEF/OWNER MICHAEL MINA

MARTIN ESTATE WINERY
P.O. BOX 390
RUTHERFORD, CA 94573
707-967-0300
MARTINESTATE.COM

Wine Making Facts :
Encépagement : 100% Estate-Grown
Cabernet Sauvignon
Appellation : Rutherford, Napa Valley
Vineyard : Puerta Dorada Vineyard Cabernet
Sauvignon Clones 4, 6 and 337
Micro-Climate : High-radiant sun exposure,
combined with cool evenings and the dusting of
early morning fogs, allows fruit to ripen steadily for
optimal color and flavor.
Average Vine Age : 12 years
Alcohol Level : 14.8%
Total Production : 483 cases
Philosophy : Hand-harvested and sorted.
Handcrafted from small lots without hi-tech
interventions, achieving the purest expression of
Rutherford terroir.
Facility : Estate grown, produced and bottled at
Martin Estate
Fermentation : Minimal handling with gentle, daily
pump-overs or punch downs
Maceration : Total maceration time ranged from 40
to 45 days
Oak Regimen: Aged 30 months
Barrels : French oak

Wine Making Facts :
Rosé of Cabernet Sauvignon
Encépagement : 100% Estate - Grown
Cabernet Sauvignon
Appellation : Rutherford, Napa Valley
Soils : Well-drained alluvial fans of Pleasanton and
Yolo loams
Elevation: Napa Valley floor
Average Vine Age : 12 years
Yield : Three tons/acre or less
Alcohol Level : 15%
Total Production : 75 cases
Winemaking: 100% Cabernet Sauvignon. Following
one night of skin contact, the chosen juice was
barreled down in neutral French oak barrels to
undergo primary fermentation, then aged sur lees in
the same barrels for one year.
Facility : Estate grown, produced and bottled at
Martin Estate
Fermentation : Minimal handling with primary
fermentation in neutral French oak
Wood Origin : France
Coopers : Demptos, Nadalié, Radoux, Saury, Seguin
Moreau, Sylvain
Bottling Format : Bottled at the estate on 6-15- 2009

"Fragrant with violet, black pepper and graphite components, which seamlessly integrate ripe blackberry and plum notes with hints of caramel and toast from French oak barrels. The wine subtly opens over time, revealing earthy elements of menthol and truffle, as well as balanced acid, tannin and fruit. It possesses a lingering, softly spicy finish. " FD

"Crafted in the style of fine wine, our Rosé of Cabernet possesses incredible structure, intense color and zero flab. Refreshing strawberry and cherry aromas a hint of exotic spice, mixes beautifully with holiday spices and autumn meals. And, when chilled, it is a refreshing aperitif that easily transitions into the first course of any meal." FD

VITIS, CABERNET SAUVIGNON WINE GLASS

MARTIN ESTATE CABERNET SAUVIGNON AND ROSÉ OF CABERNET SAUVIGNON
SLOW ROASTED KOBE BEEF ROULADE
WINEMAKER FREDERIC DELIVERT, CHEF/OWNER MICHAEL MINA

2 lb	Kobe prime rib cap, excess fat trimmed	1 c	Demi-glacé
¼ c	canola oil	1 qt	chicken stock
8	shallots, sliced	1	bay leaf
2 c	mushroom slices	2	thyme sprigs, plus more for garnish
2 T	sugar	1 ½ T	peppercorns, whole black
¼ c	red wine vinegar	tt	Kosher salt
3 c	Pinot Noir wine	tt	freshly ground black pepper

Preheat the oven to 350˚ F.

Meat:
Working from the long side, roll the cap into a tight roulade. Secure well with butchers twine.
Place a large, wide pan over high heat and get it good and hot.
Season the roulade well on all sides with salt and pepper.
Lay the beef in the hot pan and sear it all around to form a crust.
Carefully remove the tenderloin from the pan and place it on a wire rack so it cooks evenly.
Transfer the rack with the tenderloin to the oven and continue to cook for about 20 to 25 minutes for medium.
Remove the meat to a cutting board and let rest for 10 minutes before slicing.
This will ensure that the meat is not dry.
Remove the kitchen string and slice the roulade into ¼- inch slices.

Sauce:
Heat a medium sauce pot over medium-high flame, and coat with the oil.
Add the shallots and mushroom scraps and sauté until they are soft and browned, about 15 minutes.
Sprinkle in the sugar, and continue to cook and stir until the mixture is caramelized; about 5 minutes.
Pour in the vinegar and cook, stirring often, until the liquid is reduced and the mixture is almost dry; about 3 minutes.
Pour in the wine and continue to cook down for 15 minutes until the wine is concentrated and the mixture is tight and moist.
Stir in the demi-glacé, chicken stock, bay leaf, thyme, and peppercorns; bring to a simmer and cook for approximately 15 minutes more, until a sauce consistency is reached. Strain the sauce through a fine mesh strainer and reserve warm . 4 servings

MARTIN ESTATE
PO BOX 390
RUTHERFORD, CA 94573
707-967-0300
MARTINESTATE.COM

MELKA

cj

NAPA VALLEY

MELKA CJ
NEW YORK STRIP LOIN PERSILLADE, BEET TARTARE, CRISPY EGG YOLK
WINEMAKERS PHILIPPE AND CHERIE MELKA, PROFESSIONAL CHEF GARY PENIR

Wine Making Facts :
Encépagement : 97% Cabernet Sauvignon 3% Petit Verdot
Appellation : 100% Napa Valley
Soils varies from gravelly to volcanic based.
Elevation: Valley floor
Average Vine Age : 10 years
Yield : 2 tons per acre
Alcohol Level : 14%
Total Production : 1500 cases
Philosophy : CJ is made purposefully from different vineyard sources as opposed to one single vineyard. The idea of this project was to be able to create a wine that is exciting, fun and approachable, without having to age it years before drinking. Although this wine will age easily 5 to 10 years, our goal was to produce wine that was high in quality without being high in price. This is the wine you open while you're cooking and then drink the rest with dinner, burgers, pizza or filet mignon!
Winemaking Facility : CJ is produced at the Caldwell caves
Fermentation : Using wood and concrete vats
Maceration : On average about 20 -30 days
Wood Origin : France
Oak Regimen: 18 months
Coopers : Baron and Ermitage

MELKA WINES
P.O. BOX 82
OAKVILLE, CA 94562
707-963-6008
MELKAWINES.COM

VITIS, CABERNET SAUVIGNON WINE GLASS

"Lean and earthy with dark berry flavors combine with vanilla and cinder box to excite the senses. Firm yet super juicy, this succulent Napa Valley classic is a wine that never disappoints. The velvety tannins integrate seamlessly with the acidity making this wine approachable even in its youth." PM & CM

Philippe Melka has reached celebrity status in the wine world, but prefers a low profile when it comes to his own family-based wine brand. Joined by his wife Cherie, the Melkas have been quietly producing their own labels since 1996 along with a long list of high-end clients such as Roy Estate, Lail, and Gemstone. The Melkas CJ Cabernet Sauvignon, named for their children Chloe and Jeremy, derives from two Napa Valley vineyards. Using the French word for "blend," the line of Métisse vineyard-designated reds comes from single vineyards in St. Helena, Knights Valley, and St. Emilion (Bordeaux). All reflect the Melka's commitment to telling the story of the native soil, combining French expertise and tradition with the latest in viticultural techniques.

MELKA

MÉTISSE

NAPA VALLEY

Melka Métisse
Braised Lamb Shanks with Cabernet Onion Confit, Broccoli Rabe and Tuscan Beans
Winemakers Philippe and Cherie Melka, Professional Chef Peter Hall

Wine Making Facts :

Encépagement : Cabernet Sauvignon, Merlot, Petit Verdot

Appellation : 100% Napa Valley

Vineyard : Jumping Goat Vineyard

Average Vine Age: 10 years

Yield : Both are 2 tons per acre

Alcohol Level : 14%

Total Production : 450 cases

Philosophy : We produce wines of character reflecting their native soils. This single vineyard wine is planted to three varietals on a 4 acre parcel in St. Helena. The fruit is typically harvested at night in 40 pound boxes. This distinct wine is meticulously crafted fermenting some of the fruit in 59 gallon oak barrels as well as concrete tanks. Our goal is to create a wine that expresses the soil and climate of California, but showcases purity, depth and raffinity as opposed to being a wine over the top.

Fermentation : using wood and concrete vats

Maceration : on average about 45 days

Wood Origin : France

Oak Regimen : 22 months

Percentage of New Barrels : 70% new

Coopers : Baron and Ermitage

MELKA WINES
P.O. Box 82
OAKVILLE, CA 94562
707-963-6008
MELKAWINES.COM

SOMMELIERS BLACK TIE,
BORDEAUX GRAND CRU

" This wine is outstandingly rich exhibiting aromatics and flavors of crème de cassis and spice box along with vanilla and coffee bean. It displays concentration and elegance with balance and silky tannins. It is a fullbodied wine with superb richness and complex layers." PM & CM

Philippe Melka has reached celebrity status in the wine world, but prefers a low profile when it comes to his own family-based wine brand. Joined by his wife Cherie, the Melkas have been quietly producing their own labels since 1996 along with a long list of high-end clients such as Hundred Acre, Lail, and Gemstone. The Melkas CJ Cabernet Sauvignon, named for their children Chloe and Jeremy, derives from two Napa Valley vineyards. Using the French word for "blend," the line of Métisse vineyard-designated reds comes from single vineyards in St. Helena, Knights Valley, and St. Emilion (Bordeaux). All reflect the Melka's commitment to telling the story of the native soil, combining French expertise and tradition with the latest in viticultural techniques.

Melka CJ
New York Strip Loin Persillade, Beet Tartare, Crispy Egg Yolk
Winemaker Philippe Melka, Professional Chef Gary Penir

Ingredients:

½ c	golden beets tartare
3 ea	golden beet tops, sautéed
4 ea	crispy egg yolk
½ c	beet gastrique
16 oz	New York Strip Loin
½ c	persillade

Roasted Golden Beet Tartare:

4 ea	golden beets
2 T	olive oil
1 c	apple cider vinegar

Crispy Egg Yolk:

4 ea	egg yolks
1 c	Panko bread crumbs
½ c	egg wash

Red Beet Gastrique:

½ c	sugar
1 c	water
1 c	vegetable stock

Persillade:

½ c	Italian parsley
2 t	Meyer lemon, zest
1 clove	garlic, chopped fine
¼ c	extra virgin olive oil

Roasted Golden Beet Tartare:
Place golden beets in a roasting pan with vinegar. Drizzle with olive oil, salt and pepper, cover with oil. Cook for about 60 minutes until tender. After cooked, take the beets out and cool. After beets are cooled rub off the skins with a towel.
Grate beets on medium fine part of a box grater. Add some of the beet roasting liquid, salt, pepper, and extra virgin olive oil until desired flavor is achieved.
Tartare should hold together without releasing fluid when on the plate.

Crispy Egg Yolk:
Separate egg yolks from whites and place yolks on a plate. Save whites for another use. Place yolks in the freezer for 1 hour until set on the outside. Remove from the freezer, dip each in egg wash then into bread crumbs. Fry in 375°F oil until golden brown and crispy on the outside.

Red Beet Gastrique:
Roast red beets just like the gold beets above. Cool and peel, and large dice. Place beets in blender with vegetable stock and blend until smooth. Place sugar and water in large sauce pot and bring to a boil. Place blended beets in pot and reduce by one-fourth. When reduced pass through china cap.

Persillade:
Place all ingredients in a blender and purée until a thick smooth paste is achieved.
Sear Strip Loin and cook to medium rare, cool and roll in persillade before slicing.

Method:
Arrange beet tartare in a ring mold with the sautéed beet greens on top. Place beet gastrique on the bottom of the plate in a circle. Place the tartare and greens on top of the gastrique. Shingle three strips of meat on the greens with the crispy egg yolk on the meat. Allow the guest to cut through the egg yolk to reveal the running yolk in the center. 4 servings

MELKA MÉTISSE
BRAISED LAMB SHANKS WITH CABERNET ONION CONFIT, BROCCOLI RABE AND TUSCAN BEANS
WINEMAKERS PHILIPPE AND CHERIE MELKA, PROFESSIONAL CHEF PETER HALL

Shanks:

4	lamb shanks, small
1 T +1 t	kosher salt
1 t	pepper, ground
2	onions, medium, sliced
2	carrots, large, sliced
2	celery stalks, sliced
12	garlic cloves, peeled
4	tomatoes, roughly chopped
12 c	chicken stock, homemade
4 c	red wine
2	bouquet garni; thyme, parsley, bay leaf

Onion Confit:

4	onions, red, medium, cut in half, sliced
4 c	Cabernet Sauvignon
1 T +1 t	sugar
2 t	thyme, fresh

Broccoli Rabe:

2 lb	broccoli rabe, large stems discarded, blanched
3	garlic cloves, sliced thin
2 T	olive oil, extra virgin
pinch	red pepper flakes

Tuscan Beans:

1 c	Cannellini beans, dried, soaked overnight
2	bouquet garni; thyme, parsley and bay leaf
½ c	olive oil, extra virgin
4	garlic cloves chopped
1 t	rosemary, chopped

Shanks:
Preheat oven to 350º F.
Season shanks and refrigerate for at least 6 hours or overnight.
Sear shanks browning on all sides. Set aside.
Lightly sauté the onions, carrot, celery, and garlic.
Add the tomatoes, chicken stock, wine, bouquet garni and season; bring to simmer.
Add the lamb shanks, cover with lid and braise in the oven for about 2 hours or until tender.
Remove shanks from broth and set aside.
Strain the broth and discard the braising vegetables.
Let the broth settle and skim any fat from the surface.
Reduce over medium heat to four cups put through fine strainer and set aside.

Onion Confit:
Season and sauté onions in one tablespoon of olive oil.
Add sugar, wine and thyme and reduce until thick and syrupy.
Remove from heat and cool. Mixture will thicken slightly.

Tuscan Beans:
Strain beans and cover with water 2 inches and add bouquet garni. Simmer and skim off any foam.
Cook beans until tender but not falling apart; about 2 hours.
Strain and add back 1 cup of liquid; discard remaining liquid and bouquet garni.
Warm over low heat olive oil, garlic and rosemary, until the garlic is soft, about 2 minutes.
Add the infused olive oil mixture to the cooked beans; season and set aside.

Broccoli Rabe:
Sauté garlic and chile flakes in olive oil a few minutes.
Add broccoli rabe and cook over for an additional 3 minutes and season.

Serving:
Place about ½ cup of beans onto large rim bowl with broccoli rabe in center of beans.
Put shank on top of broccoli, ladle sauce on shanks, top with a dollop of onion confit. 4 servings

VINTNER'S COLLECTIVE

·P·1875·P·

1245

Vintner's Collective
1245 Main Street
Napa, CA 94559
707-255-7150
VINTNERSCOLLECTIVE.COM

MINER FAMILY VINEYARDS CABERNET SAUVIGNON AND ORACLE
STEAK TARTARE, TRUFFLE OIL, SHAVED PARMIGIANO-REGGIANO, GRILLED TOASTS
WINEMAKER GARY BROOKMAN, CHEF/ CO-OWNER TODD HUMPHRIES ~ MARTINI HOUSE

Wine Making Facts :

Encépagement : 90% Cabernet Sauvignon, 10% Cabernet Franc

Appellation : Oakville

Vineyard : Oakville Ranch Vineyard and Busceli Vineyard

Soils : Red volcanic/rocky

Elevation: 1,400 feet

Average Vine Age : 20 years

Yield : 2 tons per acre

Alcohol Level : 14.5%

Total Production : 1,360 cases

Philosophy : Old world winemaking techniques and modern technology to make wines that reflect the unique characteristics of individual vineyards or "terroir" where specific varietals grow best.

Facility : Miner Family Winery

Fermentation : 21 day primary fermentation; finished malolactic fermentation in barrel

Maceration : 19 days on skins

Oak Regimen : Aged 21 months

Percentage of New Barrels : 60% new oak

Coopers : Demptos, Taransaud, Sylvain

Bottling Format : 750 ml

Bottled : August 14, 2008

MINER FAMILY VINEYARDS
7850 SILVERADO TRAIL
OAKVILLE, CA 94562
800-366-WINE
MINERWINES.COM

VINUM XL, CABERNET SAUVIGNON GLASS

"Aromas of dark cherry and caramel segue into flavors of spicy plum, ripe blackberry with hints of cedar and coffee backed by requisite acidity and supple, generous tannins. The cooler 2005 vintage is noted for its ideal ripening conditions that allowed for incredible complexity, color and nuance." GB

At Miner Family Vineyards variety is the spice of life. The Miner label produces more than two dozen bottlings. Small lots from a single vineyard or appellation showcase each area's micro-climate. The winery's portfolio is led by its flagship Bordeaux-style blend The Oracle and the Miner Cabernet Sauvignon. But such diversity of region doesn't compromise Miner's style. "By using only ideal fruit sources combined with the best winemaking techniques available, our wines are the pure expression of both the vineyard and the varietal," says proprietor Dave Miner. The winery is also committed to being environmentally friendly, with a new waste-water recycling program and new solar-powered installation.

THE
ORACLE

MINER FAMILY VINEYARDS ORACLE
STEAK TARTARE, TRUFFLE OIL, SHAVED PARMIGIANO-REGGIANO, GRILLED TOASTS
WINEMAKER GARY BROOKMAN, CHEF/CO-OWNER TODD HUMPHRIES ~ MARTINI HOUSE

Wine Making Facts :
Encépagement : 56% Cabernet Sauvignon, 17% Cabernet
Franc, 14% Merlot, 7% Malbec, 6% Petit Verdot
Appellation : Napa Valley
Vineyard : Stagecoach Vineyard
Soils : Red volcanic/rocky, clay loam
soils with southwest exposure
Elevation : 1,500 feet
Average Vine Age : 9 years
Alcohol Level : 14.2%
Total Production : 3,306 cases
Philosophy : The fusion of superb vineyard
sites and thoughtful winemaking helps Miner
create elegant, expressive wines.
Facility : Miner Family Winery
Harvest details : Harvested October 1- 31,
2005, picked 25.5 Brix Average
Winemaking : Blended in May 2007
Fermentation : 30 day fermentation
Maceration : 28 days on skins
Oak Regimen : Aged 21 months
Barrels: French Oak
Bottling Format : 750 ml
Bottled : August 17 - 21, 2007

SOMMELIERS,
BORDEAUX GRAND CRU GLASS

"THIS CABERNET SAUVIGNON SHOWS OFF PURE, UNADULTERATED MASSES OF DARK BERRY FRUIT WITH SUBTLE MOCHA-SPICE FLAVORS WRAPPED IN WARM, TOASTY OAK. SILKY TANNINS AND A BOLD, LENGTHY FINISH COMPLETE THIS WELL-BALANCED OAKVILLE CABERNET EXPERIENCE."

WINEMAKER GARY BROOKMAN

MINER FAMILY VINEYARDS CABERNET SAUVIGNON AND ORACLE
STEAK TARTARE, TRUFFLE OIL, SHAVED PARMIGIANO-REGGIANO, GRILLED TOASTS
WINEMAKER GARY BROOKMAN, CHEF/CO-OWNER TODD HUMPHRIES ~ THE MARTINI HOUSE

1 lb	Flat Iron Steak	1T	brandy
1	shallot, finely minced	1 oz	tarragon mustard
1 bunch	chives, finely sliced	dash	Tabasco
¾ oz	capers, rised and chopped	tt	Worcestershire Sauce
¾ oz	apples, peeled and cut into a fine brunoise	tt	salt and pepper
1 ½ oz	extra virgin olive oil	2	eggs

6 slices   ½" thick French bread lightly brushed with olive oil and grilled
Shaved Parmigiano-Reggiano
Truffle oil

Method:

1. Slice beef into thin strips and then mince into a fine dice.
2. Place beef in a mixing bowl and set over another bowl with ice to keep beef chilled.
3. Add shallots, chives, capers, apples, olive oil, brandy and mustard.
4. Mix well and season with Tabasco, Worcestershire, salt and fresh ground pepper.
5. Form into 2 separate 8-oz rounds about 1" thick and place each on a chilled plate.
6. Separate the egg yolk from the white and place the yolk in the center of the beef.
7. Drizzle truffle oil over the tartare.
8. Place several shavings of parmesan cheese on top.
9. Serve with the grilled toasts. 2 servings

MARTINI HOUSE
1245 SPRING STREET
ST HELENA, CA 94574
707-963-4781
MARTINIHOUSE.COM

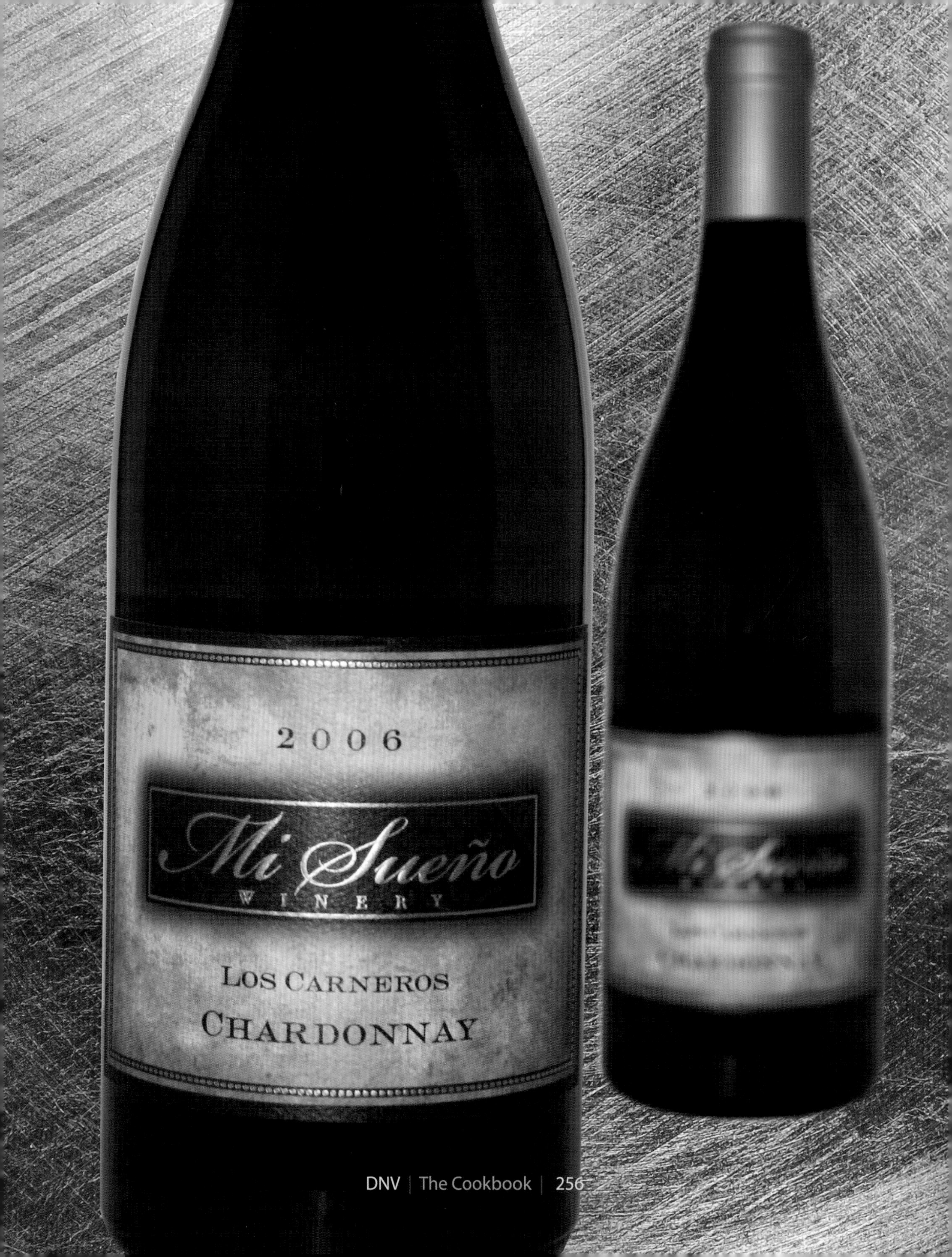
2006
Mi Sueño
WINERY
LOS CARNEROS
CHARDONNAY

MI SUEÑO LOS CARNEROS CHARDONNAY
ORGANIC FRESH CORN AND LOBSTER CHOWDER
WINEMAKER ROLANDO HERRERA, CHEF/PARTNER ANGELA TAMURA ~ ZUZU RESTAURANT

Wine Making Facts :
Mi Sueño Chardonnay Los Carneros
Appellation : Los Carneros
Vineyard : Tierra Blanca Vineyard
Elevation: Sea Level
Micro-Climate : Carneros
Yield : 2.5 pounds per vine
Alcohol Level : 14.5%
Total Production : 900 cases
Philosophy : Minimal intervention
Harvest Details : End of September to
October. 2006
Winemaking: 100% native yeasts
100% natural malolactic in primary
and secondary fermentation
Facility : Produced and bottled at
Mi Sueño Winery
Fermentation : 100% natural malolactic in
primary and secondary fermentation
Wood Origin : 100% French Oak

MI SUEÑO WINERY
910 ENTERPRISE WAY
NAPA, CA 94558
707-258-6358
MISUENOWINERY.COM

VINUM, MONTRACHET WINE GLASS

" Enticing aromas, velvety texture and long persistent finish. It offers an alluring bouquet as well as a rich, seductive mouth-feel with an abundance of citrus, honey vanilla cream and toasty oak. As in prior vintages, it strikes a beautiful balance between a lush, silky texture and crisp, lively acidity. "RH

If it's possible to put a dream in a bottle, then Rolando Herrera has done it. His young label, Mi Sueño, means "my dream" in Spanish and when you hear his story, you'll understand why. Herrera arrived in the U.S. from Mexico and under the mentorship of legendary vintner Warren Winiarski, he worked his way from "cellar rat" to cellar master, then went on to hone his boutique winemaking skills at Chateau Potelle, Vine Cliff, and Paul Hobbs. Herrera's meticulous hand in both vineyard and winery and his use of native yeasts have earned great respect for his limited production of small, handcrafted lots, and his wines have been served at White House state dinners. Located in an unassuming corporate park south of Napa, Mi Sueño Winery offers true wine lovers an insider's look at what it takes to make a dream come true.

2005

Mi Sueño
WINERY

NAPA VALLEY
EL LLANO

RED WINE

MI SUEÑO EL LLANO
BARBEQUED FLAT IRON STEAK WITH ROSEMARY CHIMICHURRI
WINEMAKER ROLANDO HERRERA, CHEF/PARTNER ANGELA TAMURA ~ ZUZU RESTAURANT

Wine Making Facts :

Appellation : Napa Valley

Vineyard : Various Vineyards (all leased and farmed by Mi Sueño Winery)

Soils : volcanic

Elevation: Valley floor in Coombsville

Yield : 6.0 lb per vine

Alcohol Level : 14.8%

Total Production : 1,775 cases

Philosophy : Minimal intervention

Harvest Details : October 27, 2005

Winemaking: 65% Cabernet Sauvignon, 35% Syrah – Minimal intervention

Facility : Produced and bottled at Mi Sueño Winery

Aging: 20 months in oak

Wood Origin : 100% French Oak

MI SUEÑO WINERY
910 ENTERPRISE WAY
NAPA, CA 94558
707-258-6358
MISUENOWINERY.COM

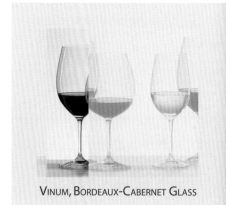

VINUM, BORDEAUX-CABERNET GLASS

" Aromas of ripe dark fruits, figs, freshly turned earth and exotic spices arrive in unison. A viscous mouth-feel leads to a rich array of dark chocolate, roasted espresso beans, mature red and black fruits and finishes nicely with a smoky, peppery, toasty quality. " RH

Chimichurri marinade:
1 c	garlic, chopped
3 c	olive oil
1	oregano, rough chop, bunch
¼	rosemary, rough chop
2	jalapeños, roasted, seeded, chopped
1 t	Piquin chili, crushed
¼ c	balsamic vinegar
½ c	sherry vinegar

Meat:
1½ lb	Flat Iron steak, cleaned
1 c	chimichurri marinade

Method:

Sauté garlic in one cup olive oil until golden brown. Add oregano, rosemary and jalapenos and cook for another minute. Remove from the heat and add remainder of ingredients; let sit overnight. The sauce keeps well in the refrigerator for two weeks. Marinate the steak in refrigerator for at least three hours or overnight (reserve some marinade separately to drizzle after cooking).

Season the steak with salt and pepper; grill to desired temperature.

Slice steak thinly against the grain and serve drizzled with the remaining sauce. 4 servings

MiSueño Los Carneros Chardonnay
Organic Fresh Corn and Lobster Chowder
Winemaker Rolando Herrera, Chef/Partner Angela Tamura ~ Zuzu Restaurant

6	white organic corn ears		1 T	butter
1	lobster tail, meat removed, shell reserved		¼ t	garlic, sliced
1 t	corn starch		¼ t	coriander, ground
1 c	whole milk		¼ t	cumin, ground
1 c	heavy cream		½ c	white wine
1 T	oregano, fresh, chopped		¼ lb	mushrooms, fresh, morel (substitute
1	Applewood smoked bacon, slice			with hen of the woods or maitake)
½	onion, yellow, diced			

Corn chowder:

Cut the corn kernels from the cobs.
Use the back of a knife to scrape the pulp and the "milk" from the cobs.
In a stock pot, put the lobster shell, corn kernels, cobs and corn milk and pulp and cover with water.
Simmer for 45 minutes and then strain; discard lobster shell and cobs, reserving the corn kernels, pulp and corn stock.
When cool, in a blender, puree 2/3 of the kernels and pulp with the corn stock and corn starch until smooth.
Put the mixture back into the pot and simmer another 20 minutes; add whole milk and heavy cream.
Add the oregano and simmer a few more minutes.
Reserve corn chowder.

Render bacon, in sauté pan, until crisp.
Place on napkin to remove excess oil; reserve bacon.

Sauté the onion in butter and bacon fat until translucent.
Add the sliced garlic, coriander and cumin and sauté for several more minutes until slightly browned.
Add the wine and reduce by half; add to corn chowder.

For a rustic chowder, do not blend and strain as described below.
Blend the corn stock with onions and spices until smooth with a blender or immersion blender.
Use a fine mesh strainer for a smooth consistency if desired.
Add the remaining corn kernels and bring to simmer.

Serving:
Sauté the morel and sliced lobster tail in butter.
Serve by garnishing each bowl of corn chowder with a generous portion of morel and sliced lobster.
Sprinkle minced bacon to finish. 2 servings

ZUZU
829 MAIN STREET
NAPA, CA 94559
707-224-8555
ZUZUNAPA.COM

MOONE-TSAI CABERNET SAUVIGNON
COLORADO RANGE FED BISON WILD MUSHROOM POTATO TERRINE, NAPA VALLEY RED WINE SAUCE
WINEMAKER PHILIPPE MELKA, CHEF/OWNER KEN FRANK ~ LA TOQUE

Encépagement : 100% Cabernet Sauvignon

Appellation : Napa Valley

Vineyard : Caldwell Vineyards blocks 13 and 15; clones 337 and 7

Soils : The Aiken soil is shallow, reddish brown in color, and laced with volcanic ash, and rock. Ideal medium for the noble Vitis Vinafera.

Elevation : 500 feet above sea level; hillside, northwestern exposure

Average Vine Age : 15 years

Yield : 2.5 tons acre

Alcohol Level : 14.2%

Total Production : 200 cases

Harvest Details : Hand-sorted both before and after de-stemming.

Facility : Moone-Tsai Winery

Fermentation : Whole-berry fermentation using native yeasts

Maceration : 30 days on-skins

Oak Regiment : Aged 22 months in new French oak

MOONE-TSAI
P.O. BOX 565
RUTHERFORD, CA 94573
707-812-8860
MOONETSAI.COM

SOMMELIERS, BORDEAUX GRAND CRU GLASS

"This elegant Cabernet Sauvignon presents seductive aromas of blackberry, black cherry, and spice. Complex, and well-structured, the wine features intense black fruit on the palate, as highly supple tannins introduce rich flavors of chocolate, tobacco, anise and spice through to a long finish characterized by muscle, finesse, and concentration." PM

The Moone-Tsai winery proudly presents its prized limited-release Cabernets – whose pedigree is rooted in a splendid combination of exceptional fruit, terroir, and artisanal winemaking. These memorable wines fulfill a vision that the co-founders, Mike Moone and MaryAnn Tsai have shared throughout a remarkable collaboration spanning twenty years in the wine industry – where they helped establish some of the most heralded wines of our time. Along with Moone-Tsai's access to some of Napa Valley's most coveted vineyard blocks, Mike and MaryAnn have enlisted the talents of renowned winemaker Philippe Melka, to craft beguiling Cabernets characterized by the subtle balance of refinement, structure, power, and finesse. These attributes are reflected in the selection of the distinctive lion on the Moone-Tsai label.

Moone-Tsai Cabernet Sauvignon
Colorado Range Fed Bison Wild Mushroom Potato Terrine, Napa Valley Red Wine Sauce
Winemaker Philippe Melka, Chef/Owner Ken Frank ~ La Toque

Meat:

8	Bison steaks, seasoned and cooked to your preference

Wild Mushroom Potato Terrine:

8	thin long slices of Prosciutto
4	Yukon gold potatoes
2 T	butter
2 c	wild mushrooms, sliced
1	onion, finely diced
2	cloves garlic, finely diced
¾ c	grated gruyère
tt	Salt and pepper

Napa Valley Red Wine Sauce:

½	strip of bacon, finely diced
3	shallots, finely diced
4 c	Napa Valley Cabernet Sauvignon
6	black peppercorns, crushed
2 qts	veal stock
tt	salt

Materials:

Small loaf pan to build the "potato terrine", 3 to 4 inches wide and about 8 inches long

Bison:
If you like steak with Cabernet Sauvignon, you will love Bison, also known as Buffalo. Top grade Bison is very tender and has a distinct meaty flavor without being gamey. It is particularly good when grilled. Season bison and grill or sear to your preference.

Potatoes:
Cook the potatoes in salted water until just barely tender to the point of a knife. Slice them into 1/8 inch thick slices. Sauté the wild mushrooms, the finely diced onion and garlic in 2 tablespoons of butter and a good sprinkle of salt until they have just begun to brown and all exuded juice has cooked away. Verify and adjust seasoning if necessary. Line the inside of the loaf pan with a big piece of plastic wrap, leaving plenty hanging over the edge to seal it up later. Then line the interior of the loaf pan with the thinly sliced prosciutto, leaving a nice flap to fold over the top at the end, as if you were lining a pate mold with back fat. Arrange a layer of potato slices in the bottom of the pan, sprinkle with some of the grated cheese and add a layer of sautéed wild mushrooms. Continue building layers like this, pressing everything together firmly, working up to the top of the mold. Fold the prosciutto neatly over the top, fold the plastic wrap over the prosciutto and bake in a 300° degree oven for one hour. Remove and chill overnight. In the morning, carefully unmold the terrine and wrap very tightly with a few extra layers of plastic wrap, this is critical for slicing and handling. Slice the potato terrine with a sharp serrated knife and arrange on a cookie sheet ready to heat in the oven before serving. Do not remove the plastic wrap until you have successfully slid the hot terrine onto the plate for serving. It will slip off easily.

Napa Valley Red Wine Sauce:
Cook the chopped bacon over moderate heat in a saucepan until it is rendered and golden brown all over. Stir in the chopped shallots but do not allow them to color. Immediately deglaze with the Cabernet Sauvignon and reduce over high heat until the pan is almost dry. Add the stock and the crushed peppercorns. Allow the liquid to come to a boil, then adjust the flame to maintain a gentle simmer. Every ten minutes, carefully skim off any impurities that collect on the surface. Depending on your taste and the richness of the stock, this will need to reduce by about two thirds until the flavors are properly concentrated. Strain and verify salt seasoning. For a truly luxurious texture and mouth feel, whisk in a small piece of fresh unsalted butter just before serving. This makes a good sized batch, 2 to 3 cups. I recommend freezing it in an ice cube tray and keeping the cubes in a zip lock freezer bag, ready to pull out "on the fly". Serves 6-8

MOONE-TSAI
P.O. BOX 565
RUTHERFORD, CA 94573
707-812-8860
MOONETSAI.COM

NICKEL & NICKEL, DRAGONFLY VINEYARD CABERNET SAUVIGNON
RIBBONED LAMB SKEWERS, MINT INFUSED MUSTARD DIPPING SAUCE
WINEMAKER DARICE SPINELLI, WINERY CHEF ABI MARTINEZ

Wine Making Facts :

Varietal: 100% Cabernet Sauvignon

Philosophy : Established in 1997, Nickel &
Nickel is based on a philosophy of producing
100 percent varietal, single-vineyard wines
that best express the distinct personality of
each vineyard. A sister winery to Far Niente,
Nickel & Nickel focuses on single-vineyard
Napa Valley Cabernet Sauvignon, and
makes select vineyard designates of other
varietals from some of the most coveted
vineyards in Napa and Sonoma valleys.

Varietal : 100% Cabernet Sauvignon

Appellation : St. Helena, Napa Valley

Acreage : 4 acres

Alcohol Level : 14.6%

Harvest Details : October 2-10, 2006

Oak Regimen : 16 months in French oak barrels

Percentage of New Barrels : 40%

Bottling Format : 750 ml

NICKEL & NICKEL
PO BOX 7
OAKVILLE, CA 94562
707-967-9600
NICKEL&NICKEL.COM

VITIS, CABERNET SAUVIGNON GLASS

*"Abundant aromas of red and black fruits are predominant on
the nose. A mixture of straw-berry and raspberry fills the glass,
with sweet vanilla and cedar adding interest. This wine has a
very silky texture that is velvety and rich across the palate. While
still retaining its usual elegance, this vintage carries the
beautiful fruit flavors into an incredibly supple finish." DS*

Lamb Marinade:

¼ c	vegetable oil
¼ c	onion, finely chopped
2 T	red wine
2 T	rosemary, fresh, leaves
2	cloves garlic
1 T	mustard, Dijon

Lamb Loin:

¾ lb	lamb loin, boneless, trimmed

Mint-Mustard Dipping Sauce:

¼ c	mustard, Dijon
¼ c	crème fraîche
2 T	mint jelly

Cooking:

1 T	vegetable oil

Serving:

24	wooden toothpicks

Lamb Marinade:

Purée oil, onions, red wine, rosemary, garlic and mustard in a blender Marinade lamb in purée and
refrigerate at least 2 hours.

Mint-Mustard Dipping Sauce:

Combine mustard, crème fraîche and mint jelly in a small bowl. Remove the lamb from the marinade
and season with salt and pepper. Heat oil in a large skillet over high heat. Sear the lamb until evenly
browned, about 3 minutes on each side. Remove from heat, let rest for 10 minutes, then thinly slice.
10 servings

NICKEL & NICKEL JOHN C. SULLENGER VINEYARD CABERNET SAUVIGNON
TOASTED PECAN AND ENGLISH STILTON DEMI NAPOLEONS
WINEMAKER DARICE SPINELLI, WINERY CHEF ABI MARTINEZ

Wine Making Facts :

Philosophy: Established in 1997, Nickel & Nickel is based on a philosophy of producing 100 percent varietal, single-vineyard wines that best express the distinct personality of each vineyard. A sister winery to Far Niente, Nickel & Nickel focuses on single-vineyard Napa Valley Cabernet Sauvignon, and makes select vineyard designates of other varietals from some of the most coveted vineyards in Napa and Sonoma valleys.

Varietal: 100% Cabernet Sauvignon

Appellation: Oakville, Napa Valley

Acreage: 30 acres

Alcohol Level: 14.5%

Harvest Dates: October 24-31, 2006

Oak Regimen: 16 months in French oak barrels

Percentage of New Barrels: 42%

Bottling Format: 750 ml, 1.5L, 3.0L

"Beautifully perfumed with aromas of dark fruits. Cherry and black cherry notes are layered with herb, spice and cedar from the oak. The most compelling element of this wine is its great middle texture. Dark and dense, the flavors expand on the middle palate with chewy tannins, resulting in a long, delicious finish." DS

NICKEL & NICKEL
PO BOX 7
OAKVILLE, CA 94562
707-967-9600
NICKEL&NICKEL.COM

SOMMELIERS, BORDEAUX GRAND CRU

3 oz	cream cheese, softened
2 oz	Stilton cheese, softened
2 t	Ruby Port
½ t	honey
Pinch	cracked black pepper
96	pecan halves, or prepared candied pecans
2 T	chives, chopped, for garnish

Method:
Cream together cheeses, port, honey, and pepper in a food processor. Transfer to a plastic piping bag. Lay 48 pecans flat side down, top with one-quarter teaspoon piped cheese mixture, then another pecan and cheese mixture again. Garnish with chopped chives. 10 servings

NEWTON CHARDONNAY
DUNGENESS CRAB WITH SHAVED FENNEL AND MADEIRA GELÉE
WINEMAKER CHRIS MILLARD, CHEF DE CUISINE PERRY HOFFMANN, ÉTOILE AT DOMAINE CHANDON

Wine Making Facts :
Appellation : Napa County
Vineyard : Various Napa and Sonoma County
Average Vine Age : 6-20
Yield : 2.5-3.5 tons/acre
Alcohol Level : 15%
Philosophy : An artisan approach that includes respecting and working with what nature provides.
Harvest Details : September to early October, multiple picking passes to select only fully mature clusters
Winemaking : Whole cluster pressing, native yeast fermentation, native ml fermentation, extensive lees stirring, aged 16 months in oak
Fermentation : Native yeast
Wood Origin : French
Oak Regimen : 100%
Coopers : Dargaud et Jaegle, Saury, François Frères
Bottling Formats : 750 ml

NEWTON VINEYARD
2555 MADRONA AVE
ST HELENA, CA 94574
707-963-9000
NEWTONVINEYARD.COM

VITIS, MONTRACHET WINE GLASS

"This rich powerful wine opens with rich crème caramel, butterscotch and vanilla bean aromas, later revealing baked apple and nutty characters. Flavors of white peach and caramel with a touch of honey round out this full-bodied, balanced wine with a lingering creamy finish." CM

Founders of Newton Vineyard, Su Hua and Peter Newton, believed in the quality, character and rich flavors of higher elevation fruit, so they set out to find the ideal hillside property for planting grapes. They found it on Spring Mountain, where they purchased one square mile of tumbling slopes overlooking Napa Valley in 1977. The Newtons were among the first to recognize the area as a prime viticultural region. Dedicated to working in harmony with nature to produce remarkable artisan wines, Newton Vineyard transforms fruit of uncompromised quality into wines of distinctive character. An early pioneer of Spring Mountain and one of the first Napa Valley wineries to craft unfiltered and naturally fermented wines, Newton Vineyard has become one of the most inspiring and fascinating wine estates in the world.

DUNGENESS CRAB WITH SHAVED FENNEL AND MADEIRA GELÉE
WINEMAKER CHRIS MILLARD, CHEF DE CUISINE PERRY HOFFMANN, ÉTOILE AT DOMAINE CHANDON

Crab:
1 lb	crab meat, Dungeness
2 T	crème fraîche
1 T	lemon juice

Salad:
1	fennel bulb, shaved thin on a mandolin, reserve fronds
1	parsnip (peeled and shaved in strips)
2 T	lemon juice
2 T	olive oil

Fennel sauce:
1	spinach, bunch
1	fennel bulb
2 T	olive oil
1 c	cream

Madeira gelée:
½ c	Madeira
2 sheets	gelatin (soaked in ice water) or use
1 T	granular gelatin

Fried parsnip:
1	parsnip (peeled and shaved with a peeler into long strips)
2 c	canola oil for frying

Plating:
½ c	pomegranate seeds

Crab:
Combine and mix crab, crème fraîche, lemon juice, salt to taste.
Mold crab into 15 – 1 ounces stacks refrigerate and set aside.

Salad:
Combine additional shaved fennel and parsnips with olive oil and lemon juice.
Season to taste.

Fennel sauce:
Blanch spinach until tender, then shock in ice water bath; drain out excess moisture.
Sweat 1 fennel bulb in oil for 20 minutes or until the fennel is soft.
Add cream and simmer until fennel is tender.
Place fennel and spinach in a blender, blend till smooth, salt to taste.
Strain through a fine mesh strainer and cool.

Madeira gelée:
Bring Madeira to a simmer and whisk in gelatin.
Place mixture in refrigerator and let cool until set.

Fried parsnip:
Heat oil to 300º F.
Fry half of the shaved parsnips until crisp.

Plating:
Place fennel sauce, top with crab, and salad on top of crab.
Pull and shred (dice if desired) the gelée into chunks and place where desired.
Garnish with fennel fronds and pomegranate seeds. 5 servings

NEWTON VINEYARD
2555 MADRONA AVE
ST HELENA, CA 94574
707-963-9000
NEWTONVINEYARD.COM

2007

Palmaz Vineyards

Napa Valley

Chardonnay

Alc. 14.5% by Vol.

PALMAZ VINEYARDS CHARDONNAY
SEARED SEA SCALLOPS AND FRISÉE SALAD WITH HOLLANDAISE DRESSING
WINEMAKERS MIA KLEIN AND TINA MITCHELL, WINERY CHEF AMALIA PALMAZ

Wine Making Facts :
Encépagement : Chardonnay
Appellation : Spring Mountain, Napa Valley
Vineyard : Rolling hills of the Napa Carneros region
and the steep slopes of the Atlas Peak
Micro-Climate : Cooler climate
Alcohol Level : 14.5%
Total Production : 694 cases
Fermentation : The Malolactic fermentation
is allowed to completely finish
Aged : Sur lies in 100% French oak,
50% new for 8 months
Barrels: 100% barrel fermented
Date Bottled : June 2008

PALMAZ VINEYARDS
4029 HAGEN ROAD
NAPA, CA 94558
707-226-5587
PALMAZVINEYARDS.COM

" Grapes are picked at full ripeness with the proper acidity to soften the palate. This adds a hint of butter to the aromas of ripe pear, tropical fruits and citrus, combined with the rich flavors and a crisp finish."   MK and TM

SOMMELIERS, CHARDONNAY WINE GLASS

16	large scallops	4	egg yolks
2 c	chicken stock	4 t	rice vinegar
3 c	frisée	2 ½	sticks butter, melted
8 t	balsamic vinegar	tt	salt and pepper
8 t	truffle oil		

Method:
Reduce the chicken stock to ½ cup, add the truffle oil and the balsamic vinegar.
Set aside.
Sauté the scallops in 4 tablespoons of butter with 2 tablespoons of olive oil.
To prepare the Hollandaise, you need a double boiler with the water barely simmering.
Place yolks with the rice vinegar on the top of the boiler and beat vigorously while slowly adding the melted butter. When it reaches the desired consistency remove immediately from the boiling part of the double boiler and set aside in a warm place. Spread a bed of hollandaise on the bottom of a salad plate. Place the frisée salad on top of the sauce, then 2 scallops and drizzle with dressing. 8 servings

Palmaz Vineyards
Napa Valley
Cabernet Sauvignon
Alc. 14.4% by Vol.

PALMAZ VINEYARDS CABERNET SAUVIGNON
SAUTÉED SQUAB BREAST WITH TALEGGIO POLENTA IN PORCINI BROTH
WINEMAKERS MIA KLEIN AND TINA MITCHELL, WINERY CHEF FLORENCIA PALMAZ

Wine Making Facts :

Encépagement : Cabernet Sauvignon, Merlot

Appellation : Napa Valley

Vineyard : Palmaz VineyardsElevation: 400, 1200, and 1400

Micro-Climate : Three separate microclimates, protected bench land, cool mountain valley, and rugged mountain top

Average Vine Age : 10 years

Yield : 2.5 tons/ acre

Alcohol Level : 14.5%

Total Production : 2,800 six packs

Philosophy : Love the land, know the grape and make a wine that honors both.

Harvest Details : Harvested from Sept 14 - Nov 10, 2005

Aged : 100% French oak for 30 months

Facility : Palmaz Winery Cave

Maceration : 4-6 weeks

Wood Origin : France

Oak Regimen : 22 months barrel aged

Fining/Filtering : Gravity flow filtration

PALMAZ VINEYARDS
4029 HAGEN ROAD
NAPA, CA 94558
707-226-5587
PALMAZVINEYARDS.COM

VINUM XL, CABERNET SAUVIGNON GLASS

"The 2005 Palmaz Estate is deep, lush and wonderfully aromatic. The palate is generous and silky with flavors ranging from dark fruits and cassis to earth and spice. This is a complete wine that drinks well in its youth and will continue to improve over the next decade." MK & TM

Squab:
4   squab breasts

Porcini broth:
4 oz   porcini mushrooms, dried
5 c   chicken stock
¾ c   Madeira wine

Soft polenta:
3 ½ c   milk
½ c   instant polenta
2 T   butter
¾ c   Tallegio cheese
4 T   parmesan cheese
2 t   truffle oil

Sauté the squab breasts in butter and olive oil leaving the center pink. Set aside and keep warm. The Porcini broth can be made ahead of time. Soak the dried porcini mushrooms in warm water, once they are soft, rinse them thoroughly and strain the juice through a cheese cloth to remove all the dirt. Place the mushroom juice, the chicken stock, Madeira and mushrooms in a saucepan and cook for 45 minutes. Strain the stock with a cheesecloth or coffee strainer, discard the mushrooms.

Polenta:
Place the milk, butter and polenta in a saucepan and start stirring well while it is cold and slowly warm to medium heat stirring constantly until it boils for one minute.
While stirring add the Taleggio cheese and the parmesan cheese, salt and pepper to taste.

In a soup bowl, place a quenelle of polenta, arrange the sliced squab breast on top and slowly pour the broth over. Garnish with a sprig of rosemary. 8 small servings

POTT WINE KALIHOLMANOK
PAN ROASTED QUAIL, OYSTER MUSHROOM FLAMBÉ AND STEAMED LEEKS
WINEMAKER AARON POTT, WINERY CHEF STEPHEN HUTCHINSON

Wine Making Facts :
Encépagement : 96% Cabernet Sauvignon,
3% Cabernet Franc, 1% Petit Verdot
Appellation : Spring Mountain, Napa Valley
Vineyard : Bel Canto Vineyard
Soils : Aiken and Kidd Complex
Elevation : 1900 feet
Aspect : Multiple exposures
Micro-Climate : Cooler days than valley floor,
warmer evenings above the fog.
Yield : 1.5 kilos per vine
Alcohol Level : 14.5%
Total Production : 50 cases
Harvest Details : Small ripe berries were harvested
under clear skies in early October.
Fermentation : High temperature fermentation in open topped
tank with swimming costume clad human body punch-downs.
Maceration : 28 days at ambient temperature
Wood Origin : 36 month, air-dried Tonnellerie Bossuet Chateau
Tradition from the forests of Cvyrais, Jupille and Tronçais France
Oak Regiment : Aged 21 months
Percentage of New Barrels : 100%

POTT WINE
2272 MT. VEEDER ROAD
NAPA, CA 94558
707-226-3277
POTTWINE.COM

SOMMELIERS BLACK TIE, BORDEAUX GRAND CRU

" Fantastic black fruit blends ideally with spice, tobacco and cedar. Great mountain fruit density with rich supple tannins and characteristic Pott Wine texture in a long finish. " AP

Aaron Pott breathes wine. In the winemaking culture of the Napa Valley he is considered a winemaker of great juxtaposition. In person, his personality is colorful and bright, and in the bottle his wines are equally as elegant in depth and beauty. For over 20 years Aaron has made wines in six different countries. His vast experience ranges from head winemaker for St. Emilion, Bordeaux Grand Cru Classé, Château La Tour Figeac and Premier Grand Cru Classé Château Troplong-Mondot and closer to home at Blackbird, Quixote and Quintessa among others. In late 2009, Aaron along with his wife Claire, will launch the inaugural release of Pott Wines including five Cabernets and one Cabernet Franc.

Wine Making Facts :
Encépagement : Cabernet Sauvignon
Appellation : Mt. Veeder, Napa Valley
Vineyard : 100% Estate vineyard, Mt. Veeder, Napa Valley
Soils : Fractured sandstone
Elevation : 1450 feet
Aspect : South facing
Micro-Climate : Cooler days than valley floor, warmer evenings above the fog.
Average Vine Age : 8 years
Yield : 1 kilo per vine
Alcohol Level : 14.5%
Total Production : 12 cases
Harvest Details : Family-harvested under clear skies in early October.
Fermentation : High temperature fermentation in open-headed barrel with excessive hand punch-downs.
Maceration : 35 days at ambient temperature
Wood Origin : 36 month, air-dried Tonnellerie Bossuet Chateau Tradition from the forest of Jupille, France
Oak Regimen : Aged 20 months
Percentage of New Barrels : 100%
Coopers : Custom made to the specifications of Pott wine by master cooper Jean-Loius Bossuet.

"Intense black color from mountain vineyards the Incubo is a model of balance and beautiful texture with silky soft tannins and great density." AP

**POTT WINE
2272 MT. VEEDER ROAD
NAPA, CA 94558
707-226-3277
POTTWINE.COM**

SOMMELIERS, BORDEAUX GRAND CRU

POTT WINE KALIHOLMANOK AND POTT WINE INCUBO
HONEY GLAZED LOIN OF LAMB, GOAT CHEESE POTATO GRATIN AND CIPPOLINI ONIONS
WINEMAKER AARON POTT, WINERY CHEF STEPHEN HUTCHINSON

Ingredients:

1	loin of lamb		1 t	thyme, finely chopped
1	Kennebec potato, medium sized		½ t	sage, finely chopped
1	yellow onion, small peeled		¼ t	rosemary, finely chopped
3 oz	goat cheese		1	small shallot, minced
2 t	goat milk, or milk		1 pinch	cumin, ground
6	Cipollini onions, peeled		1 pinch	coriander, ground
1 t	sugar		¼ t	orange zest
2 t	butter			salt and pepper
2 t	honey			canola oil
2 t	olive oil			
1 t	parsley, finely chopped			

For the Glaze:
Combine the honey and olive oil with the herbs, spices, shallot and orange zest. Finish the Glaze with coarsely ground black pepper and salt. Set aside.

For the Potato Gratin:
Peel, rinse, and grate 3/4 of it on the large side of a box grater. Soak potatoes in water and change water three or four times to remove some of the starch. Put potatoes in a dry towel and squeeze, removing as much of the water as possible. Grate the remaining 1/4 potato and the onion on the fine side of the grater. Season with salt and combine all potatoes and onion well.
Heat a small skillet; add canola oil.
Make four small cakes with the potato mixture. Drop them into the hot oil and press them flat, about ½ inch of thickness. Flip the cakes and cook until they are evenly colored on both sides. Place on a paper towel to drain and set aside. Over a low flame, melt the goat cheese and milk together to form a sauce. Keep the pan warm until plating.

For the Cipollini Onions:
Melt the butter in a small sauté pan. Add the onions and sprinkle the sugar over the top. Add enough water to cover and simmer at a low boil, adding water if necessary. Test the onions with a paring knife.

For the Lamb:
Preheat the oven on the broiler setting. Dry the Lamb by patting it with a paper towel and season it with salt and pepper. Heat a large sauté pan; add enough oil to coat the bottom of the pan and cook until both sides are well colored. Remove and rest. After the lamb has cooled for a couple of minutes, spoon the glaze over the top of the lamb. Place in a hot broiler close to the heat and place the pan of onions below it. When the glaze starts to bubble and begins to caramelize, remove the lamb. After a couple of minutes, remove the plates and place a potato cake on it. When ready to plate spoon sauce over the potato cake; place another cake on top and add a bit more sauce. Then place the onions next to the potatoes and fan three slices of lamb against the potato stack. Garnish with a rosemary flower, if available. 2 servings

Pride Mountain Vineyards Chardonnay
Bellwether Farms Goat Cheese, Roasted Marcona Almond, Blood Orange Salad
Winemaker Sally Johnson, Winery Chef Jason Skelly

Wine Making Facts :
Encépagement : 100% Chardonnay
Appellation : Napa Valley (Los Carneros)
Yield : 3- 4 tons per acre
Alcohol Level : 14.6%
Total Production : 1189 cases
Harvest Details : Picked in October of 2007 at a Brix of 24.3°, pH of 3.32 and Titrateable Acidity of 8.5 g/L.
Winemaking : Grapes were picked in the early morning and transported to the winery to be pressed while still cold. Each vineyard was picked, fermented and aged separately.
Facility : Small, family-owned winery on the Napa-Sonoma county line, at the top of Spring Mountain above St Helena.
Fermentation : After gentle pressing, the wines were fermented in French oak. Wines were inoculated with a yeast strain originally isolated from Burgundy, France.
Fermentation : Approximately 15 days
Malolactic fermentation was initiated and was stopped at 30%
Wood Origin : 3 year air dried French oak from the Tronçais forest.
Oak Regimen : 8 months in oak, racked of its lees and blended just before bottling.

PRIDE MOUNTAIN VINEYARDS
4026 SPRING MOUNTAIN ROAD
ST HELENA, CA 94574
707-963-4949
PRIDEWINES.COM

VITIS, MONTRACHET WINE GLASS

"Our Chardonnay expresses melon, green apple, star fruit and hazelnut aromas balanced with just a hint of crème fraîche. Fermenting in French oak and aging sur lees adds a roundness and depth to the palate, providing the weight to balance to the wine's bright acidity. " SJ

½ c	Marcona almonds	¼ t	thyme, plus four sprigs for garnish
¼ c	bread crumbs	1	blood orange, cut into segments
4 oz	goat cheese, preferably Bellwether Farms	2 c	micro salad greens
1	sweet baguette, cut into eight ½ " thick slices	4	honeycomb, pieces in 1- inches
4 T	Spanish olive oil, extra virgin		pieces or drizzle of honey

Preheat oven to 350° F.
Toast almonds in oven for five minutes, remove from oven and cool Pulse cooled almonds in food processor until finely chopped. Combine chopped almonds and bread crumbs. Divide goat cheese into one ounce rounds. Brush goat cheese rounds with olive oil and coat with almond/bread crumb mixture. Set aside. Brush baguette slices with olive oil and sprinkle with thyme leaves. Toast baguette slices until golden brown. Warm goat cheese in oven for 1 - 2 minutes until softened. Place one half cup of micro greens on each plate, top with one goat cheese round. Garnish each plate with two baguette slices, segment of blood orange, one piece of honeycomb and one thyme sprig. Lightly drizzle goat cheese with olive oil. 4 servings

Provenance Vineyards Rutherford Cabernet Sauvignon
Grilled Red Curry Lamb Skewers with Tomato Chutney
Tom Rinaldi Director of Winemaking and Winemaker Chris Cooney, Professional Chef Joey Altman

Encépagement : Cabernet Sauvignon

Appellation : Primarily from Rutherford, Beckstoffer Georges III and our estate vineyard.

Yield : Approximately 4 tons per acre

Alcohol Level : Average 14%

Harvest Details : After handpicking the grapes into half-ton bins, we gently destemmed them to maintain 60% whole berries.

Winemaking : Cold soaking of the must before the 2-to-3 week stainless steel fermentation.

Philosophy : Allow the wines to express the grape variety, the vintage and the region with little interference. Of course, to do that takes the best vineyards, the finest winemaking technology and innovation, premium small oak barrels and meticulous care from vineyard to bottle, but at least the philosophy is simple!

Maceration : Relatively long-term skin contact, we remove the wine from the skins and press on taste only. We put the press fraction into the blend strictly by taste to fully polymerize the anthocyanins and give "plush" to our wine.

Wood Origin : French, American, European

Provenance Vineyards
1695 St. Helena Hwy
St. Helena, CA 94574
707-968-3633
ProvenanceVineyards.com

Sommeliers, Bordeaux Grand Cru

"The wine's aromas open with lush black cherry and blackberry character, infused with subtle hints of mocha, flinty minerality and black tea. Its expansive fruit flavors are packed with ripe berry, currant and plum — with dark chocolate and toffee nuances — that persist on the palate. Balanced acidity and ripe, muscular tannins frame the midpalate flavors. This wine's graceful style and cocoa powder finish make it a truly classic Rutherford Dust Cabernet Sauvignon." TR & CC

The word Provenance is derived from the French language, and literally means "origin," or "source." In fine art, provenance is a record of authentication and, in geology; provenance is the source of materials that define the area sediment. And so, with the perfect name, vineyards and renowned wine director Tom Rinaldi, Provenance Vineyards had its origin. Tom knew this revered Rutherford bench soil like no other, having spent years as winemaker at Duckhorn Vineyards. The origin of a vineyard's soil is critical since the soil drives the wine's quality, flavors and aromas. In 1999, Provenance Vineyards launched with inaugural releases and rave reviews. Soon after, it found a home in the heart of the Rutherford appellation, having acquired the historic Chateau Beaucanon estate and massive restoration project. Provenance Vineyards produces Cabernet Sauvignon, Napa Valley Merlot, Sauvignon Blanc and recently introduced a new varietal collection including Cabernet Franc, Malbec, and a Bordeaux-style blend, duly named, The Winemaker's Reserve. "Winemaking is about expressing the character of the place. Each vineyard has its own distinct personality" says winemaker, Chris Cooney. And a sense of place always has its own provenance.

Lamb:

2 lb	boneless lamb loin, cut into 1-inch cubes (substitute well trimmed leg meat)
½ c	extra virgin olive oil
½ c	fresh lime juice (2 to 3 limes)
2 T	lemon zest (about 2 lemons)
10	garlic cloves, peeled and minced
2 T	whole cumin seed
2 T	chili powder
2 T	curry powder
1 T	kosher salt, plus additional for seasoning
1 t	cayenne pepper
2	jalapeño peppers, minced
1 lb	long beans, trimmed, cut into 3" pieces
2 t	unsalted butter
½ t	freshly ground black pepper, plus additional for seasoning

Tomato Chutney:

1	small red onion, peeled, halved and cut in thin strips
1	ginger 2-inch piece, fresh, peeled and cut into thin strips
5	cloves garlic, peeled sliced thin
¼ c	brown sugar
½ c	malt vinegar, cider or red wine vinegar
2 t	coriander seed
2 t	mustard seed
2 t	anise seed
2 t	fennel seed
1 ½ c	diced tomatoes (14 ounce can)
2 T	lime juice
2	jalapeño peppers, cut in small dice
¼ c	loosely packed chopped cilantro leaves
tt	Sea salt and freshly ground black pepper

Marinade:
Whisk together ½ cup of the olive oil, the lime juice, lemon zest, garlic, cumin, chili powder, curry powder, 2 teaspoon of the salt, cayenne, ¼ teaspoon black pepper, and jalapeños in a medium bowl. Taste and adjust salt, pepper, cayenne, and lime juice to taste.
Combine the lamb cubes and the marinade and thread 4 to 5 pieces of lamb onto each skewer. Refrigerate skewers for at least 1 and up to 4 hours.

Heat Grill:
Grill over medium-high heat, turning every few minutes, until the lamb is medium rare, about 6 minutes.

Tomato Chutney:
In a large non-reactive saucepan simmer the onions, ginger, garlic, sugar, vinegar, coriander, mustard, anise, fennel and canned tomatoes with their liquid until most of the liquid has evaporated, about 20 minutes. Turn off heat, stir in the lime juice, jalapeños, cilantro. Season with salt and pepper to taste. Serve slightly warm or at room temperature.

Plating:
Serve the lamb skewers with a mound the tomato chutney on top. 4 servings

PROVENANCE VINEYARDS
1695 St. Helena Hwy
St. Helena, CA 94574
707-968-3633
ProvenanceVineyards.com

QUINTESSA

RUTHERFORD
Napa Valley Red Wine

QUINTESSA
SEARED BEEF TENDERLOIN, BING CHERRIES, MUSTARD GLAZED MUSHROOMS, FENNEL SALAD
WINEMAKER CHARLES THOMAS, EXECUTIVE CHEF ERIK VILLAR ~ CALISTOGA RANCH

Wine Making Facts :

Encépagement : Cabernet Sauvignon, Merlot, Cabernet Franc, Petit Verdot, Carmenère

Appellation : Rutherford

Vineyard : Quintessa Estate

Soils : Five diverse soil types ranging from white volcanic ash, alluvial silts and gravel, fractured rock, shale and river cobbles, loam and clay. Five distinct microclimates.

Elevation : 200 - 450 feet

Average Vine Age : 10-15

Yield : 2.5 -3 tons/acre

Alcohol Level : 14.1%

Philosophy : Agustin and Valeria Huneeus developed Quintessa in 1990 to establish the property as one of the great red wine estates of the world. Valeria guided the 280-acre vineyard with strict criteria of care for the soil and environment through a commitment to biodynamic and organic farming methods.

Winemaking : Entirely gravity fed winery

Facility : The Quintessa winery's eco-sensitive design integrates nature and winemaking in a stunning gravity-flow winery that combines traditional old-world methods with state-of-the-art techniques.

Fermentation : Native yeast in French oak, stainless steel and concrete tanks

Maceration : 30 days average

QUINTESSA WINERY
1601 SILVERADO TRAIL
ST HELENA, CA 94574
707-967-1601
QUINTESSA.COM

SOMMELIERS BLACK TIE BORDEAUX MATURE

"Sweet and inviting aromas of bright black fruit with red fruit undertones. It has full, lush entry, developing into a broad, unrobing wine that coats the mouth with rich black fruit laced with a touch of mocha, licorice, sandalwood and vanilla spice. With tremendous density, concentration and ample fine tannins." CT

When Agustin and Valeria Huneeus discovered the land that would become Quintessa in 1989, it was the last great undeveloped property in the Napa Valley. The 280-acre estate includes a valley, a lake, a river, five hills, four microclimates, and a great diversity of soil types, all in the renowned Rutherford appellation. Using the most advanced viticultural techniques, select rootstocks and clones, and the expertise of winemaker Charles Thomas and famed consultant Michel Rolland, Quintessa produces a single extraordinary wine that expresses the diversity and elegance of the vineyard. The winery they built has won several architectural awards for it's environmental sensitivity and subtle presence.

QUINTESSA
SEARED BEEF TENDERLOIN, BING CHERRIES, MUSTARD GLAZED MUSHROOMS, FENNEL SALAD
WINEMAKER CHARLES THOMAS, EXECUTIVE CHEF ERIK VILLAR ~ CALISTOGA RANCH

Tenderloin:
4 - 5 oz   natural beef tenderloin filets

Bing Cherry Emulsion:
2 oz	olive oil
2 pt	Bing cherries, pitted
2	shallot, large, peeled, minced
24	tarragon, leaves, minced
2 oz	hot water
2 T	tarragon vinegar
8 oz	extra virgin olive oil

Mustard Glazed Mushrooms:
2 lb	wild mushrooms, sliced (substitute crimini)
½ c	shallots, peeled, small dice
¼ c	olive oil

4 T	butter, unsalted
2 oz	soy sauce
1½ c	Madeira
4 T	mustard, stone ground
2 T	extra virgin olive oil

Shaved Fennel Salad:
4	baby fennel, thinly sliced
4	shallots, peeled, thinly sliced
2 T	chives, minced
2 T	fennel fronds, sliced
4 oz	watercress
2 oz	extra virgin olive oil, lemon infused

Tenderloin:
Season beef with salt and pepper.
Sear in a small amount of clarified butter.
Finish the steak by adding whole butter and fresh thyme to the pan.
Remove from heat, tilt pan and spoon melted butter over the top of the steak.

Bing Cherry Emulsion:
Sweat cherries and diced shallots in olive oil.
Blend the cherries, tarragon, water, and vinegar on medium speed, adding in the olive oil slowly to the mixture.
Season with salt and pepper.

Mustard Glazed Mushrooms:
Sauté shallots and mushrooms in olive oil.
Add butter and deglaze with Madeira reducing liquid by half.
Add soy sauce and mustard and bring to boil and reduce to simmer.
Season with salt and pepper.
Add extra virgin olive oil to the pan and serve.

Shaved Fennel Salad:
Combine ingredients into bowl season with infused oil, sea salt and fresh ground pepper. 4 servings

LAKEHOUSE RESTAURANT
AT CALISTOGA RANCH
580 LOMMEL ROAD
CALISTOGA, CA 94515
707-254-2830
CALISTOGARANCH.COM

Wine Making Facts :
Encépagement : Petite Syrah
Appellation : Stags Leap District
Soils: Uniquely loose topsoil with
sub-soil of ash and rock
Micro - Climate : Stags' Leap
Ranch is located directly
beneath the Vaca Mountain
Range Palisades, which hold
heat during the day and release
it through the cold evenings
Yield : 2.5 tons/acre
Alcohol Level : 14.4%
Total Production : 2000 cases
Philosophy : Produce distinctive,
site-specific Petite Syrah
Harvest Details : Mid October
Winemaking : Hands-on from
vineyard to the bottle. Multiple
lots are fermented in 1 ton micro-
bins, and are hand punched for
gentle extraction. Larger lots are
pumped over through a tank
irrigator for optimal wine quality.
Fermentation : Monitored
extremes, extended cold
soaks, warm fermentation
and extended maceration.
Maceration : Typically extended
maceration, 30-60 day skin contact
Oak Regimen : 18-22
months oak aging

"Blueberries, raspberries, and black-berries intertwined with subtle aromas of violet, spice and forest floor. The palate is lush and long. Sweet mid tannins give a smooth texture and a layered lingering finish." TK

QUIXOTE WINERY
6126 SILVERADO TRAIL
NAPA, CA 94558
707-944-2659
QUIXOTEWINERY.COM

SOMMELIERS BLACK TIE, HERMITAGE SYRAH

QUIXOTE PETITE SYRAH
SPRING LAMB SHOULDER AND YOUNG PEA RISOTTO, MEYER LEMON GREMOLATA
WINEMAKER TIMOTHY KEITH, CHEF/OWNER HIRO SONE ~ TERRA

Braised Lamb Shoulder:

2 lb	lamb shoulder, boneless, cut into 5 cubes
2 T	olive oil
½ c	onion, chopped
2	garlic cloves, smashed
1 T	dried porcini mushrooms, chopped
⅓ c	red wine
2 c	chicken stock
⅓ c	tomato purée
1	rosemary sprig

Gremolata:

2 t	parsley, chopped
1 t	mint, chopped
⅛ t	lemon zest, chopped

Serving:

1 c	chicken stock
½ c	English peas, fresh, shucked, blanched
½ c	grated Parmesan cheese
2 T	butter, unsalted
½ t	chopped mint
4 T	yogurt
1 T	gremolata
4	mint sprigs

Par Cooked Risotto:

1 t	garlic, minced
½ c	onion, chopped
1½ T	butter, unsalted
1½ c	Arborio rice
¼ c	dry white wine
5 - 6 c	chicken stock

Lamb :
Preheat oven to 350 F.
Season the lamb with salt and pepper.
Sear the lamb just enough to give it color.
Add onions and garlic and sauté until golden brown.
Add the porcini and wine then bring to a boil.
Add the stock and tomato purée, return to a boil and skim foam.
Season with salt and pepper and add the rosemary.
Cut a piece of parchment paper to fit inside the pan, cover the lamb and place in the oven.
Cook until the lamb is tender; about 1 hour.
Remove the meat from the sauce and set aside.
Carefully transfer the sauce into a blender and purée until smooth.
Strain through fine sieve and return the sauce and the meat to pan.
Set aside.

Gremolata:
In a small mixing bowl, combine all ingredients and set aside.

recipe continues next page

Par Cooked Risotto:

1 t	garlic, minced
½ c	onion, chopped
1½ T	butter, unsalted
1½ c	Arborio rice
¼ c	dry white wine
5 - 6 c	chicken stock

Serving:

1 c	chicken stock
½ c	English peas, fresh, shucked, blanched
½ c	grated Parmesan cheese
2 T	butter, unsalted
½ t	chopped mint
4 T	yogurt
1 T	gremolata
4	mint sprigs

Par Cooked Risotto:
Sauté the garlic and onion in butter until translucent; about 3 minutes.
Using a wooden spoon, stir in the rice; sauté until the outside of the rice becomes opaque, about 3 minutes.
Add the wine and bring to a boil stirring constantly, until the rice absorbs almost all the wine. Season lightly with salt and pepper.
In a separate pot, bring the stock to a simmer.
Add 1 cup of the simmering stock to rice mixture; keep at a simmer but do not boil.
Stir the rice constantly until almost all the stock has been absorbed.
Continue to add the stock a ½ cup at a time and repeat the process until the rice is almost tender but still firm. Set aside.

Serving:
In a saucepan bring the chicken stock and 1 cup of the lamb sauce to a boil.
Shred one piece of the lamb shoulder.
Add the risotto and shredded meat to the stock mixture; bring back to a boil.
Add the peas, cheese, butter and mint, stirring constantly; bring back to boil.
Remove from the heat and season with salt and pepper.

Divide the risotto on four hot serving plates, place the cubes of lamb shoulder in the center of the risotto, spoon the yogurt next to the meat, sprinkle the gremolata, arrange the mint sprig on the yogurt. 4 servings

TERRA
1345 RAILROAD AVENUE
SAINT HELENA, CA 94574
707-963-8931
TERRARESTAURANT.COM

REVANA FAMILY VINEYARDS
LAMB LOIN, CARDOONS, POTATO GNOCCHI
WINEMAKER HEIDI BARRETT, EXECUTIVE CHEF ROBERT CURRY ~ AUBERGE DU SOLEIL

Wine Making Facts :

Encépagement : Cabernet Sauvignon, Cabernet Franc, Petit Verdot

Appellation : St. Helena

Vineyard : Estate Vineyard "Revana"

Average Vine Age : 9 years

Yield : 2.5 tons/acre

Alcohol Level : 14.7%

Total Production : 2,000 cases

Harvest Details : Bud break in Cabernet began around mid-March and completed in early April. Bloom was short around mid-May. Harvest began late and concluded in mid-November.

Winemaking : Heidi Barrett

Facility : Revana Family Vineyards

Wood Origin : France

Oak Regimen : Aged 18 months in all French Oak

"Dark ruby tones and deep aromas of black cherry, cocoa powder, toast, and spice. The palate is elegant and silky with bright purity of fruit and mouth-filling texture. Flavors of cherry echo the aromas, followed by layers of cassis, chocolate, black olive, crushed herb and exotic spice notes. The mid-palate is lush, with beautifully integrated tannins leading to a finish of remarkable length and finesse." HB

REVANA FAMILY VINEYARDS
2930 SAINT HELENA HWY
ST HELENA, CA 94574
707-967-8814
REVANAWINE.COM

SOMMELIERS, BORDEAUX GRAND CRU

Look closely at the logo of Revana Family Vineyards and you'll see a stylized version of the ancient symbol of Asclepius, representing the medical profession, against the background of a heart. It's no coincidence that the winery's founder is a renowned cardiologist. And when he found a small parcel of prime St. Helena land in 1997, he understood he had the potential to make a truly special wine. Revana has produced a single, estate cabernet with "backbone and tons of fruit character that will lend itself well during aging," according to Barrett, Dr. Revana calls moderate consumption of red wine "a healthful and medically defensible daily pleasure." And with the Revana Cabernet Sauvignon, that pleasure is greater than ever.

REVANA FAMILY VINEYARDS
LAMB LOIN, CARDOONS, POTATO GNOCCHI
WINEMAKER HEIDI BARRETT, EXECUTIVE CHEF ROBERT CURRY ~ AUBERGE DU SOLEIL

Potato Gnocchi:

3lb	Russet potatoes, baked in jackets, passed through tamis or ricer
7 oz	flour, sifted
1 oz	salt
3 T	extra virgin olive oil
2	eggs

Cardoon Gnocchi Ragout:

1 T	olive oil
12	pearl onions, peeled, braised in butter and stock
1	cardoon, peeled, cooked, on bias
1	clove garlic, chopped
1 T	thyme, chopped
1 t	butter
¾ t	red wine vinegar
½ c	basil, chiffonade
¼ c	Nicoise olives, pitted, halved

Lamb:

4 - 5 oz	lamb loin portions
2 T	clarified butter

Cabernet Sauvignon Jus:

1	onion, medium dice
1	carrot, medium dice
1	leek, medium dice
1	head garlic, cut in half
½ btl	red wine, plus
4 T	butter to finish
2 c	veal stock
2 c	chicken stock
3 lb	lamb bones
4 oz	olive oil

Cardoon:

1	cardoon
1	onion, diced
1	carrot, sliced
½	thyme bunch, tied
3 oz	bacon
1	lemon, halved
1 hd	garlic, cut in half
1 btl	white wine
2 T	black peppercorns
1 c	extra virgin olive oil
2 c	chicken stock
1	bay leaf
	Kosher salt

Potato Gnocchi:
In a mixing bowl make a well out of the potatoes.
Place the eggs in the well.
Drizzle olive oil over the potatoes.
Sprinkle the flour and salt on the potatoes.
Gently mix until dough comes together.
On a floured surface divide the dough into 8 pieces.
Roll the dough into ½ inch cigar shaped cylinders and cut into 1 inch pieces.
Roll each piece off fork tines onto a floured sheet pan.
Cook in non-salted boiling water until they just start to float.
Remove and set aside.

Cabernet Sauvignon Jus:
Preheat oven to 450º F.
Heat a roasting pan; add 2 ounces olive oil and lamb bones.
When bones color, place pan in the oven.
Roast the bones until golden brown.
Sauté onions, carrots and leeks, until translucent and soft.
Add the half bottle of cabernet and reduce by half.
Add the veal and brown chicken stocks.
Bring to a simmer, skimming scum off the surface often.
Add the bones to the sauce and deglaze the roasting pan with splash of wine.
Add the deglazed fond to the sauce, scraping the bits into sauce.
Reduce the sauce by half. Strain the sauce, discarding the bones and vegetables. Continue to reduce to desired consistency.
Add 2 tablespoons remaining wine. Season with salt and pepper.
Strain with fine mesh strainer.

Cardoon and Gnocchi Ragout:
Sauté the cardoon and pearl onions in olive oil until golden.
Add chopped garlic, thyme and cooked gnocchi.
Add 2 tablespoons of lamb jus, butter, red wine vinegar, basil, and olives.

Lamb:
Preheat oven to 350º.
Season the lamb with salt and pepper.
Sear lamb in clarified butter on all sides until golden.
Finish in the oven until medium rare (6-8 minutes).
Allow the lamb to rest for 10 minutes.
4 servings

Cardoon:
Place all ingredients in a small stock pot.
Cover with parchment paper.
Simmer until cardoon is easily pierced.
Remove the lemon rind and thyme.
Reserve refrigerated in liquid.

AUBERGE DU SOLEIL
180 RUTHERFORD HILL ROAD
RUTHERFORD, CA 94573
800-348-5406
AUBERGEDUSOLEIL.COM

Reynolds Family Winery

Cabernet Sauvignon

NAPA VALLEY

Estate Select

ALC. 14.6% BY VOL.

VINTAGE
2005

REYNOLDS FAMILY STAGS LEAP CABERNET
ROASTED SQUAB BREAST, BRAISED CABBAGE, SUN DRIED TOMATO BULGUR WHEAT
WINEMAKER STEVE REYNOLDS, PROFESSIONAL CHEF JOHN VLANDIS

Wine Making Facts :
Encépagement : Cabernet Sauvignon
Appellation : Stags Leap District
Vineyard : Annapura Vineyard
Micro-Climate : Warm days, breezy afternoons, and warm nights as rocks radiate heat collected during the day
Alcohol Level : 14 %
Total Production : 764 cases
Philosophy : Fruit-driven, stay true to the flavors of the vineyard, soft velvety tannins
Winemaking : Grapes are cold-soaked at 55° until spontaneous fermentation starts. Approximately 30% of the production is fermented in small bins to soften tannins and prevent over-extracted flavors.
Facility : Reynolds Family Winery
Maceration : Extended following fermentation
Wood Origin : French

"Our single clone/single vineyard Stags Leap Cabernet Sauvignon delivers big ripe plums, Crème de Cassis, and a hint of luscious cherry and dark chocolate. It's seductive, silky texture is everything you want in a Stags Leap Cabernet." SR

REYNOLDS FAMILY WINERY
3266 SILVERADO TRAIL
NAPA, CA 94558
707-258-2558
REYNOLDSFAMILYWINERY.COM

VINUM XL, CABERNET SAUVIGNON

Fourteen years ago, Steve Reynolds traded in his dental practice for the life of a vintner when he and his wife, Suzie, purchased a 100 year-old chicken ranch in the renowned Stags Leap District. Countless doctors have started wineries," he says, "but how many of them build the winery, drive the tractor, and make the wine?" This year marks the Reynolds Family Winery's tenth anniversary. Its wines have been highly ranked in the industry press, and Napa's People's Choice voted it the "Best Boutique Winery" last year. Furthermore, Reynolds was voted "Best Winemaker" three years in a row. "It's not just a hobby anymore," he says with a smile.

Reynolds Family Stags Leap Cabernet
Roasted Squab Breast, Braised Cabbage, Sun Dried Tomato Bulgur Wheat
Winemaker Steve Reynolds, Professional Chef John Vlandis

Ingredients:

4	squab
½ c	onions, diced
¼ c	carrots, diced
4	garlic cloves
2	roma tomatoes
1	bay leaf
10	peppercorns
3	thyme sprigs
1 qt	chicken stock
4 c	red wine

Tomato Bulgur Wheat:

1 c	bulgur wheat
½ c	sundried tomatoes, minced
1 c	chicken stock (for purée) plus

1 ¼ c	chicken stock
¼ c	onions, minced
1 T	thyme, minced
1	bay leaf
2 T	olive oil
¼ c	Kalamata olives, pitted

Braised Savoy Cabbage:

4 c	Savoy cabbage, julienned
6 pcs	applewood smoked bacon 2" by ½"
2 c	chicken stock

Sachet:

4 juniper berries, 1 bay leaf, 5 peppercorns and 2 sprigs thyme

Method:

Preheat oven to 425° F.

Place a roasting pan to heat in the oven. Remove the breasts from the squab, season with salt and pepper and refrigerate. Place the remaining squab legs, thighs and carcasses in the roasting pan and roast until brown, about 20 minutes. Turn the bones over and roast on the other side for an additional 20 minutes. Add the vegetables and continue to roast for 15 minutes. Remove the bones from the pan and place in a stock pot. Deglaze the pan with the wine and add to the stock pot. Add the remaining ingredients and simmer, occasionally skimming the top.

Continue to simmer for 2 hours. Strain the stock into a saucepan and reduce to a sauce-like consistency. Strain and season.

Quail:

Add a small amount of olive oil in a sauté pan and heat on high. Place the squab breasts in the pan skin side down and cook until brown and crispy. Turn them over and place in the oven for 5 minutes. Remove them from the oven and let rest. They should be cooked medium rare.

Sun Dried Tomato Bulgur Wheat :

Cook onion in oil in a 2-quart heavy saucepan over moderate heat, stirring occasionally, until golden brown; add the olives, thyme and bay leaf. Add the stock and sundried tomatoes. Bring to a boil, remove from the heat and cover. Let it stand for 25 minutes, season with salt and pepper.

Braised Savoy Cabbage:

Place small scoop of bulgur in the center of the plate, top with cabbage.

Slice the squab breast and arrange around the cabbage. Spoon the sauce around the squab. 2 servings

ROUND POND ESTATE SAUVIGNON BLANC
GRILLED FLATBREAD WITH BRIE, FRESCA PEAR SALSA, ESTATE OLIVE OIL DRIZZLE
WINEMAKER BRIAN BROWN, WINERY CHEF HANNAH BAUMAN

Wine Making Facts :

Encépagement : Sauvignon Blanc

Appellation : Rutherford, Napa Valley

Vineyard : Round Pond Block 7

Soils : Clay loam

Average Vine Age : 4 years

Yield : 6 tons/acre

Alcohol Level : 14.6 %

Total Production : 672 cases

Philosophy : Pure fruit expression with no oak influence.

Harvest Details : September 2nd, picked for ripe citrus and stone fruit flavors.

Winemaking : 100% stainless, cool fermentation, no lees stirring, two racking.

Facility : Estate Winery

Fermentation : Cool and long, no malalactic

ROUND POND ESTATE
875 RUTHERFORD ROAD
RUTHERFORD, CA 94573
888-302-2575
ROUNDPOND.COM

VIINUM, RIESLING GRAND CRU GLASS

" This wine offers aromas of white peach, Meyer lemon zest and a touch of minerality. As the wine warms up, ripe mango and Tuscan melon notes emerge and although the wine is dry, there is a perceived sweetness on the palate. With bright acid, kaffir lime and Fuji apple characteristics, this wine's balanced profile lingers on the palate long after it has been consumed. " BB

Completed in 2007, Round Pond is still considered one of Napa Valley's newest wineries but it reflects a tradition established over 25 years ago by the MacDonnell family on their Rutherford property. Since 1983, they have grown premium grapes for some of the valley's most prestigious wineries – today its 432-acre estate includes sustainably grown vineyards, biodynamic gardens, and organic olive orchards. Consulting winemaker Thomas Brown and winemaker Brian Brown employ the latest root stocks and clones and pick only specially designated vineyard rows from the very best blocks. No wonder their wines are getting buzz in the industry press.

ROUND POND ESTATE SAUVIGNON BLANC
GRILLED FLATBREAD WITH BRIE, FRESCA PEAR SALSA, ESTATE OLIVE OIL DRIZZLE
WINEMAKER BRIAN BROWN, WINERY CHEF HANNAH BAUMAN

Pear Salsa:
3	pears, ripe
3 - 4	dried pears, chopped fine
½	red onion, chopped fine
3 T	cilantro, chopped
2 T	fresh mint, chopped
1	lime, juice and zest
2 t	ginger, fresh, peeled and minced
1-2	jalapenos, roasted, seeded and minced
½ t	crushed red pepper flakes
tt	kosher salt
tt	ground pepper

Quesadillas:
½ lb	brie cheese
8	tortillas, 6 or 8 inch, flour or white corn
2 T	olive oil, Round Pond Italian Varietal honey to taste

Pear Salsa:
Roast whole jalapenos over open flame.
Remove stem, seeds and chop fine.
Core pears and cut into ¼ - ½ inch pieces.
Gently fold all ingredients for salsa.
Adjust jalapenos, salt, or lime to taste.

Place cheese in freezer for about one hour, remove and cut into cubes.
Heat skillet and brush with oil.
Distribute cheese evenly on 4 tortillas, about ½ cup each.
Spread 3-4 tablespoons pear salsa over the cheese.
Top with remaining 4 tortillas.
Cook 3-4 minutes on each side until cheese is melted and tortillas are slightly browned.
Cut into wedges, drizzle with a touch of honey and serve with extra pear salsa. 8 servings

ROUND POND ESTATE
875 RUTHERFORD ROAD
RUTHERFORD, CA 94573
888-302-2575
ROUNDPOND.COM

ROY ESTATE CABERNET
DARJEELING TEA SCENTED SQUAB, DRIED CHERRIES, BUTTER POACHED BABY RADISHES
WINEMAKER PHILIPPE MELKA, RESTAURANT CHEF CHRISTOPHER KOSTOW ~ MEADOWOOD

Wine Making Facts :
Winemaker : Philippe Melka
Encépagement : Cabernet Sauvignon, and Petit Verdot
Appellation : Napa Valley
Vineyard : Roy Estate
Elevation : 200 ft
Micro-Climate : Roy Estate is located in its own mini valley, south of Stag's Leap on Soda Canyon Road.
Average Vine Age : 4 years
Alcohol Level : 14.2%
Total Production : 585 cases
Harvest Details : September 28 to October 17, 2005
Fermentation : Malolactic 100% barrel fermentation
Maceration : 21 days
Wood Origin : New Taransaud Barrels
Oak Regimen : 24 months
Percentage of New Barrels : 100%

ROY ESTATE
122 SODA CANYON
NAPA, CA 94558
707-255-4409
ROYESTATE.COM

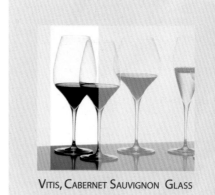

VITIS, CABERNET SAUVIGNON GLASS

" The wine shows intense ruby color. The very seductive nose reveals fresh crushed berries of cassis, rose petal, strawberry and cherry essence. The attack is dense with soft velvety texture and layered with fruits. It expresses the finesse and harmony of a "grand vin." It is very delicate on the palate and still has amazing concentration and length. Enjoy the beautiful fruit today and then watch it evolve over time. " PM

How do a civil engineer and accountant become world-class vintners? Serendipity. For Charles and Shirley Roy, this is their second venture as business partners. Their original dream was to spend time in Napa Valley enjoying its beauty, the vineyards and playing some golf. Instead, they decided to star in the wine business, and star they did, garnishing exceptional reviews for both their Estate Grown Cabernet and Proprietary Red, a Bordeaux blend. A quantum leap was taken to design a special vineyard to make these extraordinary wines. Retirement was no longer in the cards as they embarked on building a wine business. After the unexpected passing of Charles there is a huge void created by his bigger than life personality and relentless quest for excellence. His legacy, that never ending intensity of purpose and joie de vivre, continues to inspire the Roy Estate team. Shirley and winemaker Philippe Melka are dedicated to produce world-class, artisanal wines from this special vineyard. The hard work, along with the dream....continues.

2006
Estate Grown • Napa Valley
Proprietary Red Wine

ROY ESTATE PROPRIETARY RED
HERB CRUSTED RACK OF LAMB WITH ROY ESTATE EVOO
WINEMAKER PHILIPPE MELKA, WINERY CHEF SHIRLEY ROY

Wine Making Facts :
Encépagement : Cabernet Sauvignon, Merlot, Petit Verdot
Appellation : Napa Valley
Vineyard : Roy Estate
Soils : Extremely rocky, cemented ash
Elevation : 200 feet
Micro-Climate : Roy Estate is located in its own mini valley, south of Stag's Leap on Soda Canyon Road. Breezes that funnel up from San Pablo Bay moderate high temperatures, allowing the fruit to ripen more gradually producing balanced young wines with round approachable tannins and relatively low alcohols. The wines are delicious upon release and age well for 2 to 3 decades.
Average Vine Age : 5 years
Yield : 1 ½ - 2 ½ tons per acre
Alcohol Level : 14.2%
Total Production : 1020 cases
Harvest Details : September 27 to October 26, 2006
Fermentation : Malolactic 100% barrel fermentation
Maceration : 14-28 days
Oak Regimen : 18 months
Percentage of New Barrels : 100%

ROY ESTATE
122 SODA CANYON
NAPA, CA 94558
707-255-4409
ROYESTATE.COM

SOMMELIERS, BORDEAUX GRAND CRU

" Reveals aromas of dried herbs, espresso beans and chocolate. The initial push of ripe currant, black cherry, blackberry, and mocha-laced oak illustrates its depth and complexity. This uniquely elegant wine is muscular, yet seductive, intense and concentrated, yet sleek and vibrant. " PM

Lamb:
1   Rack of lamb, well-trimmed
           (with 8 bones) at room temperature
Resources:
2 T   Roy Estate Extra Virgin Olive Oil

Ingredients:
3 clove   garlic, minced
2 T   rosemary, chopped
1 t   thyme, chopped
½ t   freshly ground black pepper
1 ½ T   balsamic vinegar
1 T   freshly squeezed lemon juice
½ t   sea salt

Method:

Preheat oven to 375° F.
Place all ingredients, except lamb, together in a wide mouth jar and shake to combine.
Rinse and pat lamb dry. Generously brush lamb with mixture. Sprinkle with sea salt.
Place in roasting pan. Roast lamb 20 minutes for medium-rare. Let stand 15 minutes.
Cut lamb between bones into individual chops. 4 servings

ROY ESTATE CABERNET
DARJEELING TEA SCENTED SQUAB, DRIED CHERRIES, BUTTER POACHED BABY RADISHES
WINEMAKER PHILIPPE MELKA, RESTAURANT CHEF CHRISTOPHER KOSTOW ~ MEADOWOOD

Squab:
4	squabs, whole
2 oz	Darjeeling tea
2 T	butter, room temperature
2 c	salt
4	cloves garlic
4	bay leaves
1 liter	duck fat

Cherries:
| ⅓ c | dried cherries |
| 10 oz | ruby port |

Radish:
1	baby radish, bunch
1 c	water
3 ½ T	butter

Method:
Remove the breasts and legs from squab. Crush garlic and bay leaves and combine with salt.
Pack squab legs in salt mixture and allow to cure for 30 minutes, then rinse under cold water.
Place legs in duck fat and simmer until tender.
Remove from fat and cool.

Mix butter and tea in a food processor.
Place breasts in a Ziploc (plastic) bag with the butter mixture.

In a small pot, bring port to boil. Reduce by half. Pour over dried cherries to re-hydrate.
Once cherries have plumped, remove liquid and reduce until syrupy.

Radish:
Clean radishes, reserving tops for garnish.
Place radishes in pot with butter and water; simmer until tender and well glazed.

To Finish:
Poach squab breasts in water at 350 °F in a sauce pot until medium rare.
Remove from Ziploc bag and roast skin side down in a saucepan until crispy.
Top with cherry sauce and radish. 2 servings

Meadowood Napa Valley
900 Meadowood Lane
St Helena, CA 94574
707- 967-1205
meadowood.com

SCHRAMSBERG

J. Schram

2001

SCHRAMSBERG, J. SCHRAM
HOUSEMADE SMOKED SALMON PIEROGIES
WINEMAKERS HUGH DAVIES AND KEITH HOCK, CHEF/OWNER MATT SPECTOR ~ JOLE

Wine Making Facts :
Encépagement : Chardonnay, Pinot Noir. Sparkling Wine
Micro-Climate : Coastal Cool Climate
Average Vine Age : 11.7 years
Yield : 2.7 tons per acre
Alcohol Level : 12.6%
Philosophy : Achieving the greatest elegance and individuality possible, J. Schram epitomizes Schramsberg's philosophy to create a wine in which no effort has been spared and no care has been omitted.
Harvest Details : Harvested August 7 – October 9, 2001
Winemaking : Schramsberg's top Chardonnay based signature wine, J. Schram is made from the very best base wines from the 200 separate lots made from the over 90 different vineyard blocks from Carneros, Anderson Valley and the Sonoma and Marin coasts.
RS : 1.21g/100mL
Fermentation : 40% barrel fermentation, 60% stainless steel
Wood Origin : France
Oak Regimen : All oak is at least three-years-old or more
Aging : Six years on the yeast
Bottling Formats : 750 ml and Magnums

SCHRAMSBERG VINEYARDS
1400 SCHRAMSBERG ROAD
CALISTOGA, CA 94515
800-877-3623
SCHRAMSBERG.COM

VITIS, CHAMPAGNE GLASS

" The fruitful aromas of the wine's youth are still vibrant, with fresh green apple, lime and pineapple jumping out of the glass. Refined, bottle-aged characters of hazelnut, honey, and baked brioche chime in. A crisp entry with the flavorful essences of white peach, key lime, and juicy tropical fruit. While a creamy depth builds on the mid-palate, the wine's distinct acid backbone and a certain mineral drive stretch into a long, riding finish." HD & KH

In 1965, Jack and Jamie Davies established Schramsberg as a sparkling wine estate on the property originally founded in 1862 by German immigrant Jacob Schram. At a time when there were only 21 wineries in Napa Valley and fewer than 50 acres of California vineyard planted to Chardonnay and Pinot Noir, they set out to make world-class sparkling wine in the true Méthode Champenoise style. Theirs was the first California winery to provide a Blanc de Blancs in 1965 followed by a Blanc de Noirs in 1967. Now their son Hugh Davies, who was born the same year the Davies arrived at Schramsberg, leads the winery's management and winemaking team. The Schramsberg estate is tucked into Napa Valley's famed Diamond Mountain, a few miles south of the town of Calistoga. Tall trees and lush vegetation surround this registered historic landmark, painstakingly restored by the Davies family.

SCHRAMSBERG, J. SCHRAM
HOUSEMADE SMOKED SALMON PIEROGIES
WINEMAKERS HUGH DAVIES AND KEITH HOCK, CHEF/OWNER MATT SPECTOR ~ JOLE

Pierogies:

1	Idaho potato, large
1 T	salt
1½ c	AP flour
1¼ c	potato starch
1	egg
3 T	sour cream
5 T	melted butter

Smoked salmon stuffing:

8 oz	smoked salmon
3 oz	cream cheese
3 oz	goat cheese
1 t	orange zest
1	shallot minced
2 T	chives

Method:

Smoked salmon stuffing:
1. In a food processor combine all ingredients except chives and mix until smooth.
2. Fold in chives and reserve.

Pierogies:
1. Cover potatoes in salted water bring it to a boil and then turn the flame down to simmer.
2. Cook potato until tender about thirty minutes.
3. Peel and mash potato through a fine sieve or food mill.
4. Mix in sour cream butter and egg.
5. Add dry ingredients and mix until the dough comes together.
6. Remove from bowl onto a floured surface and knead until the dough is smooth and velvety, about five minutes.
7. Cover and let rest for about ten minutes.
8. Roll dough out to about one-eighth of an inch and cut with a three inch cookie cutter.
9. Stuff each pierogi with a good teaspoon of stuffing seal with egg wash.
10. Blanch in salted water for three minutes.
11. Drain and pat dry.
12. Heat a sauté pan over medium heat, add butter and pierogies and sauté until golden brown.
Makes 3 dozen.

JoLe
1457 Lincoln Avenue
Calistoga, CA 94515
707 942 5938
JOLERESTAURANT.COM

SILVERADO VINEYARDS SAUVIGNON BLANC
SALMON, HALIBUT, AND SCALLOP CEVICHE WITH COCONUT
WINEMAKER JON EMMERICH, CHEF /OWNER CINDY PAWLCYN ~ GO FISH

Wine making Facts:

Encépagement: 94% Sauvignon Blanc, 6% Semillon

Appellation: Yountville, Napa Valley

Vineyard: Miller Ranch

Soils: Yellow Loam with Boomer Gravelly

Loam, Clear Lake Clay Drained

Elevation: 558'

Average Vine Age: 15 years

Yield: 4.5 tons / acre

Alcohol Level: 13.6-13.9%

Total Production: 14,000 cases

Harvest Details: night pick through early morning,

generally beginning end of August

Facility: Estate Winery in Stags Leap District

Fermentation: 4-6 weeks

SILVERADO VINEYARDS
6121 SILVERADO TRAIL
NAPA, CA 94558
707-257-1770
SILVERADOVINEYARDS.COM

"Our Sauvignon Blanc has tremendous vibrancy and exotic aromatics. Our road map to creating Miller Ranch is simple: stainless steel fermentation to preserve the citrusy freshness, multiple yeast strains to enhance the aromas and enough barrel fermented Semillon to make the texture silky. " JE

VINUM, SAUVIGNON BLANC WINE GLASS

In 1981, Ron and Diane Miller established Silverado Vineyards in the heart of Stags Leap District. Over the years they expanded to include six distinctive vineyards in the Napa Valley and Carneros. The beautiful fruit from these ranches is the exclusive source of Silverado Vineyards' Estate and Single Vineyard wines. But it is Stags Leap, their golden child, where their winery estate overlooks panoramic views. It is also where viticulturists at UC Davis collected historic vines and discovered a unique clone, designating it as the "Heritage" clone. Only three Cabernets in California have this distinction, and the grapes from that clone are the origin of their flagship Cabernet, rightfully named SOLO. For those who visit, they will share in the experience of tasting several varietals, bask in the sunlight from their hillside terrace, and witness firsthand, how forward-thinking and historical preservation make Silverado a standout vineyard.

SILVERADO VINEYARDS SOLO CABERNET SAUVIGNON
MONGOLIAN PORK CHOPS
WINEMAKER JON EMMERICH, CHEF /OWNER CINDY PAWLCYN CATERING

Encépagement: 100% Cabernet Sauvignon
Appellation: Stags Leap District, Napa Valley
Vineyard: Stags Leap vineyard
Soils: Perkins Gravelly Loam
Elevation: 600-800'
Average Vine Age: 15 years
Yield: 3.9 tons/ acre
Alcohol Level: 14.6%
Total Production: 1400 cases
Harvest Details: Early morning hand picked,
mid September – late October
Winemaking: Destemmed but not crushed;
extended maceration; small fermentations
Facility: Estate Winery in Stags Leap District
Fermentation: 7-10 days primary fermentation
Maceration: Up to 30 days
Wood Origin: 100% French
Oak Regiment: 15-18 months

SILVERADO VINEYARDS
6121 SILVERADO TRAIL
NAPA, CA 94558
707-257-1770
SILVERADOVINEYARDS.COM

SOMMELIERS BLACK TIE CABERNET SAUVIGNON

"SOLO DISPLAYS ALL THE RIPE AND COMPLEX FRUIT, SUPPLE TEXTURE, AND SOLID STRUCTURE THAT HELPED DEFINE THE RENOWNED STAGS LEAP DISTRICT. THE AROMA OFFERS PURE RED FRUIT WITH LAYERS OF EARTH AND SPICE. THE PALATE IS BROAD, WITH PLUM FRUIT AND HINTS OF DRIED HERB THAT LEAD TO A FINISH WITH PERFECTLY BALANCED TANNIN."

WINEMAKER JON EMMERICH

SILVERADO VINEYARDS SAUVIGNON BLANC
SALMON, HALIBUT, AND SCALLOP CEVICHE WITH COCONUT
WINEMAKER JON EMMERICH, CHEF /OWNER CINDY PAWLCYN ~ GO FISH

Ingredients:

4 oz	scallops		2	coconuts
8-12 oz	salmon		1 to 2	avocados, sliced
8-12 oz	halibut			
1 c	freshly squeezed lime juice		Garnish:	
1 t	sea salt			cilantro sprigs
¼ t	freshly ground white pepper			extra virgin olive oil
½ t	finely chopped and seeded serrano chile			
1	red onion, minced		Secret Ingredients:	
1 c	unsweetened coconut milk			Warm fresh popcorn on the side

Method:

There's no real cooking involved when you make a ceviche, but you do need to plan ahead, as the seafood needs to marinate at least three hours but not more than eight hours. The fish "cooks" in the lime juice marinade: too long, and it will actually be overdone and mushy. Use only the freshest fish for this recipe. When it's in season, we use Pacific king salmon; it's so good! Amounts don't have to be exact, but you'll need about 10 ounces each of salmon and halibut.

For an interesting show, serve the ceviche in chunks of fresh coconut. To crack a coconut, place it on top of several layers of newspaper on a strong, stable surface—and then give it a good whack with a mallet, or some more refined hits with a pick and a hammer. You want to end up with three or four large pieces. Have some paper towels handy for the liquid that is in the center of the coconut, or catch it in a cup if you can. Some people like to drink the juice, some don't. Some people eat the coconut meat, others don't. Either way, the pieces of coconut make for a great presentation. Coconut milk is an extract of the coconut meat itself and not of the juice; you can buy cans of coconut milk at most regular supermarkets.

Slice the scallops into ¼-inch-thick circles and place in a nonreactive bowl big enough to hold all the seafood. Cut the salmon and halibut into 3 or 4 lengthwise strips about 1 inch wide, then cut these strips crosswise into ¼-inch slices to match the scallops. Add this to the scallops. Pour ¾ cup of the lime juice into the bowl and mix gently but well, making sure all the seafood gets coated with some juice. Cover and put in the refrigerator to marinate 2 hours.

Put the seafood in a colander to drain, and clean out the bowl while it's draining. Return the seafood to the clean bowl, along with the salt, pepper, chile, onion, coconut milk, and remaining ¼ cup lime juice. Mix gently but well, then cover and refrigerate at least 1 hour, but no longer than 6 hours.

When you're ready to serve, crack each of the coconuts into 3 cup-shaped pieces. Check the ceviche for seasoning and fill each of the coconut bowls with some of it. Garnish with avocado slices, a sprig of cilantro, and a drizzle of olive oil. If the coconut shells are too much trouble, just serve the ceviche in small bowls, or my favorite, in avocado halves! Serves 6

Go Fish
641 Main St.
St. Helena, CA 94574
707-963-0700
GOFISHRESTAURANT.NET

SILVERADO VINEYARDS SOLO CABERNET SAUVIGNON
MONGOLIAN PORK CHOPS
WINEMAKER JON EMMERICH, CHEF /OWNER CINDY PAWLCYN CATERING

Pork:

| 6 | pork chops, center-cut double approximately 10 ounces |

Mongolian Marinade:

1 c	hoisin sauce
1 T	sugar
1½ T	Tamari soy sauce
1½ T	sherry vinegar
1½ T	rice vinegar
1	scallion, white and two-thirds of the green parts, minced
1 t	Tabasco sauce
1½ t	black bean chile sauce, such as Lee Kum Kee
1½ t	ginger, peeled and freshly grated
1½ T	garlic, minced
¾ t	white pepper, freshly ground
¼ c	cilantro leaves and stems, minced
1 T	sesame oil

Method:

Trim the excess meat and fat away from the ends of the chop bones, leaving them exposed. Put the pork chops in a clean plastic bag and lightly sprinkle with water to prevent the meat from tearing when pounded. Using the smooth side of a meat mallet, pound the meat down to an even 1-inch thickness, being careful not to hit the bones. Alternatively, have your butcher cut thinner chops and serve 2 per serving. To make the marinade, combine all the ingredients in a bowl and mix well. Coat the pork chops liberally with the marinade and marinate for 3 hours and up to overnight in the refrigerator. You'll have extra marinade, which keeps well, refrigerated, and can be used for baby back ribs or chicken (especially chicken wings, which when smoked then grilled are great). There are two special ingredients that really make the marinade: hoisin sauce, which is a slightly sweet Chinese bean paste, and a black bean paste with chiles that is pretty spicy. Look for them in Asian markets. Try to find brands that do not contain MSG.

Prepare grill.
Place the chops on the grill and grill for 5 minutes on each side, rotating them a quarter turn after 2 to 3 minutes on each side to produce nice crosshatch marks. It's good to baste with some of the marinade as the meat cooks. As with all marinated meats, you want to go longer and slower on the grill versus shorter and hotter, because if the marinated meat is charred, it may turn bitter. The pork is ready when it registers 139° F on an instant-read thermometer. Serves 6

Silverado Vineyards
6121 Silverado Trail
Napa, Ca 94558
707-257-1770
SILVERADOVINEYARDS.COM

Wine Making Facts :
Encépagement : 85%
Cabernet Sauvignon,
7% Cabernet Franc, 5%
Merlot, 2% Petit Verdot
Appellation : Napa Valley, Atlas
Peak, Rutherford, Oakville
Vineyard : Multiple Vineyards
throughout the Napa Valley
North to South, East to West,
85% Mountain Fruit
Elevation : 200 feet – 2000 feet
Average Vine Age : Mature Vineyards
Yield : 3 – 5 tons/acre
Alcohol Level : 14.1
Total Production : 28,000 cases
Harvest Details : Hand picked into
½ ton macro bins; 24.5 °Brix, 0.59
TA, 3.60 pH (weighted average)
Facility : Silver Oak Cellars, Oakville
Fermentation : 1.5 week
primary fermentation, 86°F max
temp, 2 pump-overs daily
Maceration : 3 weeks total on skins
Wood Origin : American, Missouri
Oak Regimen : 24 months
Percentage of New Barrels : 100%

" A complex and elegant wine that balances the expression of fruity and savory elements with finesse. The wine has a dark ruby color with a purple edge and displays aromas of black plum, soy sauce, chocolate, rose petals, cedar and black olive. It has a soft, velvety attack and a fruity, floral and spicy mid-palate. The finish is long and smooth with well integrated tannins. " DB

SILVER OAK CELLARS
915 OAKVILLE CROSSROAD
OAKVILLE, CA 94562
707-942-7022
SILVEROAK.COM

SILVER OAK

— 2004 —

Napa Valley Cabernet Sauvignon

SOMMELIERS, MATURE BORDEAUX GLASS

SILVER OAK CABERNET SAUVIGNON
MOROCCAN SPICE LAMB SAUSAGE PIZZA
WINEMAKER DANIEL BARON, WINERY CHEF DOMINIC ORSINI

Ingredients:

1 ea	Napolitana pizza dough (or purchased)
½ c	herb pesto
½ c	shredded mozzarella
¼ c	feta cheese
4 oz	lamb sausage, cooked and chopped
1 T	pine nuts
1 t	preserved lemon (diced)
1 t	mint leaves, fresh

Lamb sausage:

1 lb	ground lamb
4	garlic cloves (chopped)
¼ t	ground cumin
¼ t	ground ginger
¼ t	salt

⅛ t	ground cinnamon
⅛ t	black pepper
⅛ t	ground coriander
⅛ t	ground allspice

Napolitana pizza dough:

¼ t	dry active yeast
1½ c	water (100˚-105˚F)
2 t	extra virgin olive oil
3 c	AP flour
1 c	cake flour
2 t	salt

Materials:

pizza stone

Lamb sausage:
By hand, mix together until the spices are evenly distributed throughout the meat.
Press flat onto a cookie tray and bake at 350° F. for 20 minutes.

Napolitana pizza dough:
This pizza dough recipe is not your "let have pizza tonight" recipe, but you may substitute with purchased. To fully develop the deep yeast flavor takes time, at least 24 - 48 hours. I always save some dough from the previous batch and mix it into the next batch.

In an electric mixing bowl, stir water and yeast together, let stand for 10 minutes.
Add the olive oil, flour, and salt. Using the dough hook attachment, mix the dough ten minutes.
Rest for 5 minutes; then mix an additional ten minutes.
Invert the dough; make into a ball, oil bowl and dough, cover with plastic and refrigerate overnight.
The next day punch down the dough with your fist and divide into four pieces.
Using a little bit of flour to keep it from sticking, form into 4 separate balls.
Cover the dough balls with a little bit more oil and a damp cloth.
Let sit at room temperature until doubled, 1-3 hours.
While the dough is proofing, place a pizza stone in the oven and preheat at highest setting.
Place the dough ball onto a floured work surface. With your finger tips gently flatten the dough into a disc. Press dough with palm of hand while pulling the dough outward and rotating your palm clockwise to turn dough. Continue this process until the pizza is approximately 10-12 inches in diameter.
Place the pizza shell onto a well floured wooden pizza peel. Top the pizza with ingredients and slide onto the pizza stone. Bake for 10 minutes or until the dough is crispy and golden. When the pizza is finished baking sprinkle with pine nuts, preserved lemon, and mint leaves. 4 servings

Estate Bottled

2006

SPRING MOUNTAIN

V I N E Y A R D

Sauvignon Blanc

Napa Valley

No. 13285

4 14,400 Bottles

Since 1873

SPRING MOUNTAIN VINEYARD SAUVIGNON BLANC
OLIVE OIL POACHED THAI SNAPPER, WHITE BEAN SAUCE, ARTICHOKES, CLAMS
WINEMAKER JAC COLE, ROBERT CURRY EXECUTIVE CHEF ~ AUBERGE DU SOLEIL

Wine Making Facts :
Encépagement : Estate Bottled Sauvignon
Blanc 99%, Semillon 1%
Appellation : Napa Valley, Spring Mountain District
Vineyard : Miravalle and La Perla
Elevation : 500 feet and 1100 feet above sea level
Average Vine Age : 10 years
Yield : 1.5 tons per acre
Alcohol Level : 14.6%
Total Production : 1130 cases
Winemaking : Since 1993, our estate grown Sauvignon Blanc has
been styled along the lines of a fine white Bordeaux. The grapes are
whole cluster pressed and the juice is cold settled overnight. It is
then moved to French oak barrels where fermentation is completed.
The wine is kept sur-lie for 8-10 months to marry its bright flavors
and acidity with the toasty elements provided by barrel contact.
Batonnage and extended sur lie aging create a texture that weaves
layers of fruit and vanilla into a rich and complete wine.
Winemaking : Barrel fermentation in neutral French oak. Facility :
Estate Bottled ~ Spring Mountain Vineyard
Fermentation : Neutral French oak barrels
Wood Origin : France
Oak Regimen : 6-8 months with weekly
sur-lie batonnage.

SPRING MOUNTAIN VINEYARD
2805 SPRING MOUNTAIN RD
ST HELENA, CA 94574
707-967-4188
SPRINGMOUNTAINVINEYARD.COM

VINUM XL, RIESLING-SAUVIGNON BLANC

"Effusive in its expression of the site specific soils and climate. A floral perfume enhanced by white peach, nectarine, Asian pear and Meyer lemon and a subtle herbal quality offer a mouth-watering invitation to the wine. Rich on the palate, the abundant layers of fruit, linden and minerals mirror its aromatics. A crisp acidity balances a lush mouth-feel, making its lingering impression one of completeness." JC

More than a century ago, Napa Valley's first immigrants looked not to the valley floor but to the hillsides to plant their vineyards. Among them were a German, a Frenchman, and a man of Mexican birth, each of whom built majestic wine estates on Spring Mountain. Today these historic estates comprise a single property with lavish Old World architecture surrounded by 120-year-old olive trees, gardens, and vineyards. The winery houses both 19th and 20th century caves. Guided visitors can walk through the estate's grounds and enjoy a cave tasting of current releases. Employing ancient techniques with modern technology, owner Jacob E. Safra puts his greatest passion into Elivette, a singular, Bordeaux-styled wine that expresses the soul of this special property.

SPRING MOUNTAIN VINEYARD CABERNET SAUVIGNON AND ELIVETTE
BRAISED BEEF RIBS, HORSERADISH POTATOES, BLUE CHEESE CREAM SPINACH
WINEMAKER JAC COLE, PROFESSIONAL CHEF DOUG WELDON

SPRING MOUNTAIN VINEYARD
2805 SPRING MOUNTAIN RD
ST HELENA, CA 94574
707-967-4188
SPRINGMOUNTAINVINEYARD.COM

Wine Making Facts :
Encépagement : Cabernet Sauvignon
Petit Verdot, Cabernet Franc
Appellation : Spring Mountain District
Vineyard : Estate Bottled
Soils: Elevation : 400 – 1600 feet
Aspect : Predominantly Eastern facing
Micro-Climate : Multiple
Average Vine Age : 13 years
Yield : 1.5 tons per acre
Alcohol Level : 14.7%
Total Production : 3954 cases
Philosophy : To create a bold, accessible
expression of Spring Mountain terroir.
Winemaking notes: Winemaking from a vineyard
perspective. Culturing the grapes to maturity and
concentration levels that facilitate wine production.
Fermentation : All of our Bordeaux varieties
experience a three day cold soak prior to
the start of fermentation. Each tank is then
individually managed to maximize extraction.
Wood Origin : France
Percentage of New Barrels : 80-100%
Coopers : Taransaud, Saury, Le Grand

Wine Making Facts :
Encépagement : Cabernet Sauvignon,
Petit Verdot, Merlot
Cabernet Franc 4%
Appellation : Spring Mountain District
Vineyard : Estate Bottled
Elevation: 400 – 1600 feet
Alcohol Level : 14.4%
Total Production : 3419 cases
Philosophy : To create a stylized Bordeaux blend
that expresses unique vineyard sites through the
lens of the Spring Mountain Vineyard terroir.
Fermentation : All of our Bordeaux varieties
experience a three day cold soak prior to
the start of fermentation. Each tank is then
individually managed to maximize extraction.
Wood Origin : France
Percentage of New Barrels : 80-100% new
French oak depending on lot and vintage
Coopers : Taransaud, Saury, Le Grand,
Quintessence, Darnajou

"Laden with loads of chocolate and rich, ripe fruit, specifically blackberry, cherry and plum. The palate is bright, full-bodied and balanced. Jammy fruit, toasty oak and hints of licorice and spice round out the wine. In its youth, it will benefit from decanting." JC

" Potent aromas of chocolate and raspberry jam laced with baking spices make an enticing first impression, lavishly surrounded by floral notes of lavender and violet, and supported by earthy, mineral notes. The wine offers an elegant, seamless, full-bodied attack with loads of cocoa, blackberry and black cherry fruit. Malleable tannins fill the palate and give a well-proportioned shape to the wine. Structured in the style of a classic Bordeaux, this wine will age gracefully for 10 to 20 years.." JC

SOMMELIERS, BORDEAUX GRAND CRU

Spring Mountain Vineyard Sauvignon Blanc
Olive Oil Poached Thai Snapper, White Bean Sauce, Artichokes, Clams
Winemaker Jac Cole, Robert Curry Executive Chef ~ Auberge du Soleil

4, 5 oz	Thai Snapper fillets
12 ea	Manila clams, rinsed
1 btl	Sauvignon Blanc
2 ea	shallots, peeled and diced
¾	thyme, bunch
3 cloves	garlic, 1 peeled, minced, 2 halved
1 oz	bacon
6 ea	baby artichokes
1	lemon
½	onion, peeled and large dice
½	carrot, peeled and sliced
10	black peppercorns
1	bay leaf
2 c	chicken stock
2½ oz	olive oil, extra virgin
2	tomatoes, peeled, seeded and diced
16	Nicoise olives, pitted
4	baby fennel bulb, trimmed
1	chive bunch , chopped

1 t	red wine vinegar
tt	salt
tt	black pepper, freshly ground
1 qt	olive oil, extra virgin

White Bean-Virgin Olive Oil Sauce:

¼ c	white beans, dried
¼ oz	bacon
1 qt	chicken stock
½	onion, peeled
½	carrot, peeled
10	black peppercorns
1	bay leaf
2	garlic cloves, minced
¼	thyme, bunch
2	olive oil, extra virgin
tt	salt

In a small pot add the bacon, onion, carrot, ¼ bunch thyme, 2 cloves of garlic cut in half, peppercorns, bay leaf, ½ of the bottle of wine, chicken stock, and 1 ounce of the extra virgin olive oil. Squeeze the juice into the pot and add lemon to the pot. With a paring knife remove the outer leaves from the artichokes, peel the stems and remove the tops. Add the artichokes directly to the pot and cover with a clean kitchen towel. Season with salt and bring to a simmer. Remove from the heat when a knife can go into the artichokes without resistance. Cut the artichokes in half and reserve in the liquid. In a small pot place the clams, remaining Sauvignon Blanc, thyme, one of the diced shallot, and the minced garlic. Place a lid on the pot and steam the clams over high heat until they open. Remove clams from the shells. Pass the cooking liquid through a chinois and cool. Reserve the clams in the liquid.
Bring a small pot of salted water to a boil; add the baby fennel and cook until tender.
Shock in ice water, remove from the water and reserve.

Heat olive oil to 140° F.
Season the snapper with salt and pepper. Poach the fish in one quart of extra virgin olive oil.
In a pot slowly warm the artichokes, fennel, clams and 3 to 4 ounces of the clam's liquid.
Add the remaining diced shallots, one ounce extra virgin olive oil, olives, tomatoes, chives, red wine vinegar.
Heat until hot and season with salt and pepper. Divide on four warm plates, place the poached snapper on top.

White Bean-Virgin Olive Oil Sauce
Soak beans in water and refrigerate 8 hours.
In a small pot render out the bacon, over low heat without coloring. Add the stock and beans.
Make a bouquet garni of pepper, bay leaf, garlic, and thyme, add it to the beans and simmer.
About ¾ of the way through cooking season with salt. Cook the beans until soft.
Remove the bacon, onion, carrot and bouquet garni.
Place the beans and stock in a blender. Blend until smooth while slowly adding the olive oil.
Season with salt. Pass through chinois and reserve hot. 4 servings

AUBERGE DU SOLEIL
180 RUTHERFORD HILL ROAD
RUTHERFORD, CA 94573
800-348-5406
AUBERGEDUSOLEIL.COM

Spring Mountain Vineyard Elivette and Cabernet Sauvignon
Braised Beef Ribs, Horseradish Potatoes, Blue Cheese Cream Spinach
Winemaker Jac Cole, Professional Chef Doug Weldon

Short Ribs:
4	beef short ribs, 6 oz portion
1	onion, ½ inch dice
½ c	carrot, ½ inch dice
½ c	celery, ½ inch dice
3 – 4	thyme sprigs
3 – 4	sage leaves
2 – 3	roma tomatoes, ½ inch dice
1 c	red wine
4 c.	veal stock

Spinach:
1	spinach bunch
1 T	butter
2 T	shallot

Horseradish Mashed Potatoes:
1 lb	Russet potatoes, peeled, boiled, strained, mashed
4 T	butter
½ c	sour cream
¼ c	chives, minced
tt	horseradish, prepared or fresh

Blue Cheese Béchamel:
3 T	butter
4 T	flour
1 c	milk
4 oz	blue cheese, crumbled

Preheat oven to 300º F.
Season and sear short ribs in olive oil; remove and set aside.
In same pan, sauté onion, carrot, and celery for 2 – 3 minutes.
Add thyme and sage; cook 2 more minutes.
Add tomatoes, wine and ribs; simmer and reduce by half.
Add stock, cover and braise in oven for about 2 – 3 hours or until done.
Remove ribs and set aside; strain stock, discard solids and reduce stock to sauce consistency.

Horseradish Mashed Potatoes:
Peel and boil potatoes; strain and mash.
Fold in the butter and season.
Add sour cream and chives.
Add horseradish to taste.
Add cream or milk if needed.

Blue Cheese Béchamel:
Melt butter over low heat and add flour.
Gently whisk in milk; simmer 2 – 3 minutes.
Fold in blue cheese; remove from heat and set aside.

Spinach:
Sweat shallots in butter 2 – 3 minutes.
Add spinach and cook until wilted.
Add enough blue cheese béchamel to coat.

Serving:
Mound mashed potatoes, place short ribs on top, arrange spinach to the side and top with several spoonfuls of sauce. 4 servings

SPRING MOUNTAIN VINEYARD
2805 SPRING MOUNTAIN RD
ST HELENA, CA 94574
707-967-4188
SPRINGMOUNTAINVINEYARD.COM

STERLING VINEYARDS MERLOT
WILD MUSHROOM LASAGNA WITH RICOTTA AND BELLWETHER FARMS CRESCENZA CHEESE AND SPINACH
WINEMAKER MIKE WESTRICK, EXECUTIVE CHEF POLLY LAPPETITO ~ RESTAURANT AT CIA GREYSTONE

Encépagement : Napa Valley Merlot
Vineyard : Fruit was sourced from various Napa Valley vineyards, ranging from Calistoga to Carneros, each contributing different and unique characteristics ranging from Calistoga to Carneros
Soils : Lean, rocky soils to clay loam
Elevation : Valley floor to 1,000 feet
Micro-Climate : Climatic Region III
Average Vine Age : 20 years
Winemaking : Keeping the lots separate, we put the wine to barrel, some before malolactic fermentation and some after. After 12 months of aging in a combination of new and used barrels, the various lots were blended and bottled. Small amounts of the other Bordelaise varietals add a note of complexity to the finished wine.
Fermentation : Fermented in stainless steel tanks for about 10 days
Maceration : About four-day pre-fermentation cold soak at about 50°F. No post fermentation maceration with Merlot
Wood Origin : American and French
Oak Regiment : About 12 months in barrels

STERLING VINEYARDS
1111 DUNAWEAL LANE
CALISTOGA, CA 94515
800-726-6136
STERLINGVINEYARDS.COM

VITIS, BORDEAUX WINE GLASS

"Bright ruby in color, this lovely wine offers aromas of ripe black cherries, raspberries and cedar. Luscious fruit flavors of blackberries and cherries accented by a touch of toasty oak lead to a long, silky finish." MW

Sterling Vineyards is perched high above the Valley floor and is, quite possibly, the most unique winery tour in Napa Valley. From its roots, Sterling Vineyards has had an iconic past, and from its skies provides a dreamlike exploration. Guests glide up the mountain in aerial trams to become immersed in stunning and panoramic views. The bold beauty of the winery's Greek-inspired architecture and new state-of-the-art winery sits at the summit. This is where the skilled winemaking team is dedicated exclusively to the production of Sterling Vineyards Reserve wines. "We capture the essence of each varietal and *terroir* in the bottle by creating concentrated, balanced and finessed wines. Our Reserve Merlot, for example, is harvested primarily by flavor, for its strong black cherry and berry flavors, a spicy character and ripe tannins." says winemaker, Mike Westrick. Artistic winemaking gives Sterling Vineyards Reserve wines their most profound varietal expression and allows them to honor their unique and diverse origins with great depth and complexity.

Sterling Vineyards Merlot
Wild Mushroom Lasagna with Ricotta and Bellwether Farms Crescenza Cheese and Spinach
Winemaker Mike Westrick, Executive Chef Polly Lappetito ~ Restaurant at CIA Greystone

1 lb	fresh lasagna pasta
½ c	olive oil
¼ c	minced shallot
2 t	fresh thyme leaves
½ lb	mushrooms (wild mushrooms such as chanterelles or, if not available, a combination of brown cremini and portobello), cut into ¼-inch slices
¾ t	kosher salt, or as needed
¼ t	freshly ground black pepper, or as needed
1 lb	baby spinach
15 oz	whole milk ricotta cheese (about 1 pint)

7 oz	crescenza cheese
1 c	freshly grated Parmigiano Reggianno cheese

Velouté:

1 qt	chicken stock
¼ c	unsalted butter
¼ c	all-purpose flour
½ t	kosher salt
tt	Freshly ground white pepper

Resources:
Cookbook *Seasons in the Wine Country: Recipes from the CIA at Greystone* by Cate Conniff

1. Preheat the oven to 375°F.
2. Cut the pasta into enough pieces to make three layers in a 13-by-9-by-2-inch glass lasagna pan. You may have extra pasta, as these sheets come in different sizes.
3. In a large stockpot over high heat, bring 8 quarts of salted water to a boil. Have three 13-inch pieces of waxed or parchment paper on the counter. Add the pasta sheets to the water and cook according to the package directions until just tender, about 3 minutes. Drain carefully so as not to rip sheets. Spread the drained pasta out on the waxed paper and brush the pasta with about 1 tablespoon of olive oil. Press a second piece of waxed paper on top of the pasta sheets. Turn the sheets over, carefully pull back the waxed paper and brush the other side of the pasta with another tablespoon of olive oil. Press the sheets of waxed paper back onto pasta. Stored this way, the pasta will keep at room temperature for a couple of hours.
4. In a large soup pot, heat ¼ cup of the olive oil over medium heat. Add the shallots and thyme and sauté until lightly golden, about 4 minutes. Add the mushrooms, toss to coat with the oil and shallots and sauté until the mushrooms are golden, just tender, and have released liquid, about 10 minutes. Turn the heat to medium high and cook until most of the liquid has evaporated, about 4 minutes. Season with ½ teaspoon of the salt and 1/8 teaspoon of the black pepper (8 grinds). Reserve until needed (this will make about 3 cups). This can be made up to a day in advance and refrigerated.
5. In a large stock or soup pot, heat the remaining 2 tablespoons of olive oil over medium-high heat. Add the spinach, toss to coat with the oil, and sauté until wilted, about 5 minutes. Season the mixture with the remaining ¼ teaspoon of salt and 1/8 teaspoon of black pepper. Reserve until needed (this will make about 2 cups). This can also be made up to a day in advance and refrigerated.
6. To make the velouté: In a 3- quart saucepan over medium-high heat, bring the chicken stock to a simmer.
7. In a heavy 3-quart saucepan, melt the butter over low heat. Add the flour to the butter and cook, stirring continuously, until the roux is very lightly browned and fragrant, about 4 minutes. Gradually add the stock, whisking constantly, until the stock and roux are well blended. Bring the mixture to a simmer over medium to medium-low heat, and simmer, stirring frequently to incorporate any skin that forms, until the velouté is thick enough to coat the back of a spoon, about 30 minutes. Season with ½ teaspoon of salt and a few grinds of white pepper.
8. To assemble the lasagna: Pour half of the velouté (about 1 cup) into the bottom of the lasagna dish. Gently lay enough pasta sheets to cover the veloute evenly. Evenly sprinkle half of the spinach (about 1 cup), mushrooms (about 1 ½ cups), and ricotta (about 1 cup) over the pasta, making sure to bring ingredients evenly to the edges. Drizzle½ cup velouté over the layers. Gently place another layer of pasta sheets over the ricotta. Repeat with the remaining spinach, mushrooms, ricotta, and veloute. Gently place another layer of pasta sheets. Break the crescenza into tiny pieces (this cheese is gooey, so do your best to squeeze into ½ -inch pieces) and sprinkle evenly over pasta. Sprinkle the Parmesan evenly over the dish.
9. Cover the lasagna with a piece of aluminum foil and place on the middle rack of the oven. 10. Bake for 30 minutes. Uncover and rotate the dish in the oven. Bake the lasagna until bubbly and golden, 20 to 25 minutes. Remove from the oven and let sit for at least 15 minutes before serving. Serves 6 to 8

STERLING VINEYARDS
1111 DUNAWEAL LANE
CALISTOGA, CA 94515
800-726-6136
STERLINGVINEYARDS.COM

St. Supéry Virtú White Meritage
Heirloom Carrot Soup with Crispy Carrot Confetti
Winemaker Michael Scholz, Professional Chef Gary Penir

Wine Making Facts :
Appellation : Napa Valley
Blend : Sauvignon Blanc, Semillon
Total Acidity : 5.8 g/L
Residual Sugar : 0.05 g/L
Wine Alcohol : 13.5%
History : Established in 1996 by the Skalli
Family to create the finest
White Bordeaux in Napa Valley.
Harvest Details : Harvested at night and in the cool
early morning hours of August and September
to maintain the delicate fruit flavors.
Soils : Deep sandy-clay-loam, varying
compositions valley and valley floor
Philosophy : balanced, rich and expressive Meritage
blend reflecting the terroir of the estate vineyards
with the structure for long-term aging
Fermentation : long, cool fermentation
allowed for excellent flavor retention
Barrels : predominately in French oak barrels
Facility : St. Supéry Winery
Bottling Formats : 375 mL, 750 mL, 1.5 L, 3 L, 6 L

St. Supéry
8440 St. Helena Hwy
Rutherford, CA 94573
707-963-4507
STSUPERY.COM

Vinum XL, Sauvignon Blanc Glass

"Refined and luscious with aromas of nectarines, peach and ripe cantaloupe. On the palate, the mouth-watering flavors of peaches and nectarines are joined by a subtle mineral quality. "MS

Like a good Meritage, St. Supéry's vineyards represent a perfect blend. Its Rutherford vineyard and winery reflect the long heritage of winemaking in this celebrated appellation. Its Dollarhide vineyard, located in the northeast corner of Napa Valley, is an historic horse ranch with a completely different microclimate and a diversity of soils, topography, and wildlife. Together they produce some of California's most notable, estate-bottled wines. Visitors enjoy monthly art exhibits or, on weekends, try the Divine Wine Room for selected tastings of estate wines, food pairings, and knowledgeable insights from St. Supéry's friendly, approachable staff. Outside, the shaded grounds include a parc and boules for the traditional game of pétanque.

ÉLU

NAPA VALLEY RED WINE

ST. SUPÉRY

BOTTLED BY ST. SUPÉRY VINEYARDS & WINERY

14.3% ALCOHOL BY VOLUME

CALIFORNIA 94573

St. Supéry Élu
Roasted Venison, Wild Blackberry Sauce, Creamy Porcini Polenta
Winemaker Michael Scholz, Chef/Owner Bob Hurley ~ Hurley's Restaurant

Wine Making Facts :
Encépagement : Cabernet Sauvignon, Merlot, Petit Verdot, Cabernet Franc, and Malbec
Appellation : Napa Valley
Vineyards : Dollarhide, Hardester and Rutherford Estate Vineyards
Soils : Deep sandy-clay-loam
Elevation : 80-800 ft.
Average Vine Age : 27 years
Yield : 2 tons/acre
Alcohol Level : 14.1%
Philosophy : Balanced, rich and expressive Cabernet Sauvignon reflecting the terroir of the estate vineyards with the structure for long-term aging
Harvest Details : Early morning August 31- October 5
Facility : St. Supéry Winery
Maceration : 48-hour cold soak, selected lots held for extended maceration post- fermentation for 10-20 days.
Wood Origin : 50% French, 50% American
Oak Regimen : 19 months of barrel aging.

St. Supéry
8440 St. Helena Hwy
Rutherford, CA 94573
707-963-4507
STSUPERY.COM

SOMMELIERS BLACK TIE CABERNET SAUVIGNON

"Luxurious, rich and concentrated with aromas of cherry, currant and blueberry. These are just the start of this 2004 Cabernet Sauvignon. The harmonious flavors of black cherry, anise and plush cassis explode upon tasting. This is a classic Napa Valley Cabernet which is wonderful young but has everything it needs to age beautifully."

Winemaker Michael Scholz

St. Supéry Virtú White Meritage
Heirloom Carrot Soup with Crispy Carrot Confetti
Winemaker Michael Scholz, Professional Chef Gary Penir

Ingredients:

4 ea	Heirloom orange carrots, peeled and sliced into disks
1	shallot, diced
12 ea	Heirloom baby purple carrots, peeled and cooked
1	garlic clove, chopped
2 T	butter
½ c	heavy cream
½ c	chicken stock or water

Purple Carrots:

12 ea	purple carrots
1 t	olive oil
tt	salt and pepper

Carrot Oil:

1	carrot top bunch, keep rubber band on
½ c	pure olive oil (not extra virgin)

Method:
Sweat shallot and garlic in butter until fragrant.
Add carrots and sweat for 5 minutes, add cream and stock to cover, cook until tender.
Strain carrots and reserve cooking liquid.
Place carrots in the blender with some liquid and puree; add liquid until consistency is achieved.
Season to taste with salt.

Purple Carrots Method:
Gently peel carrots making sure there is purple color left on the carrots.
Cook in boiling salted water until tender.
Strain and glaze in olive oil, season with salt and pepper.

Crispy Carrots and Tops Method:
Using a mandolin with the middle size teeth, shred carrot to achieve fine strands..
Coat strands with cornstarch and fry at 300° degrees until crispy, drain and season with salt.
Fry carrot tops in the same oil until transparent, oil will pop so be careful! Season.

Carrot Oil Method:
Blanch Carrot tops in salted boiling water for 30 seconds, shock in an ice water bath.
Squeeze all the water out of carrot tops, discard rubber band.
Blend carrot tops and olive oil until pureed, strain though a coffee filter.

Plating:
Pour soup into bowl.
Stack three purple carrots in the center of the bowl.
Garnish with crispy carrots, crispy carrot tops, and carrot top oil. 4 servings

St. Supéry Élu
Roasted Venison, Wild Blackberry Sauce, Creamy Porcini Polenta
Winemaker Michael Scholz, Chef/Owner Bob Hurley ~ Hurley's Restaurant

Venison Marinade:

3 lb	venison loin or leg
	(sinew and connective tissue removed)
10	juniper berries, crushed
2	bay leaves, crumbled
10	sage leaves, fresh, chopped
15	black peppercorns
1 c	olive oil

Blackberry Sauce:

1 t	butter, unsalted
1	shallot, peeled, fine dice
½ t	sugar
1 oz	raspberry vinegar
3 c	veal stock
1 pt	blackberries, fresh

Porcini Polenta:

2 c	polenta
8 c	water
2 lb	mushrooms, assorted wild or exotic
	(shiitake, oyster, chanterelle, etc.) sliced
2 oz	olive oil
½ c	assorted herbs (thyme, sage, and
	tarragon) fresh, chopped
4 T	shallots, chopped
2 c	chicken stock
1 oz	mushrooms, dried porcini, chopped
1 c	parmesan cheese, grated
4 T	butter

Venison Marinade:
Combine all ingredients and marinate venison for 12 - 24 hours turning once or twice.

Blackberry Sauce:
Sauté shallots in butter and cook until translucent, about 3 -4 minutes. Add sugar and cook until it begins to caramelize. Add vinegar and reduce by half. Add veal stock and ½ pint of blackberries and simmer, skimming off the impurities that rise. Reduce to one cup and strain. Put sauce back on the fire, season and add the remaining ½ pint of berries.
Let cook for 2 minutes, take off heat and reserve.

Venison:
Pre-heat oven to 350º F.
Season venison and sear on all sides in olive oil. Cook in oven until rare to medium-rare, 8 – 10 minutes (don't overcook it or meat will be dry). Remove and let rest for 10 minutes.

Porcini Polenta:
Add polenta to boiling water in a steady stream while stirring. Return to a boil, stirring constantly, until polenta begins to dissolve and does not stick to bottom of pan.
Turn heat on low, simmer and cook for approximately 20 to 30 minutes.
Add more water, if needed, to maintain a very thick consistency that pours.

Mushrooms:
Sauté mushrooms in olive oil, 2 – 3 minutes. Add chopped herbs and shallots and sauté for another minute. Add chicken stock and dried porcini mushrooms. Cook until all liquid has evaporated. Set aside.

When polenta is smooth and creamy, add mushroom mixture, parmesan cheese and butter.
Season with salt and pepper. Pour into pan ¾ inch deep or greater and refrigerate for four hours or overnight. Unmold and cut into shapes; grill or brown in a pan or bake.
Rub pieces with olive oil and place on hot clean oiled grill until grill marks appear. Set aside.
Finish in oven at 350º F for approximately ten minutes and set aside. 4 servings

HURLEY'S RESTAURANT AND BAR
6518 WASHINGTON STREET
YOUNTVILLE, CA 94599
707-944-2345
HURLEYSRESTAURANT.COM

SWANSON CHARDONNAY
SILK HANDERCHIEFS AL PESTO
WINEMAKER CHRIS PHELPS, CHEF/PARTNER DONNA SCALA ~ BISTRO DON GIOVANNI

Wine Making Facts :
Encépagement : 100% Chardonnay
Appellation : Oakville, Napa Valley
Vineyard : Oakville Estate
Soils : Clear Lake and Bale loams
Elevation : 155 feet
Aspect : 2% slope, Valley floor
Micro-Climate : Slightly cooler than Rutherford,
key marine layer influence during summer months
Average Vine Age : 10 years
Alcohol Level : 14.8%
Total Production : 396 cases
Philosophy : Sustainable farming practices,
minimalist winemaking
Harvest Details : September 9th. Very small
clusters and low vine.
Yield : Very concentrated flavors, crisp acid
Facility : Swanson, Rutherford
Fermentation : 10 -12 ° Celsius peak temperature
Wood Origin : Neutral (5-year-old)
Barrels : French oak and stainless steel barrels
Oak Regimen : 20 months in barrel,
stirring on the lees
Fining/Filtering : Unfined and minimal filtration
Bottling Format : 750 ml
Bottled : August 2008

SWANSON VINEYARDS
1271 MANLEY LANE
NAPA, CA 94558
707-967-3500
SWANSONVINEYARDS.COM

SOMMELIERS, MONTRACHET WINE GLASS

"A luxurious wine, in all senses of the term. The color is rich and golden. The nose is complex, showing Meyer lemon, minerals and a hint of hazelnut. On the palate, it is immediately succulent, with a slight sweetness upon entry, followed by citrus zest and a ripe, creamy Chardonnay texture evocative of reputable Chablis. As always, no new oak, no ML, no residual sugar." CP

In 1985, when W. Clarke Swanson, Jr. decided to develop a viticultural estate, he hired legendary vintner André Tchelistcheff as his chief technical consultant. Tchelistcheff advised him to plant the then relatively unknown varietal Merlot in his Oakville vineyard. Swanson Vineyards, family-owned and operated, has grown to become the largest single Estate producer of Merlot in the Valley, while Oakville has emerged as one of Napa's foremost red wine appellations. From the beginning, Swanson has followed the domaine model of Europe's premier wine regions by maintaining complete control over all aspects of farming and winemaking.

SWANSON
VINEYARDS
OAKVILLE
NAPA VALLEY
Alexis
2005
CABERNET SAUVIGN
SWANSON
VINEYARDS
OAKVILLE
NAPA VALLEY
2005
MERLOT
Alexis

SWANSON ALEXIS CABERNET SAUVIGNON AND SWANSON MERLOT
BEEF TENDERLOIN, MUSHROOM ORZO, CRISPY BEET CHIPS AND HORSERADISH CRÈME FRAÎCHE
WINEMAKER CHRIS PHELPS, PROFESSIONAL CHEF GRAHAM ZANOW

SWANSON VINEYARDS
1271 MANLEY LANE
NAPA, CA 94558
707-967-3500
SWANSONVINEYARDS.COM

Wine Making Facts :
Encépagement : Alexis, 90% Cabernet, 10% Merlot
Appellation : Oakville, Napa Valley
Vineyard : Schmidt Ranch
Soils : Gravelly and sandy loams
Elevation : 175 - 200 feet
Aspect : 2% slope, Mayacamas benchland
Average Vine Age : 14 years
Alcohol Level : 14.8%
Total Production : 1,817 cases
Philosophy : Sustainable farming practices, minimalist winemaking
Harvest Details : October 15 - 27
Fermentation : 30° C peak temperature
Maceration : 28 days, including initial cold soak
Wood Origin : 100% French oak
Oak Regimen : 20 months in barrel
Bottling Format : 750 ml, 1.5L, 3.0L, 6.0L
Bottled : May 2007

Wine Making Facts :
Encépagement : 76% Merlot, 19% Syrah, 5% Cabernet Sauvignon
Appellation : Oakville, Napa Valley
Vineyard : Oakville Estate, Schmidt Ranch
Soils : Bale and Clear Lake loams
Elevation : 155 - 200 feet
Micro-Climate : Key marine layer influence during summer months
Average Vine Age : 15 years
Alcohol Level : 14.8%
Philosophy : Sustainable farming practices, minimalist winemaking
Harvest Details : September 29 to October 25, fantastic phenolic maturity.
Facility : Swanson, Rutherford
Fermentation : 30° C peak temperature
Maceration : 20 days, including initial cold soak
Wood Origin : 50% French oak, 50% American oak
Oak Regimen : 18 months in barrel
Coopers : Ten different sources, barrels made to winemaker Chris Phelps' specifications.

" This wine exhibits such heady aromas of ripe black-berry, cassis, black licorice and mocha. The mouth has superb structure, with plenty of the fine-grained, round, ripe tannins we have come to expect from the Schmidt Ranch Vineyard. Lingering notes of black cherry and cassis on the palate." CP

" Smoky blackberry and black licorice aromas. Round, ripe and supple, with lingering thickness and fine-grained tannins on the palate, echoing very nicely the afore-mentioned aromas." CP

VITIS, BORDEAUX WINE GLASS

SWANSON CHARDONNAY
SILK HANDERCHIEFS AL PESTO
WINEMAKER CHRIS PHELPS, CHEF/PARTNER DONNA SCALA ~ BISTRO DON GIOVANNI

Ingredients:

½ lb	haricots verts
6	new small yellow potatoes
1 T	butter

Pasta:

1 lb	AP flour
5	eggs
2 T	dry white wine

Pesto:

2 c	basil, stems removed
½ c	Pecorino cheese
3 T	Grana Padano cheese
3 T	pine nuts, toasted
1¼ c	olive oil, extra virgin
1	garlic, clove
tt	salt

Method:
Boil new small yellow potatoes in salted water, then peel and dice when cool.

Pasta:
Knead ingredients until dough is smooth and silky.
Let rest for 1 hour.
Roll out thin sheets of dough and cut into 3-4" squares.

Pesto:
Purée basil, oil, garlic, pine nuts and salt in a blender or mortar and pestle until smooth.
Fold in cheese.

Assembly:
Cook pasta in boiling salted water.
Add potatoes and beans to the water to warm briefly.
Drain pasta, beans and potatoes and toss in a bowl. Coat mixture with pesto, butter and a little of the pasta water to emulsify the sauce. Plate and garnish with a little Pecorino cheese. 4 servings

BISTRO DON GIOVANNI
4110 HOWARD LANE
NAPA, CA 94558
707-224-3300
BISTRODONGIOVANNI.COM

SWANSON ALEXIS CABERNET SAUVIGNON AND SWANSON MERLOT
BEEF TENDERLOIN, MUSHROOM ORZO, CRISPY BEET CHIPS AND HORSERADISH CRÈME FRAÎCHE
WINEMAKER CHRIS PHELPS, PROFESSIONAL CHEF GRAHAM ZANOW

2 lb	beef tenderloin	1 lb	shiitake mushrooms
1 pt	crème fraîche	2	lemons
¼ c	fresh horseradish	3	shallots, minced
1 T	champagne vinegar	1 qt + 1 c	mushroom stock
2	large red beets	6	cloves of garlic, microplaned
2 qts	canola oil	1 bunch	chives, minced
1 lb	orzo		
1 lb	oyster mushrooms		

Preheat oven to 450 ° F.

Beef tenderloin:
Season liberally with salt and pepper. Heat a large pan over high heat with olive oil until lightly smoking.
Brown meat on all sides and place in oven for 10 minutes for medium rare.
Allow the meat to rest for at least 10 minutes.

Orzo:
In a large pot add butter, olive oil, minced shallots and garlic.
Cook until translucent.
Add the orzo and toast slightly. Add the mushroom stock and bring to a boil.
Cover and place in oven; lower temperature to 350° F bake for about 17 minutes.
Add olive oil and butter to a large sauté pan. Add the mushrooms and sauté until lightly caramelized and softened. Fold the mushrooms into the orzo and finish with lemon juice and minced chives.

Crispy beets:
Slice beets paper thin on a mandolin. Heat the canola oil until it reaches 350° F.
Place the beet slices carefully in the oil and then shut the oil off so the beets fry slowly and don't burn.
Fry for approximately two minutes or until crispy. Lay the beet chips on a paper towel to drain.
Season with salt while they are still warm.

Horseradish crème fraîche;
Combine the crème fraîche with the freshly grated horseradish and vinegar.
Mix thoroughly and season with salt and pepper.

Plating:
Slice the beef tenderloin and season the inside of the slices with salt and pepper.
Spoon the orzo in the center of the plate. Shingle the beef tenderloin slices on top of the orzo.
Spoon the horseradish sauce on top of the tenderloin medallions. Garnish with beet chips. 6 servings

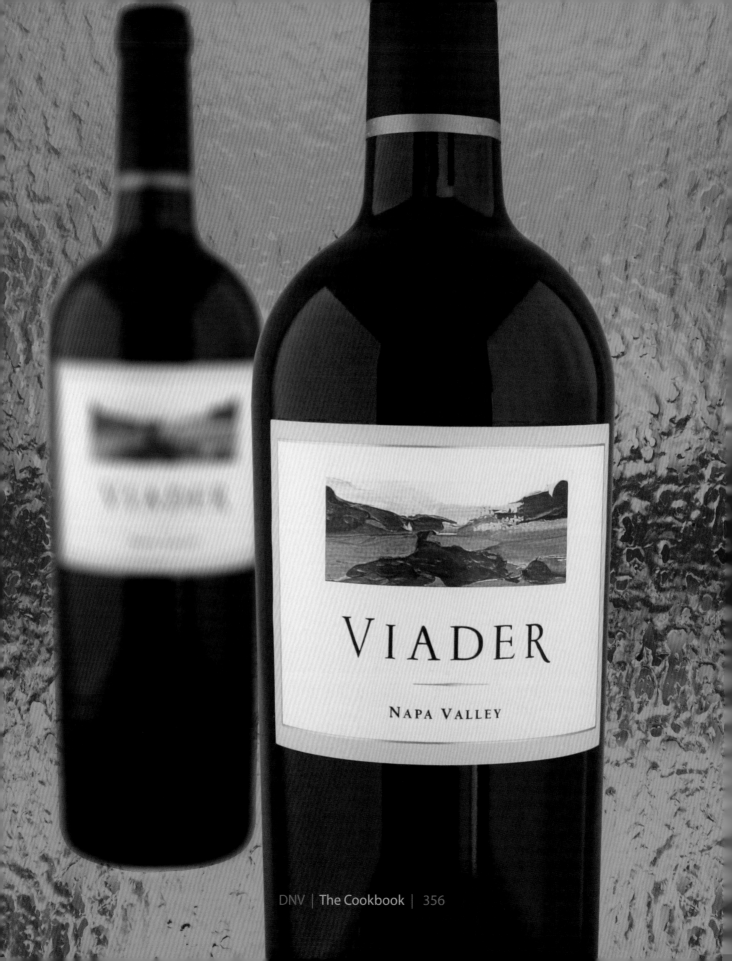

VIADER

NAPA VALLEY

VIADER
TORTILLA ESPAÑOLA WITH GARLIC AIOLI
WINEMAKERS DELIA AND ALAN VIADER, WINERY CHEF MARIELA VIADER

Wine Making Facts :

Encépagement : 69% Cabernet Sauvignon, 31% Cabernet Franc

Aspect : West facing, with vines vertically trellised down mountain

Average Vine Age : 22 years

Yield : Average 1.5 tons/acre

Alcohol Level : 14%

Total Production : 2,119 cases

Philosophy : Our vineyards are hand labored, and sustainably farmed.

Facility : VIADER Winery

Fermentation : Stainless steel and cement tanks used for fermentation. Secondary or malolactic fermentation occurs in barrel.

Maceration : About 40 days on skins

Wood Origin : France, aged 24 months

Percentage of New Barrels : 100%

Bottling : December 2007

"Exudes a sophisticated elegance, showing initial notes of mocha and tobacco leaf supporting the ripe black fruit. Enticingly sweet brown sugar notes on the nose complement currant and mineral undertones typical of wines coming from Howell Mountain's volcanic soil. On the palate, this wine shows refined, supple tannins with a persistent cashmere finish." DV & AV

VIADER VINEYARD AND WINERY
1120 DEER PARK ROAD
DEER PARK, CA 94576
707-963-3816
VIADER.COM

SOMMELIERS BORDEAUX GRAND CRU

Potato "Tortilla":		Garlic Aioli:	
¼ c	olive oil, extra virgin	3	eggs, large, yolks
12	potatoes, small white boiling, peeled, and sliced ¼ inch thick	2 T	lime juice, fresh
		1½ c	canola oil
1	onion, medium, halved, small diced	2	garlic cloves, whole
		1 t	salt
6	eggs, large		black pepper to taste

Potato Tortilla: Sauté potatoes and onion until tender but not browned; about 15 minutes. Drain oil, save and set aside potatoes. Season potatoes with salt and pepper.

Whip eggs until foamy and season with salt and pepper. Using same sauté pan, combine egg mixture, potatoes and onions and cook over low heat; about 10 minutes. Place a large plate over the skillet and carefully invert onto the plate. Add a bit of the saved oil to pan, then slowly slide cooked eggs back into the pan to cook for another 4 minutes. Remove from heat and let stand for 5 minutes. Plate and cut into wedges. Serve with the aioli on top.

Garlic aioli :

In blender, combine egg yolks, lime juice 4 tablespoons canola oil, garlic cloves, salt and pepper. Blend on high speed until creamy, about 2 minutes. Continue blending, slowly adding the remainder of the canola oil in a steady stream. 4 servings

Villa Del Lago Cabernet Sauvignon
Beef Tenderloin Wrapped in Speck with Pasticcio al Fromaggio, Chanterelles and English Peas
Winemaker Gerard Zanzonico ~ Executive Winery Chef Joshua Schwartz

Encépagement : Cabernet Sauvignon

Appellation : Rutherford

Vineyard : Pritchard Hill in Rutherford, Napa Valley

Elevation : 800 Feet

Average Vine Age : 15 years

Alcohol Level : 15.4%

Total Production : 375 cases

Harvest Details : Organic farming practices. Ground
seeded with cover crop and mowed in Spring. Green
harvest in early June followed by bunch thinning
and deleafing in September. Manual picking.

Soils : Rocky, clay-loam on both upper and lower slopes

Winemaking : Wine is drained off skins at finish of fermentation.
Only free-run is put in barrels

Fermentation : 7-10 days

Maceration : 5 day initial cold soak for more flavor development.

Wood Origin: 100% French Oak, 24 months aged with medium toast

Percentage of New Barrels: 100% New French Oak

*"Deep color, spicy bouquet, stone fruit, fleshy balanced flavors, long
finish, hint of oak, with integrated tannins." GZ*

**Villa Del Lago from
Del Dotto Estate Winery & Caves
1445 St. Helena Hwy South
St. Helena, CA 94574
707-963-2134**
DELDOTTOVINEYARDS.COM

Sommeliers Bordeaux Grand Cru

1	Filet Mignon, center cut trimmed (2.5 - 3 lb)	1 qt	milk, whole and cold	2 lb	English Peas, fresh, shucked and blanched
10	slices of speck (substitute bacon)	8 oz	Parmesan Reggiano, grated	4	garlic cloves
1 pack	Macaroni Pasticcio #2	8 oz	mascarpone	3 oz	Extra Virgin Olive Oil
4 oz	sweet butter	2 oz	bread crumbs	2 T	chopped Italian Parsley
4 oz	AP Flour	2 lb	Chanterelles	5 oz	demi glace
		½	red onion		

Beef :
Preheat oven to 350°. On parchment paper layout speck (or bacon) over lapping by a quarter inch. Season beef with salt and pepper and lay on speck. Roll the beef in the speck nice and tight then roll in the parchment and place in the fridge for at least 2 hours. Once ready pan sear your beef, rolling it slowly to get outside rendered and crispy. Place in oven and roast to desired temperature. Let meat rest for 5 minutes before slicing.

Pasticcio:
Preheat oven to 350°. Essentially Pasticcio is fancy Mac and Cheese. Bring salted water for the pasta to a rolling boil. In a sauce pot melt your butter, wisk in your flour to make a roux, cooking for 2-3 minutes then slowly incorporate the cold milk. When the sauce comes to a simmer it will start to thicken, wisk continuously. After simmering for about 5 minutes add most of the parmesan, wisk 5 more minutes then wisk in the mascarpone. Season. Cook pasta for approximately 7 minutes or el dente. Rinse pasta with cool water and place in large bowl. Add several tablespoons of cheese sauce and mix noodles to coat. Liberally oil casserole dish with vegetable spray then layer pasta noodles, trim if necessary. Continue alternating pasta then sauce until you have four layers with sauce on the top. Sprinkle generously with parmesan and bread crumbs. Bake for 25 minutes then chill in fridge till cold and firm. This will take 6-8 hours. Once chilled carefully cut out desired portions. Place on cookie sheet and reheat 5-7 minutes before serving.

Assembly:
Bring a large pot of heavily salted water to boil. Clean chanterelles by scraping the stems and brushing off any soil with a soft brush. Cut larger mushrooms in half. Dice red onion and peel and slice garlic. Sauté onion in olive oil, adding garlic and button mushrooms, let slightly brown. Add Chanterelles and sauté until tender. Finish plate with blanched peas, parsley and warmed demi glace. Serves 6

7&8
VINEYARD SEVEN AND EIGHT
ESTATE
Cabernet Sauvignon
SPRING MOUNTAIN DISTRICT
NAPA VALLEY
2007

VINEYARD 7 & 8 CABERNET SAUVIGNON AND ESTATE CABERNET SAUVIGNON
BRAISED OXTAIL, ESCAROLE AND FRENCH FINGERLING POTATOES
WINEMAKER LUC MORLET, CHEF/OWNERS CURTIS DI FEDE AND TYLER RODDE ~ OENOTRI

Wine Making Facts :
Encépagement : Estate Cabernet Sauvignon
Appellation : Spring Mountain District
Vineyard : Estate Fruit
Soils : Volcanic
Elevation : 2000 feet
Aspect : North East Facing
Average Age of Vines : 25 years
Yield : 1.5 tons/acre
Alcohol Level : 14.8%
Total Production : 600 cases
Philosophy : Focus on making wines that represent a "sense of place" and highlight the natural climate of Spring Mountain.
Harvest Details : Hand picked into small 30 pound baskets, generally beginning early October.
Facility : Estate Winery
Fermentation : Whole berry fermentation, double-hand sorting, small fermentations.
Maceration : 30 - 45 days
Wood Origin : France
Oak Regimen : 18 months
Percent New Barrels : 100%

VINEYARD 7 AND 8
4028 SPRING MOUNTAIN ROAD
ST. HELENA, CA 94574
707-963-9425
VINEYARD7AND8.COM

SOMMELIERS BLACK TIE BORDEAUX GRAND CRU

"Our Estate Cabernet exhibits a bright ruby-red color. Powerful and fruit-driven, the aromas show super-ripe blackberry, anise and cedar. The balance of ripe mountain tannins, acids and density makes a wine built to age gracefully for several decades. Each vintage, of the Estate Cabernet is made to represent the best the estate has to offer, and to remind us of a special place." LM

In the late nineteenth century, Spring Mountain district became one of the first recognized grape-growing regions in the Napa Valley. Now it's considered to be among the premier winemaking appellations in the world after a run of bad luck in the early 1900s, when Prohibition and diseased vines nearly shut it down. No wonder Launny and Weezie Steffens chose to name their new winery after two lucky numbers: "7" represents good fortune in western cultures, while "8" is lucky in eastern cultures. "There is no set formula for how we make the wine," says Winery Manager and Assistant Winemaker Wesley Steffens. "With each vintage, we let the fruit speak for itself." French-born winemaker Luc Morlet oversees a handcrafted process to produce wines that are concentrated and typical of mountain vineyards.

VINEYARD SEVEN AND EIGHT

7

Napa Valley
ernet Sauvignon
ring Mountain District
2007

VINEYARD SEVEN AND EIGHT

8

Napa Valley
Chardonnay
Spring Mountain District

VINEYARD 7 & 8 CHARDONNAY AND CABERNET SAUVIGNON
PANCETTA WRAPPED CALIFORNIA WILD HALIBUT, WARM POTATO AND CHERRY TOMATO SALAD, SALSA VERDE
WINEMAKER LUC MORLET, WINERY CHEF PETER HALL

VINEYARD 7 AND 8
4028 SPRING MOUNTAIN ROAD
ST. HELENA, CA 94574
707-963-9425
VINEYARD7AND8.COM

Wine Making Facts :
Encépagement : "8" Chardonnay
Appellation : Spring Mountain District
Vineyard : 100% Estate Fruit
Soils : Volcanic
Elevation : 2000 feet
Aspect : North East Facing
Average Age of Vines : 25 years
Yield : 1.5 tons/acre
Alcohol Level : 14.5%
Total Production : 275 cases
Philosophy : Focus on making wines that represent a "sense of place" and highlight the natural climate of Spring Mountain.
Harvest Details : Hand picked into small 30 pound baskets, generally beginning early Sept.
Facility : Estate Winery
Fermentation : Whole cluster pressed, barrel fermented with natural yeast in French oak.
Wood Origin : France
Oak Regimen : 14 months

Wine Making Facts :
Encépagement : "7" Cabernet Sauvignon
Appellation : Spring Mountain District
Soils : Volcanic
Elevation : 1600 - 2000 ft
Aspect : North East Facing
Average Age of Vines : 10-15 years
Yield : 1.5 tons/acre
Alcohol Level : 14.8%
Total Production : 725 cases
Philosophy : Focus on making a Cabernet from select growers and neighbors that highlights the natural climate and terroir of Spring Mountain.
Harvest Details : Hand picked into small 30 pound baskets, generally beginning early October.
Facility : Estate Winery
Fermentation : Whole berry fermentation, double-hand sorting, small fermentations.
Maceration : 30-45 days
Wood Origin : France
Oak Regimen : 18 months

"Exhibits a bright golden color, and displays an intense and complex bouquet of candied lemon and citrus oils, intermixed with crushed stone fruit. Full bodied with a texture that is soft and creamy, and a long finish of mineral notes that highlight the white volcanic rocky soils from the estate." LM

"Intense and rich, the 7 Cabernet displays a complex bouquet of black and red berries, intermixed with roasted and mineral notes. The youthful tannins are true to their mountain origin and will age beautifully over the next decade or more." LM

SOMMELIERS, BORDEAUX GRAND CRU WINE
SOMMELIERS, MONTRACHET WINE

VINEYARD 7 AND 8 CHARDONNAY
PANCETTA WRAPPED CALIFORNIA WILD HALIBUT, WARM POTATO AND CHERRY TOMATO SALAD, SALSA VERDE
WINEMAKER LUC MORLET, WINERY CHEF PETER HALL

Salsa Verde:

2 c	white wine
¼ c	shallots, minced
1	bay leaf
1 T	white wine vinegar
¾ c	olive oil, extra virgin
¼ c	chervil, chopped
¼ c	parsley, chopped
¼ c	chives, minced
1 T	capers, rinsed, chopped
6	anchovies, white Spanish, chopped
1	lemon, zest
1 t	thyme, minced
¼ t	white pepper, ground

Salad:

1 lb	Yukon potatoes, small, steamed or boiled, halved
2 pt	assorted heirloom cherry tomatoes, halved
2 T	olive oil
2 c	arugula, loosely packed
2 c	baby spinach leaves, loosely packed
2 c	basil leaves, loosely packed
2 c	Italian parsley leaves, loosely packed

Halibut:

4	halibut fillets, 5 ounces each
½ lb	pancetta or prosciutto, thinly sliced

Method:
Sauté shallots and bay leaf.
Add wine and reduce to ¼ cup.
Let cool and discard bay leaf.
Whisk in vinegar.
Continue whisking while slowly adding olive oil to emulsify.
Add in the rest of the ingredients, mix well and set aside.

Salad:
Toss potatoes and cherry tomatoes in olive oil.
Season with salt and pepper.
Combine with arugula, spinach, basil and parsley.
Add salsa verde to taste.
Set aside to serve at room temperature.

Halibut:
Heat oven to 350° F.
Season halibut with salt and pepper.
Wrap the middle section of the halibut fillets with one or two slices of pancetta.
Sear halibut fillets in olive oil, top side down, until lightly caramelized (about one minute).
Turn filets and finish in oven until opaque in the center (about 4 to 6 minutes depending on the thickness). Remove from oven and rest for 5 minutes.

Serving:
Divide salad onto four plates, top with halibut then spoon more salsa verde over halibut. 4 servings

DNV™ The Cookbook | 365

VINEYARD 7 AND 8
4028 SPRING MOUNTAIN ROAD
ST. HELENA, CA 94574
707-963-9425
VINEYARD7AND8.COM

VINEYARD 7 & 8 CABERNET SAUVIGNON AND ESTATE CABERNET SAUVIGNON
BRAISED OXTAIL, ESCAROLE AND FRENCH FINGERLING POTATOES
WINEMAKER LUC MORLET, CHEF/OWNERS CURTIS DI FEDE AND TYLER RODDE ~ OENOTRI

6 lb	oxtail, cut into chunks		1 c	red wine
2 c	flour		3 c	crushed tomatoes with juice
1 T	cumin		2	heads of escarole or bitter chicories
1 T	coriander		1 dz	French fingerling potatoes
1 t	cinnamon			pork stock, to cover
¼ c	extra virgin olive oil			salt and pepper
4	garlic cloves			
1	red onion, chopped			

Oxtail method:
1. In a shallow bowl, add the flour and season well with salt and pepper.
2. Dredge the meat in the flour mixture, shaking off any excess.
3. In a large stockpot over high heat, add the olive oil.
4. When the oil is hot, add the meat, and brown on all sides, about 3 minutes per side.
5. When all of the meat is browned, remove the meat from the pan and set aside on a plate.
6. Slice garlic cloves and then mashed in salt to a purée consistency.
7. In the pot, lower the heat to medium-low and add the garlic and red onion and sweat.
8. Add the wine to the pot.
9. Add the browned meat back into the pot and add the crushed tomatoes.
10. Add enough pork stock to cover the meat and then add cumin, coriander and cinnamon.
11. Add the bay leaves.
12. Bring to a simmer and cook over low heat for 2½ hours or until tender.

French fingerling potatoes method:
1. Boil potatoes in salted water for about 12-15 minutes until done.
2. When cooled, cut the French fingerling potatoes into coins.

Escarole method:
1. In a large hot sauté pan add two tablespoons of extra virgin olive oil.
2. Sauté the escarole until tender finish with a pinch of salt.

Plating:
1. Add to the potato "coins" to the sautéed escarole and finish with good extra virgin olive oil.
2. Remove oxtail from the pot to a bowl , stain sauce and pour over oxtail
3. Serve family style. Serves 4.

OENOTRI
1425 FIRST STREET
NAPA, CA 94559
(707) 252-1022
OENOTRI.COM

2007

CHARDONNAY

Indindali Vineyard

WAUGH CHARDONNAY
MAINE LOBSTER, CELERY ROOT PURÉE AND PRESERVED MEYER LEMON VINAIGRETTE
WINEMAKER RYAN WAUGH, PROFESSIONAL CHEF JOHN VLANDIS

Wine Making Facts :
Encépagement : 100% Chardonnay
Vineyard : Indindoli Vineyard
Soils : Gravel, clay and loam
Elevation : 200 ft.
Aspect : South facing exposure
Average Vine Age : 30 years
Yield : 2.5 tons per acre
Alcohol Level : 14.5%
Total Production : 400 cases
Harvest Details : October 18, 2006 harvest date,
Brix 24.9, pH 3.19, TA .57 Yeast used F10
Winemaking : Whole Berry pressing directly to
press. Never pressing all the way to 2.0 Bar.
Drop temperature to 50°F and let settle for
24 hours.
Fermentation : 14 days. No Malolactic fermentation
was done, however to create the intense mouth
feel we stir the lees very heavily.
Fermentation : Barrel fermented in neutral oak
Oak Regimen : Neutral oak

WAUGH CELLARS
P.O. BOX 3746
NAPA, CA 94558
888-883-WINE
WAUGHCELLARS.COM

VINUM XL, MONTRACHET-CHARDONNAY

" Spicy, floral and sweet on the nose, the 2007 Indindoli Chardonnay is one of the most complex wines this vineyard has ever produced. Mother nature provided us with a tremendous amount of viscosity, providing the wine with a softness and roundness on the palate not found in every vintage. Of course coupled with mouth watering acidity and wonderful citrus flavors." RW

Ryan Waugh represents the birth of a new generation in viticulture. At just 34 years old, he is one of the youngest winemakers working in Napa and Sonoma, and founded his own label in 2001. Waugh Cellars takes pride in its direct-to-consumer approach. "We know every person on our mailing list," says Waugh, "and we've tasted with about 95 percent of them." Using minimalist techniques, he strives to grow the best possible grape from each vineyard in each vintage. "We don't try to alter things if Mother Nature throws us a curve ball," Waugh says.

WAUGH PINOT NOIR AND WAUGH CABERNET SAUVIGNON
GRILLED SALMON, CRISPY RISOTTO CAKE, HARICOTS VERTS, CABERNET SAUVIGNON SAUCE
WINEMAKER RYAN WAUGH, PROFESSIONAL CHEF JOHN VLANDIS

WAUGH CELLARS
P.O. BOX 3746
NAPA, CA 94558
888-883-WINE
WAUGHCELLARS.COM

Wine Making Facts :
Encépagement : Pinot Noir
Appellation : Russian River Valley
Vineyard : Indindoli Vineyard
Soils : Gravel and loam
Elevation: 300 ft
Yield : 2 tons to the acre
Alcohol Level : 14.1%
Total Production : 150 cases
Philosophy : Natural acidity and flavors are the most important.
Harvest Details : October 11, 2006 harvest date, Brix 23.5, pH 3.19, TA .57 Yeast used F10
Winemaking: de-stemmed, but not crushed and fermented in bins, which lasted for 16 days. 2 to 3 punch downs each day depending on tasting. Extended maceration for 10 days and pressed off directly to barrel. One racking off the heavy lees during barrel aging.
Wood Origin : French oak

Wine Making Facts :
Encépagement : Cabernet Sauvignon
Appellation : Napa Valley
Soils : Rock, mixed with clay
Elevation : 1000 ft
Aspect : South and east facing
Micro-Climate : Napa Valley
Average Vine Age : 14 years
Yield : 3.5 tons
Alcohol Level : 14.5%
Total Production : 450 cases
Philosophy : Let the vineyard do the talking. Natural acidity and flavors are the most important.
Harvest Details : October 28, 2006 Brix 25.7, pH 3.60, TA .61 Yeast used D254
Winemaking : De-stemmed into bins and fermented into 8 different lots.
Fermentation : 16 days
Maceration : 10 days
Oak Regimen : French and Hungarian Oak

"Bursts of fresh raspberries and strawberries on the nose. Seductive ruby red color. Explosive fruit is the initial taste but what you find underneath is a very special wine. Its massive creaminess and rich fruit flavor is only matched by its finesse and incredibly long finish." RW

" It explodes with fresh fruit on the nose, blackberries, currants and cherries are all prominent. With some aeration you'll find plum, hints of spice and some black olives. The natural elegance of this 100% Cabernet Sauvignon gives you the flexibility to enjoy a glass on its own or to pair with most foods." RW

VINUM, BURGUNDY & VINUM BORDEAUX

Waugh Chardonnay
Maine Lobster, Celery Root Purée and Preserved Meyer Lemon Vinaigrette
Winemaker Ryan Waugh, Professional Chef John Vlandis

Ingredients:

2	Live Maine Lobsters, cooked and removed from the shell and halved
4 T	butter
¼ c	white wine

Celery Root Purée:

2 c	celery root, peeled and diced
1 c	Russet potato, peeled and diced
1 T	salt
4 T	butter, softened

Preserved Meyer Lemon Vinaigrette;

1	preserved Meyer lemon, minced, pulp removed and discarded
1	shallot, minced
4 oz	grape seed oil
4 oz	seasoned rice vinegar
2 oz	water

Method:
Heat a large pan, add the wine and reduce by three-fourths, slowly whisk in the butter. Do not boil.
Place the lobster in the pan. Heat the lobster gently.

Celery Root Purée :
Place the celery root, potatoes and salt in a sauce pot; add cold water to cover.
Bring to a boil, reduce to a simmer and cook until the celery root is tender.
Remove from the heat.
Strain well.
Place a food mill over a bowl and purée.
Stir in the butter, season with salt and pepper

Preserved Meyer Lemon Vinaigrette:
Place the shallot, oil and lemon in a blender and purée.
Slowly add the water and vinegar.
Season with sea salt, if necessary.

Plating:
Place a small amount of purée in the center of the plate, top with the half of the lobster tail and one claw. Drizzle a small amount of preserved Meyer lemon vinaigrette on the plate. 2 servings

WAUGH PINOT NOIR AND WAUGH CABERNET SAUVIGNON
GRILLED SALMON, CRISPY RISOTTO CAKE, HARICOTS VERTS, CABERNET SAUVIGNON SAUCE
WINEMAKER RYAN WAUGH, PROFESSIONAL CHEF JOHN VLANDIS

Ingredients:

4	King salmon, fillets
1 T	olive oil
8 oz	haricots verts, blanched
1 t	shallots, minced
½ t	garlic, minced
4	tomatoes, Heirloom, sliced ½ inch thick
2 T	butter

Risotto Cake:

2 c	Arborio rice
1 T	porcini powder
1½	onion, minced
2 T	butter
1 c	white wine
6 c	chicken stock, hot
½	parmesan cheese, grated
1 c	olive oil

Cabernet Sauce:

3 c	Cabernet Sauvignon
2 T	balsamic vinegar
½ c	port wine
1	roma tomato
1 ea	thyme sprig and tarragon sprig
2 T	chopped basil
5	peppercorns
2 T	shallots, chopped
1 t	garlic, chopped
1	bay leaf
12 oz	veal stock
2 T	butter

Salmon:
Preheat the grill; brush the salmon fillets with the olive oil, season with salt and pepper. Place on grill skin side up. Cook for two to three minutes on each side.

Risotto:
Melt the butter in a large sauce pot over medium heat; add the onions and the porcini powder. Stir with a wooden spoon until the onions are translucent. Add the rice and cook for two minutes continuously stirring. Add the wine and reduce by half. Add three cups of hot stock to the rice and continue to stir. Lower heat to a simmer. Add remaining stock to the rice as needed. This process will take approximately twenty minutes. When done, remove from the heat and stir in the parmesan and season with salt and pepper. Transfer to a buttered cookie sheet and allow to cool. Cover and refrigerate for one hour. Using a biscuit cutter, cut four three-inch circles. Heat one cup olive oil in a sauté pan, dust the risotto cakes in flour and cook until brown on each side. Remove and keep warm.

Haricots Verts:
Sauté the haricots verts with the butter, when hot add the shallots and remove from the heat. Season with salt and pepper. Place a slice of tomato in the center of each plate, season with sea salt and pepper. Place the risotto cake on top of the tomato and then the salmon. Spoon the sauce around and garnish with the haricots verts.

Cabernet Sauce:
Melt butter in a medium sauce pot, add the shallots and cook until caramelized, add the garlic, stir and add the wine, balsamic, tomato, herbs and peppercorns. Reduce by half and add the veal stock. Continue to simmer slowly, skimming occasionally. Reduce to one cup and strain through a fine strainer. Season. 4 servings

ZD FOUNDER'S RESERVE PINOT NOIR
GLAZED DUCK BREAST QUINOA, CIPOLLINI ONIONS, CELERY ROOT, BLACK TRUMPET MUSHROOMS
WINEMAKER CHRIS PISANI, EXECUTIVE CHEF PATRICK KELLY, ANGÈLE

Wine Making Facts :

Encépagement : Pinot Noir 100%

Appellation : Carneros

Vineyard : deLeuze Family Vineyard

Soils : Haire Series (light clay loam)

Elevation : 95ft

Aspect : North-South

Micro-Climate : Influenced by San Pablo Bay

Average Vine Age : 13 years

Yield: 2-2.5 ton/acre

Alcohol Level : 13.9%

Total Production : 765 cases

Philosophy : Through careful vineyard practices, organic farming and a gentle winemaking approach to produce a distinctive terroir driven wine.

Fermentation: in open top stainless steel fermentors. Punchdown every 6 hours.

Maceration : 7 days

Wood Origin : France

Oak Regimen : 10 months

Fining/Filtering : Unfined/Crossflow filtered

Bottling Formats: 750ml and 35 3L bottles

" The fruit for this Pinot Noir was harvested from our organically farmed vineyard in Napa Carneros. Set in motion by Norman, ZD's intensive growing techniques using deficit irrigation, crop thinning, and hand canopy management added to the natural depth and complexity of this low yielding vineyard. Aged for 15 months in French Oak, this wine would have put a sparkle in Norm's eye. CP"

ZD WINES
8383 SILVERADO TRAIL
NAPA, CA 94558
800-487-7757
ZDWINES.COM

SOMMELIERS BLACK TIE BURGUNDY GRAND CRU

Founded in 1969 by aerospace engineer Norman deLeuze, ZD Wines is family owned and operated by three generations of the deLeuze family. Norman passed away in 2007, after battling lymphoma, but his indelible legacy lives on through his wife, children, grandchildren and through ZD's passion for superior winemaking. A true pioneer in the Napa Valley wine industry (his 1969 Pinot Noir was the first wine label to recognize the Carneros region), ZD Wines continues to be at the forefront of sustainable farming practices. ZD Wines embraces biodiversity by using organic farming, solar power, and chemical alternatives. The Estate Vineyards are organically farmed and certified by the CCOF. Today, Norman's wife Rosa Lee, and their three children, are looking forward to seeing what lies ahead. With Norman's motto "Zero Defects," the future is bright!

ZD FOUNDER'S RESERVE PINOT NOIR
GLAZED DUCK BREAST QUINOA, CIPOLLINI ONIONS, CELERY ROOT, BLACK TRUMPET MUSHROOMS
WINEMAKER CHRIS PISANI, EXECUTIVE CHEF PATRICK KELLY, ANGÈLE

Quinoa:
2 c   vegetable stock
1 c   quinoa
1 T   olive oil, extra virgin
1 T   sage, fresh, chopped
1 T   thyme, fresh, chopped
1   chive bunch, fresh, chopped

Glazed onions:
14   Cipollini onions
2 T   grape seed oil
2 T   honey
¼ c   sherry vinegar

Honey glaze:
4   shallots, sliced
pinch allspice, ground
pinch clove, ground

pinch black pepper, ground
¼ c   honey
2 T   sherry vinegar
3½   sage leaves

Serving:
1 ½ c celery root batons (¼" x 2"), butter braise
1   watercress bunch, cleaned well
1 c   celery heart leaves, pick only the yellow
2 c   black trumpet mushrooms, sautéed
1 T   grape seed oil
2   duck breasts
2   sage leaves
tt   extra virgin olive oil
tt   salt pepper

Quinoa:
Cook slowly until tender, season, add olive oil, sage, thyme, and let cool.
Add chives.

Glazed onions:
Cut ends off onions and cut into quarters to allow them to fall apart while cooking.
Cook slowly in grape seed oil to caramelize.
Add small amount of honey and allow to reduce into the onions.
Add sherry vinegar to deglaze and allow to reduce, remove from pan and allow to cool.

Honey glaze:
Sweat shallots over low heat until tender.
Add very small pinches of ground allspice, clove, black pepper, and salt, stir into the shallots.
Pour honey over shallot mixture and bring to a slow boil, let reduce.
Add sherry vinegar and sage, strain.

Serving:
Sauté the black trumpets, add celery root, onions, and quinoa in grape seed oil.
Season duck, cook over medium to medium high, skin side down, to render out fat and until skin is crisp; turn and continue cooking to reach desired temperature.
While still in pan, baste it with the glaze and a couple more sage leaves.
Remove and allow to rest out of pan for 5 minutes before slicing.
Place about ½ cup cooked quinoa on plate and sliced duck over the top, small salad of watercress and celery leaves; and a drizzle of olive oil and season. 2 servings

ANGÈLE RESTAURANT AND BAR
540 MAIN STREET
NAPA, CA 94559
707-252-8115
ANGELERESTAURANT.COM

Recipe Index

DRESSINGS AND SAUCES

FRUITS AND VEGETABLES

Recipe Index

MEATS

Beef:

Game:

Lamb:

Pork:

Birds:

Seafood:

Contributors

Acknowledgements

PHOTO AND RECIPE CREDIT

CLAIRE BLOOMBERG:
111, 163, 185, 249, 347

CARYN BOSTROM : 365

BRIANA CLARK-FORGIE : 114

CHARLES O'REAR : 2, 67

JIM WHITE, NAPAMAN.COM : 143

DEBORAH JONES,
SAN FRANCISCO : 70, 284, 336

LEIGH BEISCH, SAN FRANCISCO : 86

RECIPE BY CATE CONNIFF
IS FEATURED IN *SEASONS IN
THE WINE COUNTRY: RECIPES
FROM THE CIA* : 338

RECIPES BY JOEY ALTMAN
ARE FEATURED IN
WITH RESERVATIONS : 72, 88, 286

WITH THANKS TO:

DOUG WELDON
KEVIN GEORGE ONESKO
MARY CAMMAROTA
SHARON D'SILVA
NICOLE PINKO
YVONNE LEMBI-DETERT
AND FONDLY,
DESIGN INTERNATIONAL

TO CONTACT ANY OF THE
CONTRIBUTORS IN
THIS COOKBOOK PLEASE CONTACT:
DECANTINGWINECOUNTRY.COM

INFORMATION:
CAB FOR CARE
CABFORCARE.COM

SLOW FOOD MOVEMENT
NAPAVALLEYSLOWFOOD.ORG
SLOWFOODUSA.ORG

Resources

RESTAURANT CRYSTAL CLEAN™

I WAS INTRODUCED TO RESTAURANT CRYSTAL CLEAN BY SYLVIE LALY, AFTER ONE OF OUR MANY "PAIRING SESSIONS". RESTAURANT CRYSTAL CLEAN IS AN ALL-NATURAL WASHING LIQUID FOR HIGH QUALITY STEMWARE. FOUNDER AND OWNER DOUG SAVAGE SAYS, "MY CLIENTS LOVE IT BECAUSE IT REDUCES POLISHING UP TO 97% AND LEAVES NO STREAKS, SPOTS, FILM, TASTE OR ODOR." THE UNIQUE FORMULA IS COMPLETELY 'GREEN', BIODEGRADABLE, AND PLANT-BASED. AVAILABLE AT FINE RETAILERS SUCH AS SUR LA TABLE OR ONLINE AT CRYSTALCLEANGLASS.COM.

CHEF JOHN VLANDIS

I'D LIKE TO GIVE SPECIAL RECOGNITION AND GRATITUDE TO PROFESSIONAL CHEF JOHN VLANDIS FOR CREATING PAIRING RECIPES FOR SO MANY OF OUR SMALLER PRODUCTION WINERIES. I HAVE KNOWN JOHN FOR A LONG TIME AND AM WELL AWARE OF HIS MANY CREDENTIALS: GRADUATED WITH HONORS FROM THE CULINARY INSTITUTE OF AMERICA IN HYDE PARK, NEW YORK; TRAVELS AND CULINARY TRAINING THROUGHOUT EUROPE; FORMER EXECUTIVE CHEF AT MANY OF OUR MOST POPULAR WINERIES; AND THAT HE CURRENTLY OWNS HIS OWN CATERING AND PRIVATE CHEF COMPANY IN NAPA VALLEY. BUT JOHN CONTRIBUTED MORE THAN THAT. HIS RECIPES ARE STRAIGHT FORWARD, POLISHED AND RELATIVELY SIMPLE. JOHN'S RECIPES SET THE STAGE, A SEASONED PHILOSOPHY THAT FOOD MUST "DANCE" WELL WITH WINE.

RESTAURATEUR VS RESTAURATEUR
NOUN SINGULAR RESTAURATEUR (PLURAL RESTAURATEURS) [1] RESTAURATEUR IS WIDELY USED IN MOST WRITINGS. (US) THE OWNER OF A RESTAURANT. USAGE THE OLDER FORM RESTAURATEUR (WITHOUT THE 'N'), BORROWED FROM FRENCH, IS PREFERRED ONLY FORMAL WRITING, AND ESPECIALLY IN BRITAIN. WIKIPEDIA.COM

The Riedel Stemware

Sommeliers Black Tie
Sommeliers Red
Sommeliers White
Vitis
Vinum XL
Vinum
O Series
Tyrol
FROM UPPER LEFT TO BOTTOM RIGHT

THE NAPA VALLEY AVAS

Atlas Peak AVA: Atlas Peak is the highest point in the Vaca Mountain Range at 2,700 feet, located northeast of the city of Napa. Zinfandel is emerging as the best varietal for the appellation's growing conditions, however; Chardonnay, Cabernet Sauvignon and Sangiovese are planted in this region.

Carneros AVA: Straddling the borders of the Napa and Sonoma Valleys on the north coast of San Pablo Bay is the appellation known as Los Carneros– 'The Rams'. The cool wind and fog in the early afternoon provide the ideal conditions for producing fine Chardonnays, elegant Pinot Noirs and crisp sparkling wines. In recent years, Carneros has also been recognized for the quality of its Syrah and Merlot.

Chiles Valley District AVA: This narrow appellation in the Vaca Mountains along the northeast side of the Napa Valley can be described as a 'valley within a valley'. It was named after Joseph Ballinger Chiles, who was given a land grant, Rancho Catacula from the Mexican government in the mid-1800s. The terroir is unique, as cooling bay breezes which affect the Valley floor do not reach as far inland as Chiles Valley, making the climate more continental than maritime. Zinfandel is grown here with great achievement.

Diamond Mountain District AVA: Cabernet Sauvignon is the true diamond of this AVA. Covering 5,000 rocky acres in the Mayacamas Range on the northeast side of Napa Valley, this region has just over 500 acres under vine. Unique, porous volcanic soils and extended exposure to the sun produce powerful Cabernets with chewy textures and diamond-hard tannins. Other varieties, including Cabernet Franc and Zinfandel, are being grown here with great success.

Howell Mountain AVA: The first Napa Valley sub-region to be designated an AVA in 1984. Overlooking St. Helena from the Vaca Mountain Range on the valley's northeast side, the appellation encompasses around 14,000 acres, yet possesses only 600 acres of vines. The region is rugged, with vineyards at 1,400-2,200 feet in elevation, avoiding the influences of the fog that often blankets the valley floor below. Howell Mountain is well known for its Bordeaux varieties and Zinfandels.

Mt. Veeder AVA: Nestled in the Mayacamas Mountains, this 25 square-mile appellation is situated on volcanic Mount Veeder at 2,677 feet above sea level. The slopes are steep, the soils are thin and the viticulture is back-breaking, but the result is intense, chewy wines with distinctive wild berry fruit flavors and magnificent spice.

Oak Knoll District AVA: Located toward the southern end of the Napa Valley at a relatively low elevation, this area is accessible to this climate moderating effects of San Pablo Bay. The Carneros appellation, located to Oak Knoll's immediate south, is generally the only place in Napa that can claim a cooler climate, with a reputation for a delicate and restrained style of Chardonnay. It has notable wineries from neighboring appellations choosing Oak Knoll fruit for their Chardonnays.

Oakville AVA: When H.W. Crabb planted a vineyard in Oakville in 1868, he named his chosen site 'To Kalon', Greek for 'most beautiful'. Today, this vineyard is surrounded by 5,000 acres of vines, in an appellation that only totals 5,700 acres. The gravelly, well drained soils are perfect for the world-class wines that are mostly from Bordeaux varieties. They are characteristically rich and dense, with firm tannins.

Rutherford AVA: "Cabernets need, a touch of that Rutherford dust." (Andre Tchelistcheff, legendary winemaker of Beaulieu Vineyards). The celebrated vignerons of this appellation deeply respect the unique terroir here – as they say, the "dust." The historic wineries of Inglenook and Beaulieu, as well as dozens of new houses, have proven that this six-square-mile plot of vines, halfway up the Napa Valley, rivals the best appellations of the Old World.

St. Helena AVA: The St. Helena appellation is located where the Napa Valley floor narrows, between the Mayacamas and Vaca Mountain ranges. The history of winemaking in St. Helena is legendary, as Charles Krug opened his celebrated winery here in 1861. Located in an up-valley area, the climate is quite different from the surrounding regions. The marine air that affects the lower areas of the valley is not so dominant here; however, cool Pacific breezes from the north reach St. Helena, cooling vines and deliver graceful, intense fruit with concentration and depth.

Spring Mountain District: Currently known for its mountain-grown Cabernets, this region's first premium wines were whites, particularly Chardonnay and Riesling. Vineyards here are on steep, east-facing terraces of the Mayacamas Mountain Range, situated up to 2,600 feet above sea level. Due to the higher elevations of the vineyards, fog is not a factor here like it is in much of Napa Valley. The Spring Mountain District's wine-growing history reaches back as far as the Civil War, and by 1874 the legendary Beringer brothers had a vineyard planted here.

Stags Leap District: Legend has it that a great stag, escaping a hunting party, leaped from peak to peak on palisades towering over the Napa Valley below. Located on the Vaca Mountain Range, six miles north of the city of Napa, the Stags Leap District is a mere two square-miles. Famous for Cabernets described like 'a fist in a velvet glove,' these are wines with firm tannins, yet with a sense of elegance and grace that sets them apart. In 1976, at a blind tasting in Paris, nine judges awarded first place to a 1973 Stag's Leap Wine Cellars Cabernet Sauvignon, ahead of the great growths of Bordeaux. That historic event not only put this tiny appellation on the map, but solidified California's claim as one of the world's great wine regions.

Yountville: In 1836, George Calvert Yount, one of the Valley's earliest settlers, was granted his Rancho Caymus. He soon planted the first vineyard just outside the town that now bears his name. Since then, vineyards have always existed in the appellation. The AVA has one of the valley's coolest vineyard exposures. Its long, chilly growing season produces incredibly long-lived Cabernet Sauvignon, with rock-hard tannins and deep concentration.

Wild Horse Valley: One of the Napa Valley's earliest appellations may well be its least known. The Wild Horse Valley AVA, is a mere 3,300 acres in size, with barely over 100 acres under vine, and just a single winery calling it home. Straddling Napa and Solano counties, this viticultural area enjoys many hours, as summer fogs usually stop before reaching Wild Horse's elevation. Its southerly location near San Pablo Bay exposes it to cool westerly winds from the ocean and bay, especially in the spring and summer.

By Dennis Kelly